The Ultimate Book of British Comics

a&b

The Ultimate Book of British Comics

GRAHAM KIBBLE-WHITE

First published in Great Britain in 2005 by
Allison & Busby Limited
13 Charlotte Mews
London W1T 4EJ
www.allisonandbusby.com

Copyright © 2005 by GRAHAM KIBBLE-WHITE

Cover Image: "Dennis the Menace" ®© DC Thomson & Co., Ltd.

A catalogue record for this book is available from
the British Library.

10 9 8 7 6 5 4 3 2 1

ISBN 0 7490 8211 9

Printed and bound in Wales by
Creative Print and Design, Ebbw Vale

GRAHAM KIBBLE-WHITE has been writing professionally about all aspects of popular culture for the past five years. Currently working for the Press Association as a TV writer, he provides a host of syndicated material which is, literally, read by millions. In 2005 he edited *TV Cream: The Ultimate Guide to 70s and 80s Pop Culture*. A lifelong fan of comics, Graham does in fact own that 1977 number one edition of *2000 AD*, but unfortunately he doesn't have the space spinner.

For Mum and Dad

Acknowledgements

To Jane, for her huge contribution, tactical shouting, superb organisational skills and for single-handedly keeping our life running smoothly.

Also to Roger, Gail and Jack, for letting me read their comics when I was growing up – once they'd finished with them, of course.

A special salute goes out to fellow comic readers David Oliphant and Bobby Wallace.

Thanks also to: Adrian J Andrews, Scott Andrews, Alan Barnes, Steve Berry, Cameron Borland, John Douglas, Bill Downey, Jac Farrow, Ian Gibson, Chris Hughes, Ian Jones, Calum Laird, Alistair McGown, Steve McManus, Grant Morrison, Steven Murphy, Jon Peake and Steve Williams.

Contents

Introduction

Unless you suffered a ridiculously austere childhood, comics will have played a significant part in shaping your early years. For generations, those flimsy weeklies, seemingly printed on paper normally sequestered for school toilets, populated young imaginations with wholesome – and sometimes not so wholesome – entertainment.

Some had stirring titles (*Victor*, *Valiant*, *Champ*), some excitable (*Wow!*, *Cor!!*, *It's Wicked!*), others non-threatening (*Girl*, *Bunty*, *Penny*) and a select few just plain crackers (*Krazy*, *Nutty* and *Oink!*), but common to all was a mission to entertain. And once you'd dived into that four-colour world, you were hooked.

British children in the twentieth century were unified by weekly visits to Mr Newsagent's to pick up their comic, or anxious dalliances around the letter box, waiting for the paperboy to arrive. The anticipation became almost ritualistic, but once that publication was in your hands, you were into a special adult-free zone where kids ruled, OK.

Comics were the playground currency and talking-points of our youth. As we grew up, we moved through the market to match, every few years trading in our regular title for something a little more mature and challenging. A healthy childhood for any thirtysomething male should have involved a progression through publications along the lines of *Dandy* to *Nutty* to *Victor* to *Eagle* mk II and finally *2000 AD* – at which point he'd either be hiding his weekly habit from his mates who were all freshly into indie music, or fruitlessly endorsing the escapades of his comic heroes as 'surprisingly mature allegories on racism, actually, and not just killing aliens'.

At their peak, comics in this country sold hundreds of thousands of copies, but because of their regularity and reliability, each kid's 'own' particular title felt like a personal friend. But where are they now, those pals from our past? The sad truth is, all but a handful didn't make it beyond the Eighties, and with no hint of an *Alf Tupper: The Tough of the Track* or a *Kitty Hawke and Her All-Girl Air Crew* movie on the cards, hopes of a latter-day revival look slim.

That's really not fair. US characters like Spider-Man and Superman endure not just thanks to their own publications, but also representation in films, television programmes and video games. They've even been given a veneer of pop culture respectability thanks to the squillions of weighty tomes dedicated to the American comic industry. Meanwhile, our own stock of quirkier, more eccentric, winningly daft and pleasingly low-rent heroes and heroines have failed to receive anything like the recognition they deserve and have – in the main – been consigned to history's forgotten and strangely smelling box of stuff tucked away somewhere up in the attic.

That's where *The Ultimate Book of British Comics* comes in.

What's in the Book...

This publication is a long overdue celebration of British comics.

By trawling through the biggest pile of back issues known to man, the book alights on the classic publications of the genre and tells their stories. In doing so, it also uncovers other, larger tales. You'll learn about the ups (the boom years of the Fifties and Sixties, and the second wind of the mid-Seventies) and the downs (pretty much everything since the mid-Eighties). You'll discover who appeared where (at last it can be told – was Ginger in *The Beezer* or *The Topper*?) and read a hell of a lot of 'exciting news for readers inside!' blurbs as, time after time, weak titles are forced to 'merge' with their more successful stablemates.

Alongside this, you'll also find other, subtler yarns being spun by stealth. The formation of the mighty IPC comics line and its unique obsession with a) pitting the classes against one another and b) men saved from death by bionic surgery. The rise and rise of Dundondian stalwarts DC Thomson is also charted, and their own brand of utterly safe anarchic humour (after all, this is the company that would emblazon its telephones with stickers instructing users to 'speak softly and say "yes please"'). Plus, there's the emergence of violence in the Seventies (in both boys' and girls' titles), the hope of a new wave of popularity in the late Eighties via the short-lived mania for adult publications ('Comics aren't just for kids anymore!') and the creative recycling of old material and characters across more than half a century.

...And What Isn't

By the same token, there are some things you won't find here, chief amongst them being an entire catalogue of British comics. To undertake such a project would require a book ten times the size of this, leaving scant room to note who merged with whom and what you got if you sent off a 30p postal order to join the fan club.

Adult comics of the *Viz* vein are also excluded. Although they were everywhere for about two minutes in the mid-Nineties, they weren't ever intended for kids, nor did they grow out of the lineage of children's publications. Besides, all bar Johnny Fartpants' rag were bloody awful.

Reprint titles – they don't get much of a look in either; which means bye-bye to the majority of Marvel UK's *oeuvre*. That, plus spin-offs like summer specials, pocket libraries and annuals, all worthy of a separate book in their own right, get just the occasional nod here.

And, as a general note, titles that emerged before the Sixties – bar some truly honourable exceptions – get pretty short shrift too. This is a publication unapologetically aimed at those thirty and fortysomethings who grew up in the pop culture era, and as such the austerity of the ration book years and the like are pretty much out.

Story Papers

There is one other absentee, however, that deserves more than just a passing mention: the story papers.

These were the proud grandparents of Britain's weekly comics tradition, not only establishing an appetite for old-fashioned fun on flimsy stock, but creating some of the characters who'd go on to populate their offspring for the next sixty years. However, to their detriment, they didn't actually feature any comic-strip action. In fact, it was just wall-to-wall text, meaning instant disqualification from this book.

Early fodder in this genre was *The Halfpenny Marvel*, which began in 1893, *Boys' Friend* (1895), *Boys' Herald* (1903) and *Boys' Magazine* (1922). Crammed full of tales about detectives, cowboys and hidden treasure, it was all four-square stuff – and decidedly dull from a modern-day perspective, to be honest. The big hitters in the market initially came from Amalgamated Press in the shape of *Gem* (1907) and *The Magnet* (1908), both majoring in school stories and written in the main by Charles Hamilton, better known as Frank Richards. It was the latter publication which first brought us the adventures of Billy Bunter.

Keen to get in on the market, DC Thomson soon dominated with their 'famous five' titles. First up was *Adventure* in 1921, which boasted the exploits of 'The Wolf of Kabul' amongst others. It was then followed the next year by the more working class *Rover* (with 'Tough of the Track' Alf Tupper, Sgt Matt Braddock and Morgyn the Mighty *et al.*) and *Wizard* mk I (Wilson and Limp-Along Leslie etc.). *Skipper* and *Hotspur* arrived a decade later and the quintessential quintet was established – until the former fell terminally foul of paper shortages in 1941. Nevertheless, the others soldiered on (their fortunes, in fact, boosted by the Second World War which informed much of their content thereafter) until the mid-Sixties. By now, even *The Magnet* and *Gem* were distant memories, both coming unstuck in 1940.

Times were getting tough.

With US comics beginning to flood into the market, and the arrival of television, readers were less inclined to wade through text. Pictures were the thing. As sales fell, *Adventure* was consumed by *Rover* in 1961, which two years later went on to swallow up *Wizard*. Meanwhile, *Hotspur* put itself through a major rebranding exercise, emerging from the decade as a fully fledged comic. Only *Rover* kept the faith and, incredibly, managed to limp on until 1973, at which point its eye-straining text must have looked as exciting as bible readings to its juvenile audience.

As it finally bade the world farewell, the first phase of Britain's weekly habit officially came to a close.

How This Book Works

We're nearly there now, but you just need a quick user's guide on how this thing operates before we can really begin.

The comics throughout are listed in alphabetical order, with details of which company (or companies) published them, the years when they ran and the day of the week (where given) upon which they came out. In many examples, that changed over time, so for simplicity's sake we're just listing what was the case as per issue one. Similarly, if a comic jumped between weekly, fortnightly and monthly schedules, we're only including whichever it was they plumped for first. On this latter point, however, fact fans will be pleased to note details about capricious timetables are generally incorporated into the main narrative.

One final point, comic titles that are printed in bold indicate that that publication has its own entry elsewhere in the book.

Right, that's it. You're on your own now. Prepare to reacquaint yourself with a lost world of talking bears, schoolgirl witches, killer sharks, partially crippled footballers, wholly crippled ballerinas, never-say-die paupers and loads of *Six Million Dollar Man* rip-offs.

So, what are you waiting for?! There's great news for all readers inside!

2000 AD

(IPC Magazines Ltd/Fleetway Publications/Egmont Fleetway Ltd/Rebellion, 1977-ongoing, every Saturday)

How can you not love *2000 AD*? It's the last man standing in the weekly boys' comic industry; a title that has courted controversy, suckled some of the industry's greatest talents and produced at least one genuinely iconic character (alongside literally hundreds of other hugely memorable ones).

Having had the temerity to outlive its own self-imposed sell-by date, the 'Galaxy's Greatest Comic' has enjoyed a long and eventful history.

The initial idea for a science fiction weekly came from Kevin Gosnell, who was working as a sub-editor in the competitions department at IPC. Having read a newspaper article that predicted sci-fi was going to be the next big thing at the box office (*Star Wars* was on its way), he became convinced the oncoming craze could be profitably exploited, even if it was going to prove short-lived.

Editorial director John Sanders was sufficiently impressed to set *wunderkind* Pat Mills onto the job of putting the title together. Having successfully launched *Battle* and *Action*, could the writer come up with a third hit in a row?

Despite his suspicions about the genre, Mills got to work, formulating a comic that would continue his anti-establishment themes, which were proving very popular. Heavily influenced by publications from the continent, he was determined to rope in a new wave of European artists to work on the paper, which at that time was known as *AD 2000* (a title that came from Sanders). From fairly early on the idea had occurred to lead with a new, revamped 'Dan Dare' strip. Not only had the character been a great success first time around in *Eagle* mk I, but his return would also provide the launch with a good publicity angle.

Bringing in sparring-partner and fellow *Battle* creator John Wagner, the two started thinking about possible story ideas. Wagner felt the comic needed a cop character and suggested a futuristic version of 'One-Eyed Jack', the Dirty Harry-lite he'd created for *Valiant*. In search of a name, Mills suggested 'Judge Dread', which was the title of an occult strip he'd been toying with. Changing that to 'Judge Dredd' to avoid confusion with the comedy reggae artist who was bothering the pop charts at the time, the concept was passed on to *Battle* artist Carlos

Ezquerra to visualise. Although his hugely elaborate fusion of zips, leather and chains didn't impress Wagner, it sent Mills' imagination into overdrive as he began to grasp the potential of this sci-fi lawman.

In the mean time, a chap called Paul DeSavery became interested in the duo's activities. Having bought the film rights to Dan Dare, he was checking out the possibility of buying up their comic. For Mills and Wagner this would mean they'd finally be free of in-house politics and could each expect a share in the title's profits rather than having to accept a miserly £10 page fee. Unfortunately for them, the IPC board rejected the deal and now thoroughly disgruntled with the whole thing, Wagner quit, leaving his partner to soldier on alone.

Writing dozens of potential strips for a dummy issue that was required to secure the backing of the company's head honchos, Mills agonized with finding the right artists for his creations, trying out three or four on some stories. Painfully slowly, things came together, the mock-up ('action-packed stories from outer-space!') found favour, and gradually a first issue line-up began to emerge. However, relatively late in the day there was a sudden panic when *Action* was withdrawn from sale in October 1976 following complaints about its violent content. Anxious not to fall foul of our 'moral guardians' again, IPC scoured *2000 AD* (as it was now known) for traces of Whitehouse-baiting gore – and found plenty.

Strips had to be re-drawn, or at the very least treated to a liberal dose of Tipp-Ex, and all the while, Mills was still struggling to finalise who was going to write and illustrate what. Days before the printing presses were due to roll, there was one last problem – Sanders had developed cold feet over the depiction of Russian soldiers invading Britain in the Nineties, and art assistant Kevin O'Neill was given the job of removing all traces of the hammer and sickle from their uniforms, to replace them with the symbol of the newly created Volgan Army.

That first issue hit the news-stands dated 26 February, 1977. As Mills had guessed, the return of Dan Dare had provided the publication with some pretty decent newspaper coverage (a trick later repeated by *Eagle* mk II), and IPC had even shelled out for a spot of TV advertising.

Arriving with a free space spinner (*née* 'a frisbee' – another trick to be repeated by *Eagle* mk II), the first issue may have sported space-age dinosaurs and the adventures of *The Six Million Dollar Man*-influenced MACH-1 whose 'incredible hyper-power will amaze you!', but there was one thing it didn't have: Judge Dredd. Due to the continuing difficulties in finding a suitable writer and artist for the strip, the Lawman of the Future's first story just wasn't ready in time. It wasn't seen as a huge problem, however, as a certain Pilot of the Future was considered the big draw.

The first tale, 'Invasion', brought us that Volgan army parachuting into London with guns blazing as 'War with the East!' was declared in the media. Even Angela Rippon was roped in, telling readers via a 'stereopanorama' television set: 'For the first time in a thousand years – *Britain has been invaded!*' Worse was to come as just a couple of pages on, poor old Ange herself fell foul of the attacking squad who stormed BBC TV Centre. '*The last free broadcast is over!*' While the army failed to withstand the onslaught, there was one man who wouldn't be messed with – lorry driver Bill Savage. 'I ain't running from dirty Volgans!' he exclaimed as he unloaded two barrels into an enemy patrol vehicle.

Next up was 'Flesh', the story of Earl Regan, a cigar-chomping hunter from the twenty-third century, an era when animals had been made extinct and man lived on synthetic foods. Nevertheless, it seemed we still had an appetite for blood, and thus Earl and pals travelled back in time to hunt dinosaurs for grub.

On the centre pages we had – in colour – the new Dan Dare. Set in the year 2177 AD, the hero some might have remembered from the Fifties had undergone some serious changes. Existing in a grim, sinewy world drawn by Italian artist Massimo Belardinelli, the character had developed a constant scowl, a nasty buzz-cut hairstyle and – cripes! – a line in bad language. 'Drokk it!' he exclaimed as he railed against his deskbound boss at the Solar Astronautical and Space Administration HQ.

'MACH-1' was next out of the bag. 'Not so much a secret agent, more a secret weapon!', it brought us the adventures of John Probe, a spy whose physicality had been augmented by 'compu-puncture hyperpower' and thus now exhibited superhuman abilities.

Finishing off the issue was 'Harlem Heroes', another spin on *Action*'s 'Death Game 1999'. Here we found ourselves in the year 2050, enjoying the futuristic, jet-powered sport of Aeroball. Inevitably, violence formed part of the playing tactics: 'A perfect 80mph kung-fu drop kick from Hairy!' announced a delighted commentator. 'He's punched the ball out to Louis!'

Helming this fine mix of futuristic action was the alien Tharg, who introduced himself to readers on page 20. We were advised his spaceship was 'cunningly disguised as a thirty-two storey office block in London'

(IPC's King's Reach Tower), and in a neatly typed missive he advised us: 'From the heart of the Galaxy, I, Tharg, have journeyed many light years to bring you *2000 AD* – your planet's first comic of the future,' before signing off with the baffling 'Splundig vur thrigg!', which seemed to be alien-speak for 'cheerio'.

The following week brought us our first encounter with Judge Dredd. Part of a breed of twenty-second-century lawmen who'd been empowered to deliver instant sentences on the spot, here he tackled the gun-happy Whitey, who was blasting futuristic cops for fun with his laser cannon.

The comic proved to be another smash for Mills, with Dredd quickly becoming the standout character. From issue nine, Wagner took over the scripting duties, having swallowed his pride about that earlier walkout, and things went from strength to strength as the bizarre world of Mega City One took shape.

A year on from launch, IPC produced sister title *Starlord*, while *2000 AD* found itself getting into trouble thanks to a series of Dredd strips featuring futuristic versions of Ronald McDonald and Burger King battling over the state of Kansas. If that wasn't bad enough, Colonel Sanders then showed up, using the likes of the Michelin Man and the Jolly Green Giant to do his bidding. The latter's creators in particular, were very upset – resulting in an out-of-court settlement with the character's creators and a dumb half-page strip in which Dredd feasted on sweetcorn and spelt out clearly that the malevolent emerald-hued character they'd tangled with previously wasn't the real Giant.

In October 1978, the title merged with *Starlord*, which, after five months on the shelves had been pulled, despite strong sales. 'Two sci-fi greats united in a giant leap for mankind!' ran the cover blurb, as mutant bounty hunter 'Strontium Dog' Johnny Alpha, and put-upon robot rescue squad 'Ro-Busters' joined the paper's line-up with 'prog' (the comic's sciffy take on 'issues') eighty-six.

Into 1979, it was becoming increasingly obvious the new Dan Dare just wasn't cutting the mustard, and the character was given a super-hero makeover as he donned a cosmic claw that blasted 'some kind of electro-magnetic beam!' Meanwhile, another new title came and went as *Tornado* tried its luck with more down-to-Earth action. Again, just five months later it merged with *2000 AD*, but its earthier brand of characters didn't last long. By now, Mills (who was still producing scripts for the comic) was really getting into his stride, bringing us 'Ro-Busters' spin-off strip

'The ABC Warriors' which focused on robot Hammer-Stein's war years fighting the Volgan empire. Yep, the same baddies Bill Savage had locked horns with, albeit hundreds of years in the future. This cross-pollination of ideas was rife, and gradually built up the impression of a shared *2000 AD* universe in which all the characters existed (Dredd's earlier encounter with the evil tyrannosaur Satanus from 'Flesh' also feeding into this notion).

And so the hits kept on coming. By the time the title reached prog two hundred in 1981, we'd been introduced to the whimsical private dick Sam Slade in 'Robo-Hunter', Dredd had replaced Dan Dare on the centre pages (whose strip was suddenly abandoned altogether partway through a story) and bizarre alien anti-hero Nemesis the Warlock had made his debut in a tale inspired by the Jam song 'Going Underground', and was now contemplating a full-scale assault on mental-case ruler of the earth Torquemada in his own self-titled strip, which began in prog 222.

The Eighties really saw the comic achieve greatness – despite the mixed blessing of 'Tharg's Future Shocks'. Emerging in this decade, these one-off twist-in-the-tale stories were blatant space-filler material, but proved an important training ground for untested newcomers. As such, they were often as brilliant as they were dire, but helped wean the likes of Grant Morrison and Alan Moore onto more substantial offerings.

Indeed, in 1983, the latter's first regular series, 'Skizz', arrived telling the story of an alien stranded on Earth. While it might have owed something to *ET*, it was a minor classic – Moore's work owing as much to Britain's own kitchen-sink dramas as Spielberg's imaginings. That same year the writer would go on to bring us out-and-out humour with delinquent teen extra-terrestrials DR and Quinch ('S'right') before his best work for the publication arrived in 1984, in the form of 'The Ballad Halo Jones', a superior slice of sci-fi following the adventures of an ordinary fiftieth-century girl. Designed as a contrast to the hardcore macho action found elsewhere in the paper, it was something of a slow-burner to begin with, but gradually found critical acclaim.

In December 1986, there was really something to shout about as *2000 AD* clocked up its five-hundredth prog. Sporting a glossy wrap-around cover for the occasion, it showcased the comic's fine array of characters, which by now included blue-skinned genetically engineered soldier Rogue Trooper (he'd arrived in 1981), Celtic, axe-wielding barbarian Sláine (1983), the flat-headed super deadly infantryman Kano from the strip 'Bad Company' (1986) and former psychic sidekick to the mighty Dredd turned leading lady Judge Anderson (who went solo in 1983).

As the US comic giants began poaching *2000 AD*'s star players, the hunt was on for the next generation of talent, and in August 1987, the brightest star from the new wave was revealed. 'Zenith' was a mould-breaking British superhero strip which told the story of a vain and materialistic nineteen-year-old who used his special powers as we all would: to become famous. Crime-fighting was hardly his bag when he could be out clubbing with some Page Three girl, but nonetheless, he reluctantly found himself engaged in a fight to the death with – well – a super-powered Tory.

'Zenith' felt young and fresh, and came from the imagination of former *Starblazer* writer Grant Morrison, who'd more recently been plying his trade on a Marvel UK Zoids spin-off title.

Having grown up with comics, he had a desire to play around with the genre in the same way Dennis Potter had evoked old songs in many of his TV dramas, and thus, as the series developed, he played self-consciously with the conventions and lineage of the medium. This reached its apex in 'Zenith's' third phase, when a huge war across parallel universes gave him the excuse to not only unearth *Lion*'s Robot Archie (reinvented here as a tin-plated acid house freak) but pretty much everyone else from the Fleetway/IPC back catalogue.

The week after 'Zenith' started, another change hit the paper. IPC had sold their youth group to Maxwell Communications who were now publishing the comic under the Fleetway banner – the name the Mirror Group had used in the Sixties for their juvenile division.

In 1988, the comic adopted glossy covers full-time, and there was a sense that the next phase of its life had now begun. With adult spin-off *Crisis* making a splash and *Judge Dredd Megazine* and *Revolver* soon to follow, the good times were surely here. Added to that, in 1990, the newly appointed managing director at Fleetway, Jon Davidage, consented to redraft the agreement the company had with its creatives following a confrontation with Wagner.

Full colour throughout arrived in 1991, but despite the impressive production values, there was suddenly a sense that *2000 AD* was running on empty.

Something had to be done, and in July 1993, the comic launched its 'summer offensive'. Handing over control of the title for eight issues to Morrison and fellow bright young thing Mark Millar, the campaign's name had a double meaning: not only was it supposed to represent a relaunch of *2000 AD*, it was also designed to – well – offend. The chief exponent of this was 'Big Dave', a beer-swilling, Rottweiler-owning, tabloid-reading hard nut who, in his first story, decided to help 'our boys' by nutting Saddam, in 'Target: Baghdad', before later jumping into bed with Fergie and Di at Buckingham Palace.

During this run, Morrison also wrote 'Really and Truly' (the tale of a couple of ditsy female drug couriers) while Millar brought us big robot action in 'Maniac 5'. Meanwhile, *Crisis* writer John Smith also got a look-in, producing 'Slaughterbowl' – yet another futuristic sports strip.

Although none of the above would turn into long-running properties, this had been the most overt acknowledgement yet that the comic's readers were no longer eleven-year-old boys. In fact, it was now the case that a significant percentage of the audience had been following the title since the Seventies.

As the Nineties continued, *2000 AD* never quite recaptured the sparkle of its early years, but did its best to capitalise on the excitement of the 1995 *Judge Dredd* film. Aside from launching another spin-off title, *Judge Dredd: Lawman of the Future*, the paper received something of a makeover – the distinctive logo being ditched for a far less impressive version. With even Dredd himself subject to a merry-go-round of writers, was *2000 AD* set to snuff it before the end of the millennium arrived?

Thankfully not, and as that fateful year beckoned, the paper was still hanging on in there. Well aware that it had now pretty much survived all its rivals, it celebrated the fact with a fantastic cover drawn by fan favourite Brian Bolland. Based on the famous photo of the US Marines raising the American flag at the top of Mount Surbatchi in Iwo Jima, it depicted old hands Dredd, Nemesis, Johnny Alpha, Rogue Trooper and relative new boy Nikolai Dante, plunging the *2000 AD* banner into a mound of deceased comics. Yes, they were all there, from **Deadline** to *Valiant*, a literal heap of history upon which Tharg's boys were now standing tall.

Some favourite creators who'd long ago opted to take the US dollar returned to the fold to mark the occasion, with artists Dave Gibbons, Mike McMahon, Brett Ewins and Kevin O'Neill coming back to the strips that made their name. As if things weren't exciting enough, this edition also saw the death of that alien Warlock, who was melded together with arch-enemy Torquemada to form a ghostly spaceship fated to loop the Earth for all eternity.

However, for lapsed readers lured back in, this shock would have paled alongside the glimpse of – gasp! – bare naked boobs in Dante's story!

The following year, it was announced Oxford-based computer games company Rebellion had purchased *2000 AD* from Fleetway. Their arrival coincided with another new look for the paper, but also brought about a sense of optimism for its future.

The new bosses were aware that while the publication was now a luke-warm seller, there was still money to be made in licensing the characters for other projects, particularly video games.

In 2001, the comic thankfully reverted back to its former logo ('If it ain't broke, don't fix it...creep!' said a truncheon-wielding Dredd to a perp about to dismantle it) and began billing itself as 'the UK's award-winning cult weekly'. And indeed, that's what it was and still is. Long gone are the days when comics could sell in their hundreds of thousands, but thankfully under its current owners, it seems *2000 AD* is happy to accept it's no longer on regular order with the majority of the nation's boys. Instead, it's courting an already devoted audience who tuned into its thrill-power some twenty-odd years ago and have stuck around since. Recent issues have seen the rise of popular hit-man double-act 'Sinister Dexter' and yet another futuristic sports tale, 'Second City Blues', while 'Russia's greatest love machine' – that certain Mr Dante – is up there with any of the comic's greats from yesteryear.

Glossy from start to finish, far more adult than ever before and Britain's only remaining all-new action weekly – in many ways *2000 AD* has never had it so good.

As for Tharg, the green-skinned fella is still hanging on in there giving it a 'Borag Thungg, Earthlets!' at the start of every edition and promoting each 'new thrill!' with the same recognisable chutzpah he'd employed to big-up Dan Dare and MACH-1.

Zarjaz!!

2000 AD's Diceman
(IPC Magazines Ltd, 1986, monthly)

You had to hand it to Pat Mills – he was all for experimentation. The driving force behind *2000 AD*, the man who beefed up girls' comics with his contributions to the likes of *Tammy* and *Misty*, and also the chap who tried to introduce photo-strips to boys' publications (alas, a papier-mâché Nemesis the Warlock strolling around Forbidden Planet didn't go down so well with readers), here he was again, mucking about with the form.

As the Eighties unfurled, it was becoming increasingly clear comic reading was turning into something of a hobbyist's pursuit. There was some logic, then, in trying to fuse the genre with the pastime of another interest group – role-playing. First he dabbled with the concept in a 1985 fifteen-part 'Sláine' strip he'd written for 'The Galaxy's Greatest Comic'; then came the full explosion in a Mills-devised spin-off, *2000 AD's Diceman*.

Plump and glossy, on first appearance it looked like a summer special, but as the opening spread explained inside, readers were about to enter some 'savage, phantom worlds' where cause and effect were decided upon the role of a die. Editor Simon Geller explained the title was 'a new concept which puts together the best of fantasy gaming and the ultimate in graphic action'. With stories that put you in charge of Judge Dredd, Nemesis and Sláine, they were bringing out the big guns here. In fact, not only were *2000 AD*'s top characters made to jump through hoops, some of its best creators were too – Kevin O'Neill designing the publication and drawing Nemesis, Glenn Fabry contributing a fully painted front cover, Bryan Talbot depicting Dredd's adventure and *Warrior*'s David Lloyd providing some quality etchings for 'Sláine'.

It was certainly a neat concept – one that would doubtlessly be described as interactive nowadays – but the problem with this *Choose Your Own Adventure*-style stuff was the amount of preparation required by the reader/player. 'The only essential weapon you'll need is a pair of sacred ivories…a brace of the blessed bones themselves – *two six-sided dice*,' came the insincere instruction. And then: 'You'll also need some scraps of paper, a pencil and a rubber.'

Even more off-putting was a full page of instruction that then had to be digested before we could take on the mantle of Judge Dredd. The last thing kids needed before embarking on some innocent mega-violent escapism was a page entitled 'Rules'.

Things got even worse with issue two's 'Rick Fortune' strip, which expected the reader to consume six pages of preamble before getting to rattle those bones. Making up for that, however, was the ace exhortation for people to contribute to the Letter Rack! page: 'Every reader on the rack wins a really good feeling inside!'

'If you prefer to steer clear of political shenanigans, simply skip the Ronald Reagan story,' began the editorial in issue five, as Mills evidently grew sick of wrapping up his politicking in sword fighting and snot-spewing aliens and went straight for the jugular. Doubtlessly embold-ened by the success of *Spitting Image* on TV, this strip – illustrated by prodigious cartoonist Hunt Emerson – presented what was then a famil-iar take on the US president, depicting him as a gormless, trigger-happy buffoon, terrorising the developing world ('It's time we stood up to the bully boys of Central Africa!') and shafting Britain through his special relationship with Maggie Thatcher ('Your cute little island's our biggest aircraft carrier!'). It was unsubtle, clumsy satire for sure but, hey, this was the Eighties, everyone was at it.

As it happens, issue five would prove to be the last edition of *Diceman*, despite the comic suggesting readers keep up to date with *2000 AD* to find out when the next one was coming out.

Still not completely finished with the concept, in 1987 Pat Mills and Hunt Emerson created *You are Maggie Thatcher: A Dole-Playing Game* for Titan Books. At last it seemed as though he'd scratched that itch – the role-playing aspect of it at least. But the tub-thumping was set to contin-ue in a big way in *Crisis*...

Action
(IPC Magazines Ltd, 1976-1977, every Monday)

'A giant shark snaps off a man's head in one crimson-splashed chomp. Then it tears apart another victim, limb from trunk. An international diplomat dissolves in agony as sulphuric acid gushes from his bathroom shower. They could be X-certificate, adults-only scenes from a thriller combining the worst violence of *Jaws* and James Bond. But they are not. These are just two scenes from *Action*, a lurid new 7p British comic.' So reported the *Sun* on 30 April 1976.

In the world of UK weeklies, the rise and fall of *Action* is probably the biggest story there is. It's a tale that takes in young bucks intent on mak-ing their mark in the world of comics, a thrill-seeking bloke called Steve, *Nationwide*'s Frank Bough, mega-violence, and Mary Whitehouse and the Responsible Society. And it all rose out of the desire to revitalise what kids were picking up off the news-stands.

By the Seventies, many were feeling the stalwarts of British comics were looking dated. DC Thomson's response was to create the gritty and violent *Warlord*, a title devoted to war and nothing but. Immediately it proved a huge success and prompted IPC into coming up with *Battle*, its own realistic and critically acclaimed look at men killing other men.

It too enjoyed healthy sales, but formed something of a schism inside IPC. The editorial director, John Sanders, had employed two freelancers, Pat Mills and John Wagner, to create the title, feeling the majority of staff in the company's boys' comics division were too rooted in the old ways to produce something truly modern.

At the end of 1975, Sanders formulated the idea for a new project (working titles: *Boots* and *Dr Martens*) which would appeal to streetwise kids who had forsaken comics. It would be modern, edgy and – again – overseen by Mills. The *wunderkind* appointed the former *Lion* editor, Geoff Kemp, to actually edit the comic, and together the two put together something that screamed of contemporary culture – particularly because it ripped off so much of it.

'You've never seen stories like these before!' ran the promotional pull-out featured in the likes of *Buster et al.*, as it bigged up the arrival of the title. In truth, readers kind of had – particularly if they were regular cinemagoers – but not in British comics.

Issue one of 'the sensational paper for boys!' gave some small indication of the furore that was to follow. '*Action* is deadly!' ran the editorial. 'You are about to experience the toughest stories ever – *Fast! Fierce! Fantastic!*' Here the paper introduced us to future *2000 AD* and *Crisis* editor Steve McManus, its very own Action Man! He was appealing for readers' correspondence, offering to pay out a fiver for anything they printed, but later on in the issue he'd live up to his exotic *nom-de-plume* by blowing fire for the sake of some excitement. As the photographs showed the bearded real-life hero expelling flames from his mouth, he confessed, 'at one stage my face fungus nearly caught alight.'

So to the strips, and it was here the extent of *Action*'s pilfering became obvious. Leading the pack was 'Dredger', a *Dirty Harry* variant about a hard-nosed cop ('You're dead, pal! Dead!') and his by-the-book partner, Breed. 'Hellman of Hammer Force' was rather more original. Even though it was a war story, the hero was a German panzer commander who had no truck with the Nazi party or the SS. Instead he just wanted to fight a good clean battle, declaring, as he bore down on a

Belgian convoy, 'we kill tanks – not men if we can help it.' Naturally, this meant he got up the nose of his superiors and some readers too, who couldn't quite handle the concept of 'your favourite squarehead' being a goody: 'How is it that a German can be a hero?' wrote one.

Following on was a thinly disguised version of boxer Mohammed Ali, in the form of 'Black Jack'. Up-and-coming heavyweight Jack Barron dreamed of being world champion and, in this first instalment, showed off his prowess by dancing around pugilist 'Irish' Tom Tully in the ring. A rags to riches tale, it didn't shy away from portraying the racism the hopeful experienced, his opponent here declaring, 'I'll teach you your place, ye black ballet dancer.'

By contrast, 'Play Till You Drop!' (a footballer who is blackmailed into throwing matches), 'The Coffin Sub' (standard 'Men at War' stuff, following the fortunes of the HMS *Conquest* in the waters of the Mediterranean) and 'Sport's Not For Losers!' (a tale of a fag-smoking layabout dragooned into joining Barcastle Harriers, and written by Action Man McManus himself) were disappointingly run-of-the-mill and could have conceivably appeared in the likes of *Lion*.

Far better was 'The Running Man' (also penned by McManus), the comic's own take on *The Fugitive* TV series, with athlete Mike Carter set up via plastic surgery to look like Don Scarlatti's son, who was on the run from the authorities for killing a policeman. 'Don't know why the cops want me dead,' declared the patsy as he speedily legged it from the strip, 'but I've got to run like I've never run before.'

Despite the exploits of Carter, Hellman, Black Jack and company, *Action* had one unarguable standout star – and again it came in the form of a movie rip-off. *Jaws* was still fresh in readers' minds; now, the Great White would produce an unofficial heir, in the form of 'Hookjaw'. So named because he had the blade of a game fisherman's harpoon lodged in his chin, readers were advised, 'when Hookjaw strikes – you only scream once!' The killer concept here was that the story was told from the shark's point of view, as it toured the seas mauling boats, men and other fish alike, and generally ensuring the strip's artist regularly ran low on red ink.

The first issue over, the comic exited with the line: '*Warning* to nervous readers – *don't* buy *Action*!' No one could claim they hadn't been sufficiently advised.

Almost immediately, trouble brewed up. After the edition hit the streets, the *Evening Standard* ran a story on the publication, entitled 'Aargh lives – but the blood is printed red'. Describing the comic as a 'deliberate, calculated and commercially minded attempt to cash in on What the Kids Want', it painted a picture of John Sanders as an uncaring mogul, 'unbuffetable by criticism'.

Two months later, the *Sun* took an interest, calling the publication 'the sevenpenny nightmare', but the comic continued unbowed.

Reflecting its unpopularity with readers, 'The Coffin Sub' was first to be dropped, making way for another war story, 'Green's Grudge War', a slightly more inventive tale of a soldier whose lust for glory regularly endangered his colleagues. Alas, the strip didn't quite come up to scratch, with Green finally copping a fatal bullet and being left face down on a German beach in September.

In May, the final under-achiever, 'Sport's Not For Losers!' was superseded by 'Death Game 1999', a re-working of the film *Rollerball*, featuring prison inmates playing the deadly sport of Spinball, a motorcycle-bound hockey game where body-count mattered as much as goals. Then, come September, 'Black Jack' bowed out. He may have finally won that championship, but he lost his sight in the process. Taking the strip's place was 'Kids Rule OK' (no relation to the later *Champ* story of the same name), an *über*-violent tale of a dark future set in 1986, where a plague had wiped out all the adults, leaving warring tribes of juveniles to fight it out on the lawless streets of Britain.

By this stage it was the *Daily Mail* that was now bristling, objecting to an edition of football strip 'Look Out for Lefty!' which depicted the hero's girlfriend flinging a bottle at a player on the pitch. To make matters worse, Lefty himself was seen to be endorsing her actions, declaring, 'Good ole Angie!' The paper brought in Football League secretary Alan Hardaker to exclaim: 'It is really appalling that there are people so brainless as to sell comics to children with stuff like this inside them. The man responsible ought to be hit over the head with a bottle himself.'

The outcry rumbled on, with John Sanders called to account on the teatime news programme *Nationwide*, where Frank Bough attempted to wrong-foot the exec by suddenly jettisoning the agreed line of discussion to launch an all-out attack on the comic, while questions were asked in the House, prompting a meeting between Sanders and Home Secretary Willie Whitelaw.

The heat was certainly on, and now Mary Whitehouse's National

Viewers and Listeners' Association, and the Responsible Society joined in to also pour scorn on the endeavour. Meanwhile, pressure group The Delegates Opposing Violent Education festooned issues of the comic with stickers declaring, '*Caution*. This is a *blacked* publication.'

But it wasn't to be any of the campaigners who struck the fatal blow. In fact, it was the high street newsagent chain WH Smith who – legend has it – made disquieting rumbles about possibly refusing to stock the comic. Reaction to this was immediate, with IPC pulling the title in October while the editorial team were instructed in no uncertain terms to dim down the violent content. When it returned in December claiming, 'We're back! We're sensational!' it couldn't have been further from the truth. With no acknowledgement made to the reasons behind its hiatus, 'Kids Rule OK' and – another strip – 'Probationer' (more urban-set ultra violence, this time written by the Money Man himself, Stuart Wales) were dropped without explanation, while bland racing story 'Roaring Wheels' and safe sporting yarn 'Double Dynamite' took their place. 'Death Game 1999', meanwhile, had been renamed the rather-less-exciting 'Spinball', while Hookjaw took to chomping on his victims off-panel.

Surprisingly, the comic continued in this emasculated form for nearly a year – but it was all too clear the sparkle had gone. From being one of IPC's best-selling titles, it went on to stink the place out in terms of sales. In November 1977, the 'exciting news inside' arrived – the title was to be swallowed up by big brother *Battle*.

Thankfully, by this time there was something new on the scene, another comic created by the *Action* team which, over the years, would establish its own reputation for violence and mayhem: *2000 AD*.

Battle
(IPC Magazines Ltd, 1975-1988, every Thursday)

War and boys' comics had been a winning combination since, well, the war, really – but never was the connection so expertly essayed than in the Seventies. DC Thomson had been the first to hurl a grenade into the market with the dynamic *Warlord* in 1974, but IPC were commendably quick to respond by bringing out its own guns 'n' guts publication just six months later.

Although the title's stories were mainly rooted in the Thirties and

Forties, it displayed modern sensibilities (the only thing remotely old-fashioned about it being the initial addendum of 'Picture Weekly' to the name) that were driven by an uncommon desire to display, unflinchingly, the shit side of combat.

The first issue arrived on 8 March 1975, with a fully painted front cover featuring two soldiers emerging from flames to deliver leaden-death to an off-page enemy.

Inside, the drama proved to be bone-crunchingly good right from the off, as 'D-Day Dawson' introduced us to the titular sergeant who turned into a one man killing machine of gay abandon when he learnt that, thanks to a bullet near his heart, he only had one year to live. Other stories included the imaginative 'The Flight of the *Golden Hinde*' in which a bunch of Navy personnel set sail in a replica of Sir Francis Drake's ship only for war to break out while they were in the Indian ocean – whereupon they found themselves declared a legitimate target by the Germans; silky secret agent action in 'Day of the Eagle'; the kitchen-sink drama of short-arse marine Danny Budd in 'The Bootneck Boy'; and the hell-for-leather action of the 'Jap' killing 'Rat Pack'. This strip was particularly notable for the first time partnering-up of Wagner with *Wizard* mk II artist Carlos Ezquerra, forming what would become a formidable double-act – two years later the duo would create 'Judge Dredd' for *2000 AD*.

Alongside this, the issue's other highlight had to be 'The Terror Behind the Bamboo Curtain'. Set in 1942 in a Burma-based Japanese prisoner of war camp, captured British troops were forced to build a bridge across the Benwaddy River. Overseeing the construction was the aptly named commandant Colonel Sado who delighted in whisking ailing Tommies through those eponymous wooden drapes to try their luck in a booby-trapped filled assault course. 'The British pig no build bridge fast enough!' he reasoned here. 'Must be punished as example to you all!' Unfortunately for the bully-boy, newcomer 'big' Jim Blake was determined to smash the sadist's regime, and submitted himself for the treatment.

All in all, it had been a strong start but better stuff – much better – was waiting in the wings. On 10 January the following year, another Ezquerra-illustrated strip debuted on the centre pages. 'Like him – hate him! You can't ignore Major Eazy!' we were advised, as the laconic rifling-wielding former member of the Long Range Desert Group in Africa rode into battle in a chauffeur-driven Bentley.

Meanwhile, other characters came and went in a haze of gun smoke, few making as much of an impression (the schoolboys of 'Operation Shark', anyone?) until 'Darkie's Mob' appeared on the scene. Appropriately enough, one of the darkest strips to feature in the comic, it followed the fortunes of a ramshackle group of British soldiers behind Japanese lines in Burma (again), led by the obsessive Captain Joe Darkie, a half-English, half-Burmese approximation of Colonel Kurtz who was described by one of his own men as 'a hard, cruel son of Satan who led us into the very pit of hell.' 'They feared the Japs,' ran the strip's tagline, 'but they hated Darkie!' Written by John Wagner, who by then had stepped down from a short stint as *Valiant* editor, it was here readers came face-to-face with all manner of cruelty, including dysentery and crucifixion at the hands of the Japanese. The story was told via the blood-stained journal of Private Richard Shortland, and when it reached the conclusion ten months later, it didn't end prettily.

In October 1976, the title absorbed the free-falling *Valiant*, allowing 'One Eyed Jack' to continue policing the mean streets within its pages for a while – despite the fact his wasn't a war story (although he was an ex-marine) – and, rather more ludicrously, inviting the comedic Captain Hurricane to host its letters page, even though his blustering war effort stood for pretty much everything *Battle* didn't.

The following year brought the comic's hundredth issue in January, an event celebrated by the serialisation of a 'fantastic' A to Z pull-out booklet on war. Inside, the Rat Pack licked their wounds following a disastrous mission that had left their leader, Major Taggart, seemingly fatally wounded. In stepped none other than Major Eazy to take over the top job in their party for the next four months.

That same issue also saw the start of 'Johnny Red', the tale of a former RAF pilot who, via a series of accidents, ended up leading a Russian fighter squadron, the Falcons, on missions against the Germans. Thanks to a close encounter with a booby-trapped stove, he'd also developed the annoying habit of occasionally losing his vision (usually when he was involved in some piece of airborne devilment) meaning readers quickly grew to fear those panels featuring our man rubbing his eyes in anguish: 'I can hardly see. The control panel! What's happening to me?'

In November, the title merged with the now troubled *Action*, announcing 'it's all systems go in the new...*Battle Action*.' With 'seven big stories' every week, the appropriated title contributed *Rollerball*-esque feature 'The Spinball Wars', relatively unusual German war hero 'Hellman of Hammer Force' and tough cop 'Dredger' (who made One Eyed Jack look like a right wuss) to the mix.   However, for many, all of the above had been just an extended preamble to the arrival of what would become the title's most respected and best-loved strip. As issue two hundred arrived at the start of 1979, readers were introduced to 'Charley's War'. 'He was a boy soldier pitched into the horror of the World War One trenches!' ran the billing on the cover. Inside, we met sixteen-year-old Charley Bourne, an idealistic dreamer who lied about his age to join the army. Written by Pat Mills, it was nothing less than a sustained anti-war polemic, the title character finding his naïve expectations of honour and adventure being overturned by the reality of senseless killing and inept leadership. Skilfully depicted by original 'Roy of the Rovers' comic-strip artist Joe Colquhoun (who'd been pulled off 'Johnny Red' to work on this new venture) it was grim stuff indeed, but supremely moving, more than living up to the film, *Oh! What a Lovely War*, which had inspired it in the first place.

Battle – © Egmont UK Ltd

As the Eighties arrived, *Battle* was firing on all cylinders with a strong mix of blood, guts, flying lead and – against all the odds – thoughtful pieces on the nature of combat. However, change was on the cards, and in February 1982, the comic unveiled a new look that would see its remit extend to include generic adventure stories. 'Tom Turpin drives into a lot of danger when he takes on a trucking job in the USA!' was the premise behind the *BJ and the Bear* rip-off, 'Truck Turpin', while another TV series – *The Professionals* – got a rather more imaginative reworking in 'The Hunters: SI6'. Here we were introduced to Larry Fox and Ned Hare who, rather neatly, played the part of two cops in a TV series, but were also undercover agents in real life. Meanwhile, in 'The Fists of Jimmy Chang' a Bruce Lee lookalike tangled with a bunch of Triad heavies who were leaning on his poor old granddad.

Although the three newcomers were pretty exciting, you couldn't escape the feeling that from hereon in, that special *Battle* bullishness was being diluted, the comic now having little to differentiate it from other run-of-the-mill boys' titles. And, indeed, that proved to be the case as things rapidly took a turn for the worse. In 1983, the title was changed to *Battle Action Force*, IPC having done a deal with Palitoy to promote their dinky Action Man-esque range of dolls. The result was the inclusion of three new strips, all emblazoned with the toy line's logo and set in the present day. This quickly turned into a sixteen-page pull-out supplement as commercialism bit deeper.

Then, in 1985, things got worse as Pat Mills opted out of writing a new 'Charley's War' strip set during the Second World War when it became clear the company wouldn't be willing to pay him to research the subject matter. Scott Goodhall took up the scripting reins – in the main because Colquhoun was keen to keep the story running – but it was never the same.

As the comic's tenth anniversary arrived, it celebrated by devoting a page to ten classic covers of years past, while Captain Hurricane proclaimed on his letters pages: 'Let's look forward to many more years of exciting reading in *Battle Action Force!*' As it happens, 'many more years' was looking a bridge too far for the paper, and Hurricane in particular. In 1986, Marvel UK acquired the rights to comic-strip adaptations of Action Force, which meant *Battle* had to revert back to its original title in December 1986, as the junior Action Men shipped out *en masse* for their own self-titled weekly publication from the 'House of Ideas', which would run from 1987 to 1988.

Robbed of its team of heroes, the comic's creators simply came up with their own, and thus, at the start of 1987, we had *Battle with Storm Force*. A suspiciously similarly named troupe of teeth-gritting toughies ('The most exciting fighting team in the world'), they were led by The Mole, a beady eyed, bald-headed, wheelchair-bound character, on missions against various evil-doers, plus regular clashes with the nefarious Tarantula and his hoard of baddies, the Web Masters – a name doubtlessly less thrilling now than it was in its day.

Alongside this proto-Power Rangers stuff, the Captain was finally pensioned off from correspondence duty, and the comic became content to lay on a whole host of reprint action as Charley found himself back in the First World War, while Johnny Red and Vietnam strip 'Fighting Mann' also made a return. Rather more interesting was 'Invasion!', which detailed the fairly recent Falklands War from the point of view of young islander Tommy Baker – 'It...it's like a scene from a war film...only this is for *real*!'

Come January 1988, it was all over for the once great boys' comic, which was now submitting itself to the tender mercies of *Eagle* **mk II**. Combined, the two titles promised 'war in the future!' and 'war in the past!' as the 'Charley's War' and 'Johnny Red' reprints continued, along with the inevitable nonsense from the Storm Force crew.

For the first eight years of its life, *Battle* was undeniably a fantastic publication, but everything that had happened since the Action Force invasion had left the paper looking progressively weaker and insipid. Nonetheless, it had been responsible for bringing Pat Mills and John Wagner in from girls' papers – and that was a huge achievement indeed. It's fair to say that without this publication, the British comics industry would have been significantly different: we certainly wouldn't have got the mega-violence of *Action*, and its doubtful whether *2000 AD* would have toddled along in 1977 without the crucial groundwork laid down by the Rat Pack, D-Day Dawson and chums.

The Beano
(DC Thomson, 1938-ongoing, every Tuesday)

'Two big comics every week from now on!' ran the publicity campaign. '*The Dandy*'s new companion paper is coming!'

Despite being *The Dandy*'s little brother (it turned up eight months down the line), *The Beano* has to be Britain's most influential and best-known comic ever. Its roll call of stories ('Dennis the Menace', 'Biffo the Bear', 'The Bash Street Kids', 'Jonah', 'Minnie the Minx', 'Roger the Dodger' *et al.*) presents a veritable greatest hits package of well-known characters, many of whom have cross-pollinated into other titles and media for a life outside the confines of the comic.

And – like younger siblings everywhere – throughout its life, the publication has been that little bit cheekier and more effervescent than its slightly staid brother. There's a sparkle about *The Beano* which no other comic has ever managed to replicate (although **Nutty** came close).

That said, upon its launch it was saddled with one of the dopiest characters ever.

Dated 30 July 1938 and sporting a mascot in the shape of a dungaree-clad black youth (who looked like he'd just come off the plantation) chomping on a melon, it led with 'Big Eggo'. This featured a yolk-obsessed ostrich ('Someone's taken my egg again,' although how a male bird managed to produce such a thing in the first place was glossed over) whose long hairy neck and legs hardly made for a cute and cuddly character. With no real story to drive him – although sometimes it was hinted he was in charge of some sort of bizarre zoo – the big bird had an occasional penchant for cruelty. In issue eighteen, he donned a spiked helmet with which he menaced a bear whose only crime had been to rebuff his offer of a bun. And then, much later on, he force-fed a rugby ball to a snake, before affixing the creature to the ground by driving a pitchfork around its neck. Oh yes, Big Eggo could certainly be a big bastard when the mood struck him.

Packed with a free 'whoopee mask', inside *The Beano Comic* (as it was called up until 1950) sported what now seems like an uncharacteristic mix of text stories, picture-strips with text underneath and kosher comic-strip fare. Sticking out like a sore thumb – and proving that even in its early days DC Thomson wasn't averse to turning its characters into comic ringers, shunting them from title to title – was *Rover*'s (DC Thomson, 1922-73) leopard-skin-wearing Tarzan wannabe, Morgyn the Mighty. Here, the presumably Welsh (if the spelling of that name is anything to go by) muscle man stepped out for a written yarn full of derring-do.

Meanwhile, in the comic-strip realm we had 'Ping: The Elastic Man' which introduced us to an always chipper but grotesque-looking little chap who was blessed/cursed (it depends on how you look at it, really) with a body that had the qualities of Stretch Armstrong. 'Helpful Henry' was a hapless young chap whose efforts to assist people always backfired, while 'Contrary Mary' was a clued-up donkey who generally had the last laugh. 'Wee Peem' gave us a mischievous little lad with an oversized head whose future adventures would be pepped up no end thanks to some magic pills, and 'Big Fat Joe' ('He hasn't been weighed since the age of three – the weighing-machine always broke, you see') brought us good-natured laughs with the morbidly obese juvenile.

However, it was to be a happy little chap from a rather different stock who'd provide *The Beano* with its first real superstar. Marmaduke, the young Lord of Bunkerton, was 'son of a duke but always pally with the beezer kids of Ash-Can Alley' (they were big on rhyming couplets back then). This blue-blooded whippersnapper in his Eton suit lived a privileged life and no mistake. The opening episode took place on his birthday and revealed a huge stash of presents had been deposited for him, including a box of Meccano, various sporting gear and a train set. But, news that Algernon, Percival and Vernon Tootle were on their way to present him with a further gift left 'Lord Snooty' (as he was known by his chums) decidedly down. Opting to sneak out of the building to meet up with his real pals in that under-privileged street, he donned a standard-issue ragamuffin costume (including a conspicuous patch on the arse of his trousers) and opted for a bit of goat-drawn go-kart tom-foolery instead.

A clear message that life on the breadline was actually far more worth-while than an existence spent in ivory towers, it was doubtlessly hugely comforting for readers whose dads had gone on the Jarrow March just two years previously.

All in all, it wasn't a bad debut, and for the next few months *The Beano* carried on rattling out the fun stuff. Alas, it wasn't long before dark shadows were on the horizon as the comic found itself plying its humour against a backdrop of war. Like *The Dandy*, the title quickly proved itself ready and willing to do its bit for the nation's morale. While the mightily bearded Hairy Dan used some of his face-fuzz to mend a tank's caterpillar tracks, the big-eared Rip Van Wink ('He's 700 years old') joined the Navy, Pansy Potter ('The strong man's daughter' who'd arrived during Christmas 1938) duked it out with a U-boat, and Big Eggo unveiled a Japanese secret agent ('Here's the spy – he's no Chink, he's a Jap!'). Alongside that, the comic also went straight to the top, with

'Musso the Wop', a thick-lipped parody of a hapless Mussolini – much in the same vein as *The Dandy*'s crack at Hitler in 'Addie and Hermy: The Nasty Nazis'.

But, out of all these characters, Lord Snooty was the one who really went to town over the conflict. First mentioning the situation in his strip on 6 January 1940, he and his pals made life hell for the Evil Axis. 'With Snooty and the gang at war – those Germans really get what for!' indeed, causing merry hell for parachuting Jerries with their hoard of giant moths, teaching seals to catch bombs, sending overgrown measles germs into Berlin and coaxing the enemy into dropping propaganda pamphlets over Bunkerton castle so that the paper could be fed to Gertie, who needed fattening-up prior to entering a goat show at the town hall. Not for nothing did The Führer kick himself in the backside, declaring: '*Der dinsniggled* Lord Snooty has fooled me again!'

Now appearing fortnightly (it had been alternating weeks with *The Dandy* since 1941, in an effort to save paper stock), *The Beano* nonetheless came out of the war years in fairly good shape. But better was yet to come. In January 1948, it was 'Hip hurrah! Hip hooray! Biffo Bear is here today!' as the famous black, hairy mammal supplanted Big Eggo on the cover – the ostrich being demoted to a half-page black and white strip, before being ditched altogether, save for a regular gig standing guard over the comic's logo; that melon chomper now consigned to history.

In 1949, Lord Snooty took a break from the publication, to return the following year with a new line-up for the gang. Happy Hutton, Hairpin Huggins, Skinny Lizzie and Gertie the Goat were all brought back for one last hurrah, before being replaced by new chums drawn from other less prestigious strips. The comic's original gut-bucket, Big Fat Joe, was in, as was the wide-eyed star of 'Doubting Thomas' and the vain lead character in 'Swanky Lanky Liz'. In addition to these three, the new crew also consisted of twins Snitch and Snatch (who'd jumped on board near the end of 1938), Rosie (who'd long since gone blonde) and the redoubtable Scrapper.

However, an even bigger event in the comic's history would not only bequeath it with its most famous character of all, but also throw up a curious footnote in the annals of funny paper history. In the issue dated 17 March 1951 we met a scowling, jaggy haired troublemaker who baited his dad by constantly walking on the grass in the park, despite signs declaring such a practice was forbidden. Drawn by Davey Law, 'Dennis the Menace' was a partial reworking of 'The Wee Fella', which he'd created for *People's Journal*. On the same day this new character's debut issue went on sale, in America cartoonist Hank Ketcham premiered his comic-strip about a rabble-rousing child, also titled 'Dennis the Menace'. It had to be serendipity, and while both would go on to win fans on either side of the Atlantic, 'our' Dennis was by far the stronger personality.

Originally clad in shirt, tie and shorts, it would take a couple of months before the official uniform of menacing – that hooped sweater – was established. But, right from the off there was something special about this strip; its juvenile lead living in a very real recognisable world, less whimsical than the savannahs stalked by Biffo and the like. Immediately, Dennis caught children's imagination and – perhaps more importantly – stoked the creativity of reader Leo Baxendale, whose jaw had dropped when he'd first clapped eyes on the character. Prompting him to send off samples of his work to DC Thomson, his eventual involvement would result in the creation of a fleet of stalwarts for the paper.

1953 was a good year for the comic. First, Dennis was promoted from a half to a full page strip, before being given the colour back page. Then, in April, the comic ran a trailer for a new feature: 'Roger the Dodger'. 'Is Roger really a dodger?' it asked, accompanied by a couple of panels from what would be his debut appearance. 'These pictures are only part of a funny story told in pictures next week…and the story tells you why Roger is the world's craftiest dodger. He is trickier than a cageful of monkeys.' And, indeed he was. The slacker kid who'd continually conspire to shirk his duties and get things done the easy way was another instant hit.

In September young Jumbo Johnson hoofed his football into a scientist's garden and came face-to-face with a legion of miniature troops. Taking command of the tiny army, he became 'General Jumbo'.

October then brought Baxendale's first original work (until then he'd been filling in on various established strips), 'Little Plum'. Created as a Red Indian version of Dennis (the artist admits to even giving him the Menace's distinctive mouth), 'your redskin chum' was notable for sporting a bright white nose (despite the rouge colour of his skin) and the regular 'um' in his speech pattern.

Two months later, another Menace-inspired character made her first appearance, also coming from Baxendale's pen. At the suggestion of editor

George Mooney, Minnie the Minx was as visually near to Dennis as possible. She too wore a hooped sweater, while her black beret was supposed to mirror her inspiration's famous shock of hair. Slightly less intent on causing mayhem, she was more interested in beating up boys (using her patented 'double whammy' punches) and was – in the artist's words – more 'an Amazonian warrior' than an out-and-out trouble-maker.

And still, the hits kept on coming. In 1954, 'When the Bell Rings' began. Yet another Baxendale-drawn strip (prompting the artist to move up to Dundee to be near the DC Thomson offices) it detailed the mayhem caused by Class 2B, and generally culminated in a large chaos-packed panel by way of a finale. The first characters introduced were Danny, Toots and the caretaker, but as the weeks passed a full cast was built up, Toot's brother Sidney joining the crew, as did Fatty, Wilfred (who was always half hidden inside his roll-neck jumper), 'Erbert, the pug-ugly Plug, deeply stupid Smiffy and, finally, Spotty. In 1956, the story was retitled 'The Bash Street Kids' and *The Beano* had yet another success on it hands.

Before the decade was out, there was just time for another iconic character to enlist, as the calamitously cursed Jonah ('Arrgh! It's 'im!') signed on for his nautical tour of duty. During this era, the comic still sported regular adventure strips, but their time was fast running out.

When 16 September 1961 arrived, *The Beano* celebrated its thousandth edition with an oversized cake on the cover. The impressive array of personalities who were all competing to nab more than their fair share of the concoction (Dennis characteristically shoving a stick of dynamite into it, musing: 'This'll be quicker than cutting it') would mostly still be recognised by kids of today. Newcomers to the party were 'The Three Bears', yet another strip visualised by Baxendale, and inspired by the furry creatures he'd taken to drawing in the 'Plum' strips.

As the decade continued more notable features arrived – although none would prove to be anywhere near as illustrious as the creations of the Fifties. Billy Whizz was a super-fast egg-headed boy whose curious haircut made him look as though he had antenna growing out of his forehead; Billy the Cat was a lad who fought crime in the town of Burnham while clad in black and wearing a crash helmet suitably modified to look like a feline's head; and 'Pup Parade' translated The Bash Street Kids into canine form. There was a significant change afoot for Dennis too, who on 31 August 1968, acquired pet pooch Gnasher.

But there was an ever bigger development to come for the young anarchist. As the Seventies arrived, it was becoming increasingly clear poor old Biffo was looking a tad old-fashioned, and couldn't really compete with the Menace's charm. It was inevitable, then, that he'd finally make his move, booting Biffo off the front of the 14 September 1974 edition. Still, the furry fella had enjoyed a reasonable innings, having had the cover to himself for the last twenty-six years.

By the mid- to late Seventies, a standard issue of *The Beano* would lead with Dennis on the front and back and boast inside a mixture of 'Pup Parade', 'Minnie the Minx', 'Lord Snooty', 'Ball Boy' (the football-mad chap who'd arrived in 1976), 'Baby Face Finlayson' (the superbly ugly infant bandito whose adventures started in 1972) 'The Bash Street Kids', 'The Three Bears', 'Billy Whizz', 'Roger the Dodger', 'Biffo the Bear', 'Little Plum' and three other sundry strips (such as 'Wee Nevis', 'Grandpa' and 'Tom, Dick and Sally'). Pretty much everyone a winner, it was a seriously impressive line-up.

The 5 June 1976 brought the arrival of the 'Dennis the Menace Fan Club', *The Beano*'s own answer to *Warlord*'s 'Secret Agents' loyalty scheme. For a mere 30p postal order readers would be sent an official fan club badge, a furry Gnasher button (which, brilliantly, had moveable googly eyes), a membership card, 'club secrets' and a smart wallet. Who could refuse all that booty? The mandate for bashing softies everywhere was quickly taken up.

With the Dennis franchise ever-expanding, in 1979 he acquired a new pet, a disgustingly hairy pig by the name of Rasher, with hooked teeth and a habit for ramming people.

Into the Eighties, the onslaught of notable new characters was drying up a little, although the filthy fingered Smudge wasn't half-bad, nor was the tearaway tot 'Ivy the Terrible'. Rasher got his own strip in 1985 ('A lot of readers have said they want to see more of my pet pig…' explained Dennis), while 'The Bash Street Kids' Smiffy briefly went solo in 1986.

That was also the year the comic courted publicity by having Gnasher go 'missing' for a brief period. In later years they'd repeat the trick by fooling the media into thinking Dennis was set upon trading in his sweater and shorts for a 'trendy' tracksuit.

On 26 June, 1990, the comic celebrated its 2500th issue with Dennis doing a 'twenty-one catty salute!' With children's weeklies finding life increasingly tough, *The Beano* was adapting to survive. That same year witnessed the launch of a 'Dennis the Menace' cartoon on the Children's Channel and then, in September 1993, *The Beano Video* arrived. The following month, the comic went full colour and glossy for the first time, as Dennis deluged his co-stars (which included The Numskulls, who'd fled from the closure of *Beezer and Topper* just a few weeks previously) with paint.

When the comic's sixtieth birthday came round in 1998, it celebrated in fine style, bringing General Jumbo out of retirement and reworking that original 'Big Eggo' strip to include a cameo from Gnasher. Then, a month later, Dennis was endowed with a menacing little sister, Bea, and the all-new *Beano* Club was launched, charging a tenner for a poster, T-shirt, mini torch and a fun-sized edition of the comic.

With the arrival of the new millennium, *The Beano* even embraced the World Wide Web, launching *beanotown.com*, while further videos and merchandising followed. In 2003, there was more cause to celebrate as the comic turned sixty-five. 'We may be entering the ranks of the grey brigade,' confessed its current editor, Euan Kerr, 'but there is life in the old dog yet.' Aside from publishing a replica edition of issue one, the regular comic invited back some of the characters from that first number 'for one week only'. Thus, when Dennis' gran gave him a pair of shorts originally owned by the star of 'Jimmy and his Magic Patch', the lad was whisked back in time to 1938. Once there, he promptly hooked up with a black and white array of chums, and dragged them into the present day.

'Come on, join us in the rest of the comic for some laughs,' suggested Minnie the Minx to Ping as she took him by the arm.

The result was a supremely good-natured, nostalgic mix ('Ivy the Terrible' even adopting the old pictures-with-explanatory-captions format of old) which must have truly baffled the comics' current readership. 'Toddle-pip! We're off back to jolly old '38' declared Lord Snooty as the worlds-collide experiment reached its conclusion.

And so *The Beano* continues to this day, resisting the pressure to turn itself into the feature-packed organ that represents the content of most of its peers on the shelf. Nope, it's still wall-to-wall comic-strips thankfully, although the empire now also encompasses DVDs, *Classic Comics* reprints, new fun-size editions, calendars and even novels.

In January 2005, readers were invited to phone in votes for a new 'Comic Idol' competition to decide which out of three prospective characters should be given their own full-time strip in the paper. The winner was Zap Zodiac, 'a miniature alien on a mission to study human life.' How long his endeavour lasts is up for grabs, but here's hoping he gets a decent crack of the whip as he tries to follow in the footsteps of the comic's many greats – Big Eggo not withstanding.

Beeb
(Polystyle Publications Ltd, 1985, weekly)

You had to hand it to Polystyle, they weren't quitters. Following a failed attempt to steal *Look-in*'s crown with *Target* in 1978, the publishing company were back at it again, despite the collapse of its own *TV Comic* and the failure of DC Thomson's *Tops* the previous year.

As the name suggests, *Beeb* was created in co-operation with the BBC, and packaged as nothing less than the official young person's organ for all things pertaining to buttons one and two on the telly. As such, this not only gave it a huge cache, but also put it in direct opposition to the ITV-centric Junior *TV Times*.

To capitalise on the corporation's backing, issue one triumphantly led with a montage of logos and photos from BBC television shows carefully arranged to appeal to both boys and girls. Yep, all your faves were here, including Janet Ellis and a *Blue Peter* ship; dull mid-Eighties *Doctor Who* wannabe *The Tripods*; Janet 'Ro-land' St Clair, Julie Marchant and some other spods in a *Grange Hill* classroom; the *Saturday Superstore* gang; crap but ubiquitous cartoon series *The Family Ness*; a picture of Kenny Dalglish (just to offset Janet and those *GH* girls, presumably); and US import, the *Tron*-lite crime-fighter, *Automan*. A dizzying array of talent indeed, and nicely capped off by a free 'popchart' – a calendar detailing the birthdays of such luminaries as Michael Sundin and The Thompson Twins' Joe Leeway.

So what about the comic strips? From the off, the adaptation of *One by One* was a bit of a puzzle. This teatime, middle-class, plodding drama series about 'zoo vet' Donald Turner was surely not the sort of thing to get the kiddies fired up. Rather closer to the mark – even if it was drawn from an equally dull source – was 'The Tripods'. OK, so the actual TV series was no great shakes, but at least this was proper sci-fi action, and superbly illustrated to boot. As the series continued its run in *Beeb*, a new character in the form of a young woman called Fizzio was introduced, to appeal to the publication's female readers. Similarly well-suited was *Automan*, which translated into a perfectly serviceable strip, albeit without the thrill of actually getting to see his car do that great right-angle turning thing. And then there was 'Grange Hill' which in the main covered the comings and goings of Zammo, Fay and company – as had *School Fun*'s own *GH* strip the previous year. With all the teachers from Bullet to Bronson present and correct and even proper Grange Hill uniforms hoving into view in later weeks, this was probably the famous school's best-ever representation inside a comic.

Fulfilling the requisite humour role were adaptations of *The Family Ness* and *Bananaman*. The latter was clearly a specific take on the fruit-based superhero's TV series rather than a straight port over from his *Nutty* strip, with the copyright note ('Bananaman Productions Ltd') being a real signifier of how huge the character had now become.

A potpourri of famous faces, issue sixteen arguably had the most infamous line-up ever. Not only did it sport latter day conspiracy theorist and lapsed Son of God David Icke doing his regular sports stuff, but on the front of the publication we had a worlds collide meeting between Erkan Mustafa, aka *Grange Hill*'s Roland Browning, and Gary Glitter headlined, somewhat unfortunately, 'What's Eating Roland...?' Inside, things stepped up a notch as the bewigged glam rocker was photographed threatening the child with a brandished chair. So: Ike,

Glitter – could things get any worse? Of course they could, because also on show was Michael Jackson who was reportedly interested in appearing in an 'all black' version of *Oliver!* and, apropos of absolutely nothing, a big picture of Jonathan King on page 23. It's a line-up of personalities you probably won't be seeing in any other 'junior' publication ever again.

Despite *Beeb*'s unique access to BBC stars and rather nice production values, the paper just didn't work out. Across town, *Look-In* editor Colin Shelbourn had followed its progress with interest but never really felt his paper was under much threat. According to him, *Beeb* was never afforded the sort of onscreen advertising its Polystyle overlords had expected from the corporation, and so withered on the vine.

Whether that's correct or not, the publication didn't see out the year and after just twenty issues, the whole thing ground to a halt amid rumours a *Tripods* special was set to follow. However, nothing materialised. Nonetheless, the publication did provide the impetus for what Sherbourne would describe as 'the first real head-on challenge *Look-In* had ever had,' *Fast Forward*.

The Beezer
(DC Thomson, 1956-1990, every Tuesday)

See: *The Topper*.

OK, not quite – but it is true that the history of *The Beezer* is so tied-up with the fate of its big brother comic as to make them almost indivisible from one another. Let the record state, then, that *The Beezer* was the one with Ginger in it.

Following hard (well, three years later) on the success of *The Topper*, *The Beezer* was a similarly formatted tabloid-sized paper that even bandied about the same free gift its sibling had used upon its own arrival, namely a paper 'Whizz Bang!' (although *The Topper* had referred to its own by the equally exciting name of a 'Big Crack Bang'). That first issue sported the new DC Thomson mischievous child character Ginger on the front. Drawn by Dudley D Watkins (who was also turning out 'Mickey the Monkey' for the other paper) it was finely rendered stuff, although it seemed that the USP here was simply the fact our hero had red hair. Nevertheless, who could deny a character who – after struggling to get warm all day – retired to bed with a load of hot water bottles and bid us, the readers, a cheery 'good night chums!'

Bringing up the rear inside, there was a familiar mix of serious and not-so-serious fare. Stories such as 'The Voyage of the Bushwhacker', 'Mick on the Moon' and 'Lone Wolfe' were beautifully detailed pieces, not dissimilar to some Victorian etching from the pages of *Strand Magazine*, while the fantastic 'Pop, Dick and Harry' (accurately billed as 'laughs with a dad and his tricky twins'), 'Calamity Jane', *Rover* (DC Thomson, 1922-73) refugee 'Nosey Parker' and 'The Hillys and the Billys', amongst others, secured the guffaws. But it was the back page which really made readers fall in love with this new venture.

Legendary comic artist Leo Baxendale (who originally drew the likes of 'Little Plum' and 'The Bash Street Kids' for *The Beano*) claims that when he was first asked to pen 'The Banana Bunch' he thought it was a new feature for *The Topper*. However, after delivering some weeks' worth of work, it was revealed his strip was actually destined for the nascent *The Beezer*. According to the pensmith, it soon became the comic's most popular feature, with its huge (half-page) intricately detailed scenes of mayhem. There was no denying this was top stuff; issue three's was a doozy as said Bunch got up to all sorts of mischief in a train station, including stealing the numbers off the carriages, plugging the guard's whistle with chewing gum and blowing hot steam into the face of an army officer and down the pants of a fat commuter. Hooray!

However, for some reason the powers that be decreed the strip was not suitable back page fodder and it was quickly demoted to the comparative ignominy of just two colours on the inside of the paper. Readers wrote in their droves to complain, but the decision had been made, and that's where the fruit-themed friends stayed.

Despite these shenanigans, the format had been put in place (once 'Baby Crocket' from *The People's Journal* jumped on board) to take the comic through the decade and into the Sixties. Along the way there was some excitement as the publication – rather incongruously – took the decision in 1966 to run an adaptation of US puppet sci-fi series *Space Patrol*.

In 1976, *The Beezer* swallowed up the ailing, and relatively short-lived *Cracker* ('More Laughs! More Fun! in this great new two-in-one' it assured us) to form an equally transient pull-out section, and did much the same three years later when *Plug* ran out of steam, meaning the loafing 'supergoon' was appearing both within its pages, and those of 'The Bash Street Kids' in *The Beano*. Confusing.

By the start of the Eighties, *The Topper* had switched format, dropping down from tabloid to A4 size and, following in its sister's footsteps as ever, *The Beezer* did the same in 1981 without so much as an 'important news for all readers inside'-style warning. New, more overtly modern characters such as 'Beefy Dan: The Fast Food Man' and a revamped 'Banana Bunch' appeared, but when the likes of Harry 'Loadsamoney' Enfield were creeping inside the paper and Ginger was booted off the front by Johnny-come-lately 'Tommy Britain', the end was suddenly looking all too inevitable.

When it came, it wasn't as bad as all that. Logically enough, DC Thomson merged *The Beezer* with its sister paper and formed a new publication *Beezer and Topper* (1990-3).

Buddy
(DC Thomson, 1980-1983, every Saturday)

As *Hotspur* began its steady descent into merger death with *Victor* – having recently taken the short-lived *The Crunch* with it – DC Thomson launched a new title aimed at 'boys who like action, adventure and sport!'

Buddy – © DC Thomson & Co., Ltd

Buddy was themed around the titular freckled scamp, and made for a publication which somehow seemed that little bit more 'street' than a lot of its stable mates.

This was the comic that boasted the adventures of the BMX-ing junior crime-fighters 'The Q-Bikes' (patrolling the city of Limethorpe on their specially equipped bikes, 'ready to help anyone in trouble'), the *Grange Hill*-esque activities of 'Tom Smith's Schooldays' ('The true-to-life story of one of Britain's top public schools') and 'Tuffy', the tale of a football-mad, caravan-dwelling orphan and his continual clashes with The Man (best personified by a rival mobile home-dwelling family who trashed his ramshackle abode declaring, 'Now we'll have a nice site all to ourselves! That was a mouldy old caravan, anyway!').

The front cover of that first issue sported a denim-jacketed Buddy gleefully firing off his 'pop pistol' to illustrate the comic's free gift ('comes with two plastic bullets'), which spoke volumes about the venture's loutish ethos. This was less true stories of men at war and more dispatches from the front line of urban Britain. Alongside the new crop of characters were a fleet drawn from the DC Thomson back catalogue, presenting comic-strip outings for 'Limp-Along Leslie' and 'The Wolf of Kabul' (both of whom had their stories originally delineated in text form inside *Wizard* mk I, (DC Thomson, 1922-63), new, very Eighties adventures for *The Beano*'s 'General Jumbo' and 'The Iron Fish', and what would become a regular back page berthing (and therefore in full colour) for some of its old 'Jonah' strips ('the biggest jinx on the seven seas').

But, *Buddy* still had more to offer. Alongside the excitement of continually rotating cover stars (Billy the Cat one week, The Huddersfield Hackers the next), the comic had an additional ace up its sleeve in the form of its 'Super Personality Series'. Two pages of real-life biogs told in comic-strip form, famous faces honoured included Andy Gray (in issue one), Daley Thompson, Ronnie Corbett, Ringo Starr ('I'm going to be a drummer when I grow up!' says the proto-Beatle at age thirteen, spying a kit in a shop window), Glenn Hoddle and Paul Daniels (culminating in the diminutive magician's appearance on *Blankety Blank* where he 'practically stole the show').

Alongside that, the inside back pages brought a treasury of educational goodness in the form of 'Buddy's World of Knowledge'. Building week-by-week to create a veritable junior encyclopaedia, this good-natured feature armed boys with 'facts you can baffle your pals with and impress your teacher!' Did you know that on 16 February 1980, 26-year-old Doris Rogers of Scarboro, Ontario set a new world record when she high-kicked 8,491 times in four hours, twenty-two minutes?

The first *Buddy* of 1983 brought changes as the comic got a minor makeover with the informal looking red-with-yellow edges logo (a DC Thomson staple, that) turned into a rather more staid effort. 'Stone-age soccer star' Klog also began gracing the publication doing a *Where's Wally?* by hiding in various locations on the front cover. What Buddy himself made of this incursion by a new mascot was left unrecorded. Photo content began creeping in too, with regular sports spreads and, somewhat improbably, a 'News Desk' ('if it's happening...we'll tell you about it!').

Unfortunately, it wasn't enough to save the comic from its own merger nightmare, and on 6 August of that year our freckle-faced friend had the ignominy of having to announce his own title was set to be consumed by, yup, *Victor* the following week. But it wasn't all bad news. The spirit of *Buddy* lived on in the newly launched *Spike* (a comic *Buddy* had been faithfully promoting since its inception in 1983) which would continue to essay the juvenile editor shtick into 1984.

Bullet
(DC Thomson, 1976-1978, every Tuesday)

DC Thomson were never slow at recognising when they were onto a winner. *Warlord* had quickly established itself as a smash hit, with its gritty (some might say unrelenting) tales of bloodshed pushing boys' comics to a rather edgier place than ever before. It was perhaps unsurprising, then, when Lord Peter Flint's nephew arrived to cut himself a hefty slice of the high-octane action.

The result was a new 'rough tough action story paper for boys!' which followed very firmly in its uncle's footsteps, to the point of affording its spokesman a luxurious nine pages of self-contained story every issue.

But, who was this exciting new chancer? If Flint was the John Steed of boys' comics, Fireball (as he was rather confusingly codenamed – surely Bullet would have been neater?) was the Jason King. Resplendent in his luxury-issue moustache, wavy hair and medallion, he wore his shirt open to the navel and travelled the world on the back of his steely business card: 'Fireball for hire – Mysteries solved, problems licked, lost things found, crooks straightened out, any time, any place: but...only tough jobs accepted.' A jack of all trades, he not only beat people up and, er, located missing property, he also hosted the 'Fireball Club' page (wherein, if you sent a postal order for 25p, you could get a wallet, a pendant, an identity card and – best of all – learn the secret of how he came to be so great) and still found time to boast to readers, 'what a punch-up I'm having in Paris – see centre pages'.

Bullet – © DC Thomson & Co., Ltd

A tremendously exciting and glamorous character, his connection with Flint wasn't made explicit at first, and despite his various references to 'Uncle Peter', the readers were slow to catch on and remained desperate to know what the smooth operator's real name was ('That, of course, is top secret! I've too many enemies who would like to know that'), how many Fireball agents there were ('Thousands') and, most importantly of all, what he liked to eat ('Food, mostly – but I've had to eat my words once or twice!'). When he started appearing in photo form on the letters page (a stagy looking male model, with 'tache and fringe visibly penned in) boys just went mental. 'A lot of you have been asking – am I just a drawing on a few pages in *Bullet*...or am I real?' he boomed. 'Well, the editor has decided I should answer – *so judge for yourselves!*'

Across weekly run-ins, often with a villainous woman named Cat, and high-kicking adventures around the globe, we gradually learned more and more about the hirsute harbinger of havoc, until finally it was time to tell all. By the end of 1977, 'Cadet Fireball' was revealing everything about our hero's younger years being educated by Flint as – moustache-less (but not medallion-less) – he picked up the art of kicking people in the throat.

In comparison to the loud-mouthed troubadour, *Bullet*'s supporting cast couldn't help but pale. 'Smasher' was a *Valiant*-style outing for a nasty big robot controlled by the evil (as if you needed telling) Doctor Doom (no relation to *The Fantastic Four*'s nemesis). 'Survivor' told the tale of Dick Arnold, whose plane crash-landed in the desert, 'Wonder Mann' was standard computer-augmented action man stuff, while 'Vic's Vengeance' was a dark yarn about a young lad trying to avenge his father's death at the hands of a gang in east-end London.

Naturally, stories came and went. 'Swooping Vengeance' was pretty good as Doctor Doom (him again) got his hands on a giant eagle and, yes, wrought chaos. 'Hunted' wasn't a bad effort either, a *Fugitive*-inspired strip following Benny Regan's efforts to evade an erroneous murder charge and track down the man with a missing finger who actually did it. However, the less said about 'The Killer Kangaroos' ('The terrors of the Outback!'), the better.

Bullet – which happened to hit the news-stands on the same day as IPC's *Action* – outlasted its rival by a clear year, but when times got rough it couldn't hack it, despite the tough-talking of its main character. As a result, Fireball was sent back into Uncle Peter's guardianship in 1978 as the whippersnapper's comic was engulfed by *Warlord*.

Bunty
(DC Thomson, 1958–2001, every Tuesday)

It may appear distinctly whitebread when we look back on it now, but *Bunty* was a pretty nifty read in its time. Indeed, some of its stories were positively ground-breaking, but, that said, there were still oodles of pages devoted to those girls' comic staples of ballet, horses and animals – as the first issue proved.

Coming with a free ladybird ring, and a Scottie dog positioned by the logo (because girls like Scottie dogs), it promised to be both 'the paper with topping picture stories' and 'the snappy picture story paper for girls'. A tall order, indeed.

Bunty – © DC Thomson & Co., Ltd

What the comics' creators were unaware of was the fact that within this first number, they'd stumbled upon the title's defining strip: 'The Four Marys'. 'Fun at boarding school with a frolicsome foursome' it may have been, but the adventures of the omni-named quartet (those surnames: Radleigh, Field, Simpson and Cotter) at St Elmo's School for Girls would provide *Bunty* with a perennially popular strip across its forty-three-year run. Forever stuck in the third form, the foursome would see off original head teacher Dr 'The Squawker' Gull, persevering with her replacement, the comparatively glamorous Miss Madeline Mitchell, while feuding with bullies, The Snobs and arranging the occasional innocent liaison with the chaps from the neighbouring boys' school.

Over the years, it may have seemed as though the girls were slow to change with the times – although flinging out reprints of 1969 strips ten years later couldn't have helped – but by the early Eighties the quartet had received a welcome image overhaul, even if they were still most likely to exclaim 'golly!' in moments of stress. Proof, if proof be needed, that their own brand of Enid Blyton-style adventures were impervious to age.

Other strips during *Bunty*'s run may have come and gone, but according to one-time scribe Bill Downey, they often shared a common theme. Apparently, what girls really liked was a 'waif-life creature' as the main character. The more winsome and fragile the better – witness the crushingly lonely 'Second-Hand Sue'; painfully thin street kid Winnie Johnson in 'Maid to be a Lady'; enslaved orphan Jenny Lane from 'Ballerina on a String'; 'Ragamuffin Queen' Nina who was even described as 'a twelve-year-old waif'; and thousands of others.

However, it would be grossly unfair to suggest all *Bunty* had going for it was 'The Four Marys' and a hefty dose of cruelty (besides, *Mandy* did the latter far more successfully). 'The Taming of Teresa' was a veritable 'Tarzan' for girls, detailing the exploits of the titular girl who'd been raised by wolves but was now being rehabilitated into polite society ('W-what's she doing?' 'She's getting to know you by your scent.'). And, who could resist the latter-day look at post-relationship bitterness, superbly titled 'When Harry Dumped Sally', 1974's exposé of the pop scene, 'My Brother's a Pop Star', or the tales of 'Balloon Girl', alien Nandi who – as a punishment for bad behaviour – was sent to the planet Earth to bring harmony to its people?

In 1987, *Bunty* swallowed up the relatively glossy *Suzy* (DC Thomson, 1982-7) and two years later did the same to *Nikki*. It was a chilling portent of things to come as times were getting hard for girls' comics. By the mid-Nineties, the publication was sporting photographic covers and stories in a bid to appeal to the now prevalent appetite for magazines, but it could never be enough. Unable to sustain itself, the weekly folded in 2001 (having clocked up an impressive 2249 issues), whereupon it turned into a monthly reprint magazine, 'for girls who love reading'.

This, in turn, lasted a desultory five months – a poor finale for what became Britain's last remaining girls' comic. Don't remember it this way.

Buster
(Fleetway Publications/IPC Magazines Ltd, 1960-2000, every Monday)

In the world of weekly humour comics, *Buster* rises tall, a monolith that ate up all other publications in its path – and that made for a hefty feast. During its near forty-year run, it consumed an incredible twelve titles, making it the comic where others went to die.

Of course, that means that by the end of its life, the paper was a hybrid of all sorts of different publications, a jackdaw creation taking the best from each corpse it plundered. If you think tracing the lineage of the **Whizzer and Chips** (which did the merger thing a fair few times in its life) cast list is a daunting prospect, this one requires a family tree etched out on a roll of wallpaper if you want to stand a chance of untangling the parents of Joker, Gus the Gorilla, Jack Pott, Pete and his Pimple *et al*. But, putting it simply, *Buster* was there before the rest of the Fleetway/IPC gang showed up, and still around after they'd all gone away again.

In 1959, Fleetway pissed off rival publishers Odhams Press by beating them to the draw and acquiring Amalgamated Press (Odhams would take out their bad mood on relative minnows Hulton, instead – see **Eagle** mk I, **Girl** mk I, **Robin** and **Swift** for more on that). Suitably emboldened by its new catalogue of titles, which included *Knockout* mk I (1939-63) and *Radio Fun* (1938-61), the company launched its own new kids' comic as it eyed up rivals DC Thomson.

Intended to take the wind out of **The Topper** and **The Beezer**, *Buster* was a tabloid-sized affair to begin with. However, it didn't just draw inspiration from those two publications – it also capitalised on the success of the *Mirror*'s 'Andy Capp'. With Fleetway being part of the Mirror Group, it was quite acceptable for the comic to claim its title character was the son of the light-hearted wife-beating drunkard. The fact that carnal intimacy between Andy and Flo always seemed a no-no was neither here nor there. Decked out in a flat cap that – much like his pop's headwear – covered his eyes, the youngster ambled into his new publication with a familiar air of nonchalance and talking in a very particular dialect ('Garn!'). All that was missing was the tab dangling from his mouth.

The first issue came free with 'Buster's Balloon Bleeper', and, surprisingly when we look back on it now, was absolutely stacked with adventure strips such as 'Sea Hawk', 'Warlord of the Sioux' and 'Phantom

Force Five'. In fact, during these early years the humour content made up only about twenty-five per cent of the comic's sixteen pages. Not the best of starts, maybe, but the title quickly picked up speed.

The following year, original 'Buster' artist Bill Titcombe was replaced by Hugh McNeill, and the character's look significantly changed, his eyes now visible and references to his famous father phased out.

By February, the comic acquired its taste for blood, as it devoured *Radio Fun*, transplanting the likes of 'Whacko!', 'Charlie Drake' and a reprint of the US *Superman* comics into its own line-up.

In 1962, the cloth-capped predator pounced upon another *Fun* prey. This time it was the antiquated *Film Fun* (Amalgamated Press/Fleetway Publications, 1920-62) that proved to be a little too slow on its feet. *Buster* still being new at this merger game, the comic made no song and dance about the acquisition (nor had it done so the previous year). Instead, it was far more interested in bigging up the free 'flying model' of the Vicker VC10 plane it had on offer inside, and *Film Fun*'s name was incorporated into the comic's logo via the smallest font possible. That's despite the fact the fallen title had brought along a fabulous Bruce Forsyth strip.

By the time of its third merger, the comic had reduced its paper size, increased its page count and weaned out most of the colour. Leaner and meaner, it now eyed up the bizarre *Big One* (Fleetway Publications, 1964-5). 'Britain's Biggest Comic for Boys and Girls' had been a rum venture all told – the dimensions of a broadsheet newspaper, it was home to a host of reprints taken from the Amalgamated Press archives. The fact it was running some of the same strips its new home had acquired from the *Fun* titles made the fusion all the more painless, although it was at least able to donate 'Sinbad Simms' (the adventures of one boy and his shark) to the mix.

As with the last merger, the bitter pill (at least for the fallen comic's readers) was sweetened by another aeronautical themed free gift – a construct-yourself 'Zoom-a-Jet' ('It soars! It loops! It climbs! It swoops!'). And this time, *Big One* got a pretty good crack of the whip as far as its share of the front page billing was concerned.

Still hungry for more, *Giggle* (Fleetway Publications, 1967-8) was the next to hove into view and, on 20 January 1968, the maw of *Buster* opened wide. With another humour comic digested, at long last it looked as though the cloth-capped lad's organ was finally turning into a presentable funny paper. In terms of comedy, it could now boast the latest twist in the 'Buster' saga, 'Buster's Dream-World' (the little chap suddenly developing narcolepsy and falling asleep in various locations which then informed his dreams); 'Freddie "Parrot Face" Davies' (a strip vehicle for the bowler-hatted raspberry-blowing comic who'd found fame on *Opportunity Knocks*); 'Captain Swoop: He's Half Man, Half Bird, Half Wit' (the bird-brained superhero whose arch-enemy was, inevitably, Catman); 'Tin Teacher' (*Hotspur*'s Iron Teacher's stupider little brother, perhaps); super-powered invertebrate 'Wonder Worm'; 'Mervyn's Monsters' (a bespectacled chap who ran Mervyn's Undercover Monsters – or MUM – who battled the Crafty Rascals' Union of Saboteurs and Hoodlums – CRUSH); Cruncher ('The tiny termite with the big appetite'); and Professor Nutcase (an inventive fella whose creations always backfired).

Of course, there was still adventure to be had. 'Galaxus: The Thing From Outer Space' was fine fare, detailing the woes of an ape-like alien stranded on Earth. Meanwhile, 'Fishboy: Denizen of the Deep' brought us H_2O infused excitement with a scantily clad web-handed lad, and was notable for one episode featuring an equally near naked leather-masked torturer whipping the unfortunate hero, providing an unlikely S&M thrill for a small portion of the readership.

Best of the batch had to be 'The Astounding Adventures of Charlie Peace'. It told the story of a Toby Jug-faced scoundrel who, after being transported from Victorian times to the present day, made numerous doomed attempts to carry on his criminal career: 'Now I'll make a quick snatch at somethin' and scarper!'

Around the start of 1969, keen-eyed (or maybe just anal) readers would have spotted an alteration in the small print on the front cover of the comic as '© Fleetway Publications Ltd' changed to '© IPC Magazines Ltd'. This wasn't the result of a buy-out, just the Mirror Group consolidating its juvenile branches under the one name.

Aside from that, things remained pretty much unchanged as *Buster* entered the Seventies. Doubtlessly feeling a bit peckish again, it was time another comic was sacrificed to its insatiable appetite. The poor sap this time was *Jet* (IPC Magazines Ltd, 1971), another stunted publication that couldn't cut it in the big bad world. The high-octane boys' paper only notched up a measly twenty-two issues before waving the white flag in the form of a 'There's some sensational news inside, pals!'

announcement in its final issue in September 1971.

When it sloped into *Buster* the following week, it received a warm welcome with a full front cover promoting its arrival. Its contribution to proceedings included a fantastically mental strip ('Von Hoffman's Invasion') about a disgruntled German scientist who'd created a gas that could enlarge creatures to a super size. He would then use them to 'attack anything symbolic of Great Britain's pride' which, in one instalment, meant him riding to war against the England football team while sitting astride a giant budgerigar. Luckily, brothers Barry and Joey Drake were always on hand to foil his efforts with their convenient can of shrinking spray.

As much fun as all this was, it couldn't hold a candle to 'Faceache', Ken Reid's brilliantly drawn strip about a boy who could 'scrunge' his features into a hundred different faces – all of them hideous.

By 1974, reprints were beginning to seep into the comics' pages. As a sense of ennui crept over the paper, a pick-me-up was required. What to do? How about a merger?

Cor!! had been launched in 1970. A pretty solid humour title, it was now being put out to pasture. The new injection brought Gus the Gorilla in to helm the joke page, class warfare courtesy of 'Ivor Lott and Tony Broke', magical graffiti artist Chalky, soccer-themed fun in 'Football Madd', ghostly quality assurance courtesy of The Spectre Inspector and invisible hi-jinks in 'Val's Vanishing Cream'.

These were exciting times. Not only was there a fresh influx of characters, but TV funster Dick Emery was now appearing every week to host 'The Airfix Modellers Club'. An unlikely project it may have been (although presumably remunerative for both the personality and the publishers, who also carried it in various other titles), his grinning face was there every week, accompanying his regular letter to all his Spitfire-constructing pals. Even though *Buster* was supposed to appeal to both sexes, it's doubtful anyone was really excited when, in January 1975, Dick revealed the launch of the company's new series of period figures with a 1:12 scale construction kit of Anne Boleyn.

But enough about that – who was next on the paper's hit list?

Monster Fun had proved an even bigger flop than *Shiver and Shake* and, obviously, *Buster* couldn't just stand back and do nothing. In November 1975, our cover star swapped his regular head attire for a top hat to welcome pathetic shark Gums, mollycoddled Mummy's Boy, Kid

Kong and the others in from the cold to join his circus of fun. Not only that, there was also a special 'funny monsters' competition laid on in which readers could potentially get their hands on a metal-detector (always big on hobbies, *Buster*).

By the mid- to late Seventies, the comic was firing on all cylinders, with some top stories including 'The Spritely Lads' (two chucklesome pals, one Asian, which was a rarity for British comics of the era, and therefore all the more welcome), 'Teddy Scare' (a toy that would turn into a fearsome grizzly when it came into contact with water) and 'Terror TV' (spooky spoofs of favourite telly programmes as suggested by readers).

Adventure stories still had their place too, but were becoming quite a marginal concern. Nevertheless, it was during this era one of the very best began its run.

'The Leopard of Lime Street' arrived in 1976. 'After being scratched by a radio-active leopard, young Billy Farmer found that he had somehow developed the strength and agility of the mighty jungle cat.' Following this incident, the Selbridge-based lad turned into a crime-fighter who would supplement his income by taking photographs of himself in action and selling them to a newspaper editor who was, perversely, leading a campaign to have the spotted vigilante brought to justice. Thankfully, Spider-Man's lawyers weren't looking in.

Interestingly, over the years there'd be some real development in Billy's character as he'd become increasingly feral in appearance and developed a liking for raw meat, suggesting the animal instincts were taking over.

Into the Eighties, *Buster* freshened up its look with a larger logo and a splash of red to liven up the previously monochrome 'Ivor Lott and Tony Broke' on the centre pages. Its next acquisition came in 1982, as *Jackpot* fell on its sword after a run just short of three years. 'There's so much fun for you inside!' declared our man, peeling back the cover of *Buster and Jackpot* to reveal a plethora of chuckles. Now, the super-lucky family The Winners, 'Kid Kong', *The Good Life* rip-off 'It's a Nice Life', 'Laser Eraser' and Jack Pott himself joined the fold. Of special note, however, was the incorporation of 'Milly O'Naire and Penny Less' into the comic – they now received second billing after messrs Lott and Broke in a strip that combined all four financially obsessed characters.

In that same issue, readers also came across a fateful announcement. 'Big, big, *big* news – Big Daddy joins *Buster and Jackpot* next week in a

great new fun strip!' 'It'll be a *big hit!*' chipped in the rotund erstwhile
Shirley Crabtree. 'Easy!' Not without precedent – after all, *Buster* itself
had been running strips featuring real-life personalities before now – it
was still a little bit odd to see the large grappler hanging out with kids and
using his prodigious belly to get up to mischief. Nevertheless, this was
the year in which the wrestler had intended to move into children's TV
(his plan to host a Saturday morning show on ITV in October was
shelved at the last minute due to ill health) so it all made some sort of
weird sense.

Buster – © Egmont UK Ltd

By now, the aforementioned Lime Street crime-fighter represented the
only remaining adventure strip in the comic. Meanwhile, Buster himself
found he was often giving up half the front cover to promote other stories, or even being booted off altogether, such as the time Big Daddy
decided to dress up as a giant Suchard's egg to celebrate Easter.

There was another minor overhaul of the logo in 1983 (which also
served as a good excuse to drop *Jackpot* from the billing), but otherwise it was business as usual. Its merger with **School Fun** in June 1984
was probably its most perfunctory union yet, leaving *Buster*'s pages all

but unaffected.

By 1985, the logo had changed again into a kind of hand-written affair, while *School Fun*'s 'Young Arfur', 'Walt Teaser' and 'School Belle' finally turned up in their new home. The last new 'The Leopard of Lime Street' graced the pages of the comic in May, Big Daddy's adventures had by now been dropped and – most importantly of all – Buster received a makeover at the hands of artist Jimmy Hansen. It was out with the shorts and in with long trousers, trainers and an overactive thyroid if those bulging eyes were anything to go by. Full colour also returned to the centre pages on occasion, making this version of the paper one of the most handsome yet.

Buster's tenth scalp took the form of the rubbish *Nipper* in September 1987, bringing with it the likes of the morbid 'Brad Break' (a kid with brittle bone syndrome) and the eponymous child himself. It also coincided with a further ramping up of production values. However, despite the obvious benefits, this wasn't a good sign. With other IPC titles dropping all around it, the paper was now fighting for survival. The following year, yep, there was another revamp which saw the creation of more obviously modern characters such as 'Vid Kid' rubbing shoulders with reprints of *Krazy*'s 'Birdman and Chicken the Boy Blunder'. Then, the seminal *Oink!* fell under the juggernaut in 1988, bringing with it 'Pete and his Pimple', 'Tom Thug's Skooldayz' and 'Weedy Willy'.

As the Nineties arrived, *Buster* went full colour, continuing to essay a mix of reprints and an impressive amount of new stuff (such as the missing-the-boat film parody 'Nightmare on Erm Street'). The start of the decade also brought the most shocking acquisition of all and, fittingly, it was to be the comic's last. After a glorious innings of twenty-one years, *Whizzer and Chips* finally faltered, leaving our man to pick up the tab. The union between the two left *Buster* as IPC's sole children's humour weekly on the shelves. A sad day indeed.

From hereon in, it got decidedly depressing. By the mid-Nineties, *Buster* had turned into a fortnightly comic, desperately launching spin-off reprint titles in an effort to keep some cash flowing in, but the whole comics market was buckling fast.

Nevertheless, it did well to limp its way through to the end of the decade. That final issue was dated 22 December, 1999 to 4 January, 2000, meaning it could stake its claim to having survived into the twenty-first century. In a last show of greatness, it went out with a thoroughly self-obsessed final number. Different representations of Buster over the years informed readers: 'Sadly this is the very last issue of *Buster*. It started in 1960...since then there have been more than two thousand issues.' Meanwhile in the main story, the character wept openly as his old nursery school was symbolically destroyed. 'Sniff! Some of my earliest adventures were in that building!'

But the tour-de-force came on the back cover, a fantastic one-page strip which provided a spate of conclusions to the unfolding stories of many of the comic's favourite characters from the last four decades. Thus, Joker was revealed to be Jeremy Beadle in disguise, Sweet Tooth lost his one remaining nasher to dental decay, Ivor Lott's dad went bust 'investing in *Buster* comic' and Chalky was arrested for scrawling on walls. Best of all, though, was the revelation as to what Buster looked like under his cap. With the famous headgear removed, we finally learned that over the years he'd been hiding a Dennis the Menace-style mop of black spiky hair. 'I couldn't take off my cap...I have the same hairstyle as a certain other comic character!' he explained mischievously.

And so the curtain came down on a long and noble lineage of kids' comics. *Buster* had seen it and done it all, spectacularly mugging its way through the funny-paper library, outlasting nearly all competitors. DC Thomson's *Dandy* and *Beano* were – and are now – the only two humour titles left in the game.

'Special thanks to all our loyal readers!' ran the text at the bottom of that final page. '*Don't* place a regular order with your newsagent! (We've waited years to say that!)'

Buzz
(DC Thomson, 1973-1975, every Monday)

A tabloid-sized comic (as were *The Topper*, *The Beezer* and *Buster* upon launch), at first glance *Buzz* looked very similar to contemporaneous copies of the *Sun*. Don't worry, the publication was a strictly straight down the line laff-o-rama.

Blessed with a huge masthead, the paper had plenty of room to big up what was going on inside, making it seem like there was always something happening, whether that was the excitement of the standard issue 'pop pistol' free gift with number one ('craack!'), a giveaway 'whoopee whistle', a £50 treasure chest up for grabs in a Funny Faces competition or the chance to nab 'pocket-money prizes' (a £1 postal order) on the letters page – which was superbly titled 'Postman Knox' and helmed by the mail-delivering bloke himself.

Buzz – © DC Thomson & Co., Ltd

Beneath this regular promotion ran the exploits of three likely lads, Hop, Skip and, er, Jock (doesn't quite work, that). A trio of undistinguished generic comic chancers (one had a skinhead, one wore a striped sweater and the other a tartan bonnet), initially their stories would culminate in a huge, meticulously detailed panel brimming with incident – such as the time they opened up their own barbershop. Then, we had Hop running a lawn-mower over a line-up of sailors' heads ('I'm giving the crew a crew cut!'); Jock peering at a baldy's bonce with a magnifying glass ('Listen mister! It's 1p for the haircut an' 24p for findin' the hairs!'); various other kids getting up to locks-related hi-jinks; and a smiling Skip brandishing a comb towards us ('Any of you readers fancy a haircut?'). It was inventive stuff, certainly, and made good use of the extra room afforded by the comic's dimensions. However, for some reason along the way, the threesome lost that big finish effect and had to make do with a normal, multi-paneled layout like everyone else. Shame.

In fact, looking inside *Buzz* it would be fair to say that while the publication was entertaining enough, it wasn't really big on innovation. 'Nobby' was a bit like a watered-down Ginger from *The Beezer* (red sweater, shorts, outrageously untidy hair), 'Wig and Wam' felt just too 'Little Plum'-ish (although, to be fair the characters had originally appeared in *The Dandy* some twenty years before our 'Redskin Chum' came on the scene), 'Skookum Skool' dealt out 'Bash Street'-style kids versus teacher fodder, 'Big Bad Moggy' was far too much Mr Jinks the cat from the *Pixie and Dixie* cartoons (swapping bow-tie for a trilby and waistcoat, and fixating on 'them burds' rather than his counterpart's nemesis, 'those meices') and as for 'The Rooky Racers' and their crackpot automobiles...

Of course, being derivative in British comics is no crime (the witness for the defense, *Action*'s amped up *Jaws*-wannabe, 'Hookjaw') but it just didn't feel like *Buzz* was doing it with much zest. Nevertheless, the title did become home to a few truly great stories, such as the exploits of crap crook 'Fred the Flop' ('I tried a smash-and-grab, but the jeweler's window was unbreakable glass!'); the brilliantly surreal 'Olly's Occy' (boy and octopus scampering around together causing mischief); inveterate liar 'Billy the Kidder'; the constantly warring Weeble-esque 'The Buzzies and the Fuzzies'; and 'Big Fat Flo' (the high concept of which you can work out for yourself).

However, none was finer than 'Jimmy Jinx and What He Thinks' which detailed the continuing turmoil felt by a young lad whenever an opportunity for mischief presented itself. It was at this point that both an angelic and demonic version of himself would appear above his head in a couple of thought balloons. While the former would extol the virtues of not letting a clockwork mouse loose during 'Mum's sewing bee' (and in a nice touch of characterisation refer to the titular kid as 'James') the latter would gleefully endorse all and any bad behaviour that crossed 'Jim's mind. The absolute best moments were when angel and devil actually interacted with each other, the saintly apparition delivering his dark counterpart a swift kick in the rear by 'order of the boot' when that week's devilish activity resulted in their host ending up over Mum's knee.

It was entirely right, then, that when *Buzz* folded one issue shy of its second birthday and was absorbed into the pages of fellow outsized paper *The Topper*, Jimmy's strip was maintained and he continued to be tormented by what surely must be the finest representation anywhere of the illusion of choice.

Captain Britain
(Marvel Comics Ltd, 1976-1977, weekly)

To be honest, *Captain Britain* weekly shouldn't really be in this book, with only a third of its content being non-reprint stuff. However, not only does it give us a good excuse to get to grips with Britain's very own 'newest and greatest superhero of all!', but we can also cast an eye over the bonkers world of Marvel UK during the Seventies.

For some time, the 'House of Ideas' had been assailing the British market with various repackaged reprint titles, which mixed together chunked up stories from the US in an effort to emulate the UK appetite for weekly anthology titles. The granddaddy of them all was *The Mighty World of Marvel* mk I (1972-9), which fulfilled a kind of *Buster* role for the company, merging with its many failed titles over the years. From the start, this featured a veritable *Who's Who* of characters, a can't-go-wrong mix of the Hulk, the Fantastic Four and Spider-Man; all reprints from the Sixties, repackaged onto traditional A4(ish) sized paper and transformed into two colours.

Lending his endorsement to the exercise was Stan 'Excelsior!' Lee, Marvel's slightly sinister (roll-neck sweaters, huge moustache etc.) founding father, who'd regularly interrupt the 'zingy excitement' to share insights from the 'batty Bullpen in the halcyon hall of Marvel'. That events depicted on the front of some editions (the Fantastic Four battling some kind of giant lizard thing on issue six) failed to transpire inside was neither here nor there for Stan's 'True Believers'.

But, that wasn't enough for the company, who were keen to establish a proper presence in the UK market. And so, a scheme was formed even more elaborate than swapping all the 'thru's for 'through' and color's for 'colour'. *'It had to happen!'* railed Lee from the pages of *Captain Britain* number one. 'Even though Marvel's heroes are the world's most popular comic book characters, the time has come for a new superhero – one who will be *Britain's own!*' But, there was more: 'Month after month you have demanded him! Comicdom has needed him! All of

Britain has been waiting for him! And now, he's here at last!'

Yes, indeed. Here was Marvel's first effort at creating a character especially for the Brits, and by gum should we be grateful ('Imagine – specially written and drawn for you!'). Nevertheless, lest anyone got the idea Lee was investing in UK-based talent (and, to be fair, in his editorial he did give a nod of thanks to Brits George Mina, Alan Murray and Pet Shop Boy-in-waiting Neil Tennant who were all employed in the company's Kent offices) the whole thing was put together by a pair of Yanks. Chris Claremont was given the job of writing it, thanks to the fact he apparently had relatives in the UK, while Herb Trimbe took on the main art chores because he'd once had a holiday in the country.

That premiere number arrived with a free Captain Britain mask, and depicted the hero giving a bunch of hi-tech knights what for on the cover as he flailed around with his magical quarterstaff.

Inside, it was all too obvious this was a version of Britain very much via the Big Apple. Unassuming physicist Brian Braddock was working temporarily at the Darkmoor Research Centre until a new term started at Thames University. When the place was suddenly attacked by criminal mastermind the Reaver, Braddock made his escape on a motorbike, but ended up pitching himself over a cliff. In truth, he should have been dead, but instead came face-to-face with a vision of Merlin and his slightly less well-known friend, the Lady of the Northern Skies, who told him: 'Thou must choose either the amulet or the sword...life or death for thee...and mayhap for thy *world* as well!' At this point the first episode was over. 'Continued next week!' ran the rather brilliant caption. 'Thou shalt not miss it!'

Depicted in full colour, no less, these seven pages could have been culled straight from an American source. Despite the spurious Anglicisms, nothing here felt especially British.

Backing up the Cap, we had the usual suite of reprints, a black and white 'Fantastic Four' story and a 'Nick Fury: Agent of SHIELD!' strip, which was also rendered in full colour. Was this really the best it was going to get?

As the weeks rolled by, policeman Dai Thomas embarked on a J Jonah Jameson-esque campaign to unmask the Captain as a menace to society, and readers became familiar with the olde worlde take on Britain with vague approximations of red London buses driving the wrong way down roads and Dick Van Dyke dialogue plopping from characters' mouths ('Look what's happened to the boss! He looks like some bleedin' knight in shining armour!' 'I feel rather chipper for a lad who spent the past three days battling the Red Skull! But I won't think of battles today! It's Sunday!' 'Hey! Coppers from Scotland Yard no less!').

It was a mix that never came close to convincing (particularly when all colour was removed from inside the title) and didn't seem sufficiently different from Marvel UK's other round of weeklies. At the time, those included *Super Spider-Man* (which originally started out as *Spider-Man Comics Weekly*, in 1973); *The Titans* (1975-6); the aforementioned *The Mighty World of Marvel*; the crap take on British war comics *Fury* (1977) – which included a story entitled, simply, 'Fokker!' in its first issue, and would eventually be succeeded by the equally poor *Forces in Combat* (1980-2); and the unique combo of *Planet of the Apes and Dracula Lives* (which started out without the fanged chap in 1974 and folded into *Mighty World*... in 1977). Despite getting official endorsement from Marvel's US characters (Captain America and Nick Fury showing up in one story), Captain Britain always remained the poor cousin.

Nine months after his launch, the UK's own superhero (who, remember, we demanded) was out on his ear, the title falling foul to poor sales. In an issue which led with the character in a trance-like state, hurling himself at Queen Elizabeth ('Down with the female tyrant who misrules our British realm!'), the news arrived that the publication was to merge with Spidey's comic to form *Super Spider-Man and Captain Britain* – 'and if that ain't the best line-up for a Marvel weekly, we don't know what is!'

However, the Cap's career didn't grind to a halt there.

First he made an official crossover into US comics, turning up in New York in January 1978 inside two issues of the American *Marvel Team-Up* ('At last! Marvel's *British* superhero sensation *explodes* on the stateside scene!' was the disingenuous billing) and then he enjoyed a brief sojourn in another ostensible UK reprint title, *Hulk Comic* (1979-80), which had been launched to capitalise on the success of the TV show starring Bill Bixby.

It would be just enough to keep the character ticking over until the Eighties arrived, whereupon he'd receive a rather miraculous rehabilitation at the hands of some British-based talent.

Captain Britain Monthly
(Marvel Comics Ltd, 1985-1986)

With the juvenile weeklies feeling the pinch by the mid-Eighties, the likes of *2000 AD* and *Warrior* were putting together a pretty convincing case that, in order to survive, comics had to go upmarket.

Thus, 'exploding from the *Mighty World of Marvel*' came *Captain Britain Monthly*, a credible attempt by Marvel UK to inject some original, more adult-orientated material into the industry.

Up until fairly recently, the character's history was pretty ignominious, but in 1980, he started off on the road to rehabilitation as some actual Brits finally got their hands on him. First, writer David Thorpe and artist Alan Davis ditched all of his US-bound continuity, gave him a brand new Union Jack-themed costume (first seen in September 1981, fact fans) and set him in a world outside the influence of Spider-Man and company. Northampton comics magus Alan Moore then pitched the character into some increasingly multi-layered stories. All this was going on in the pages of Marvel UK's ostensible reprint titles *Marvel Superheroes* (1979-83), *The Daredevils* (1981) and then *Mighty World of Marvel* mk II (1983-4) where the creators had to cut corners wherever possible to gather together cash to produce new stories, rather than just flinging out reruns of American stuff.

Thus, by the time Cap's new self-titled comic arrived, he was actually quite a sturdy, complicated character, well suited to the company's flirtation with mature readers.

'Britain's only active superhero has finally made it back to his own title,' ran the editorial in issue one, wilfully invoking memories of the original, woeful, *Captain Britain* weekly. Right from the off, this was sombre, serious stuff, opening with perennial thorn-in-the-Captain's-side Chief Inspector Dai Thomas holding a conference with his superiors in which he posited, quite correctly, that the superhero's secret identity was Brian Braddock. Alas he was laughed out of the room. Nevertheless, he would go on to pursue his suspicions over the coming months, while the Captain himself battled with all manner of crazies from other dimensions (The Crazy Gang for one, a bunch of *Alice in Wonderland* characters brought to life), battled alternative versions of himself (one of whom would attempt to rape his sister, Betsy), hooked up with a nubile shape-changing gypsy (who in one memorable instance, transformed into a wizened old reptile while the Cap's tongue was half-way down her throat) and travelled back to fourteenth-century Peru to encounter an obese alien killer with parasites nesting in her gut.

Weird and wonderful it may have been, but throughout it was infused with a particularly British sense of realism that would see the hero squabble with his sibling while taking his elevenses, or appear inside the pages of the *Guardian*. Plus, the realistic art of Alan Davis (who was still sticking with the character) gave everything a pleasing kitchen sink quality.

However, this being a British comic, the title character wasn't going to get the full run of the publication to himself. Nope, the anthology still ruled and so backing up the Union Jack-clad crime-fighter were a host of B-features. Both 'Abslom Daak: Dalek Killer' and 'Warworld: The origin of the Free-Fall Warriors' owed their existence to *Doctor Who Weekly*, but whereas the former was just a straight reprint of the chainsaw-wielding nutter's campaign of vengeance against the Skaro-based bastards ('Ha ha! These tin freaks are dumber than I thought'), the latter presented all new adventures for the motley intergalactic soldiers of fortune.

Elsewhere, 'The Mysterious Night-Raven' from *Hulk Comic* (Marvel Comics Ltd, 1979-80) stepped out in a series of *film-noir-esque* strips drawn by 'V for Vendetta' artist David Lloyd and, rather less promisingly, 'Paragon of Painthorpe Street' brought us four text story pages of superhero parody featuring the self-deluded Redmond Jonah Pringle.

Yep, the back-up features weren't a patch on the main event, particularly when the Free-Fall crew got dropped in favour of the less idiosyncratic 'Space Thieves', but those dozen or so pages of CB at the front were well worth the 50p entrance fee on their own.

Nevertheless, with Marvel UK always ultimately reliant on reprints rather than original material, few people were surprised when – thirteen months after its launch – the Cap was stepping out into his own title for the last time. Perversely, the comic had done quite well in the US, it was just the domestic market that had let the side down.

Thus, there was barely enough time for the Captain to make his peace with Dai Thomas before it all came crushing down around him. 'Never the end' ran the pay-off in the final panel of his strip – and indeed that proved to be the case.

Two years later, the run of *Captain Britain Monthly* stories were collected into one colour volume, designed specifically to appeal to the

American market. Then, shortly afterwards, the character made his return to comics, spearheading the US series *Excalibur* which teamed him up with both *The X-Men*, and the writer who'd originally scripted his stories back in 1976, Chris Claremont.

All those years spent keeping his distance from the rest of the Marvel squad, and now here he was, going with Americanised spellings and having his adventures counter-stamped by the Comics Code Authority. Against all the odds, it looked like our own superhero was actually going to make the grade.

Champ
(DC Thomson, 1984-1985, every Saturday)

The final part of DC Thomson's ill-fated (but rather good) trilogy of new boys' comics from the start of the Eighties (the other two being *Buddy* and *Spike*), *Champ* also holds the distinction of being the company's last ever attempt (to date) to come up with a new publication for this market. From hereon in, British boys' comics were just to become one long depressing series of mergers and cancellations.

However, *Champ* wasn't half bad, particularly as it contained one of the best soccer strips ever.

Issue one, which came with a free Super Soccer Slide Guide ('a t'rific two-in-one finger fingertip fact file' was the nicely alliterative description), proclaimed itself to be 'a winner for boys!', featuring 'creepy tales, comics capers, school shocks and much more!'

Like *Buddy* and *Spike*, this translated into a mixture of old and new content. The headline act here was unarguably 'We Are United', the comic-strip tale of a former top-flight team struggling to recapture the glory years after 'a disastrous run of bad luck and injury' sent them plunging into Division Two (nowadays known rather disingenuously as 'The Championship', of course). One of the most realistic football stories around, the opening episode was appended with a list of stats and figures about the club's fortunes and a picture of its home ground, the Mill. In this opening instalment, United's board broke the news that the side had run out of money and was going to have to transfer off some of its more lucrative players. A dead cert for the knacker's yard, however, was aging captain Joe Pearson – 'Your first-team days are numbered, old man!' mused talented-but-lazy Welsh midfielder Terry Evans in a particularly malicious thought-balloon. By the end of the issue, the team had been asset-stripped, but Pearson, rather than being consigned to the scrapheap, was offered the role of manager when the board decided they could no longer afford the present incumbent's expensive boozing and cigar-chomping ways. 'This is what I've always dreamed about,' declared a fist-clenching Joe, 'My life-long ambition.'

With players like burly defender Tug Wilson ('cop that!'), punk Alex 'Hedgehog' Jones, going-to-seed journeyman striker Willy Barnes and the callow Benny Grainger on the side, Pearson's inspirational brand of leadership ('Don't stand like a bunch of dummies! We've got to *win* this match! *Move*!!') and inevitable last minute clearances from the goal line, reignited the side's fortunes. That, and various superstar signings, including Scottish talent Kevin Nicklish (a compound of Kevin Keegan, Charlie Nicholas and Kenny Dalglish) from rival side Southpool, Charlie 'Iron' Barr from *Spike* (inherited when the two titles merged in 1984) and 'Limp-Along' Leslie Thompson, last seen playing in the pages of the now dead *Hotspur*.

All of this helped give the strip a kind of soap opera feel, and in its time 'We Are United' tackled realistic issues such as merchandising, the stars' private lives and football hooliganism.

Absolutely playing second-fiddle to Joe Pearson and company was 'Kids Rule – OK!' No relation to *Action*'s yob-athon of the same name, this focussed on the antics of a group of working-class lads (Junkyard, Smudge, Danny, etc.) who were determined to stop their school closing down. That their number was later also bolstered by refugees from *Spike*'s similar 'The Bleak Street Bunch' just compounded the impression that all DC Thomson comic-strip adventures were really just taking place two doors away from each other. Then there was 'The Sinister World of Mr Pendragon', creepy 'Future Shock'-style tales told by a Satanist Patrick Stewart lookalike and 'Mike's Mil££ions', the story of a young tyke who was bequeathed control of a multi-million pound business by a deceased tycoon.

Meanwhile, the centre pages were devoted, rather oddly, to 'Dennis the Menace's Fun Section'. Here, old humour strips like *The Topper*'s 'Send for Kelly' and *Sparky*'s 'Puss 'n Boots' were given another airing.

The publication's aforementioned absorption of *Spike* in May 1984 should have indicated that things were on the up, but in fact it was really a sign of the increasingly tough time comics were having in the Eighties. Despite remaining a bracing Second World War-free read throughout most of its life, *Champ* lasted less than two years and, in October 1985, went the way of all boys' comics by merging with *Victor*. One year later, that venerable title would be the only DC Thomson boys' weekly left on the shelves.

Cheeky
(IPC Magazines Ltd, 1977-1980, every Monday)

It could have been billed The Battle of the Overbite. In one corner we had moonlighting, toothy Bash Street Kid Plug and his self-titled publication. In the other an ex-Krazy Gang member gone solo, the equally orthodontically cursed Cheeky. The former had hit the newsagent's shelves a month prior to his rival, but that didn't stop the oddball turning on the charm when he finally arrived.

Cheeky – © Egmont UK Ltd

With his pet snail exclaiming 'fame at last!' on the front cover of 'my own comic' (a spin-off from *Krazy*, no less), *Cheeky* wooed readers with a free gift of a 'Red Jet Rattler' (a build-it-yourself model plane), and then got straight to the point on the inside page. 'Hiya! I'm Cheeky...and I know we're going to be good mates,' promised our new leader, before going on to reveal the comic's rather unusual, freewheeling format. Every issue was presented as a week in the life of the titular character, who would wander from an adventure with 'The Skateboard Squad!' set on Sunday morning, into an encounter with 'Walter Wurx' (whose ace character trait was a constant need to rush off to have a piss) which took place on Sunday evening, and so on.

This was practically stream-of-consciousness stuff, and unlike anything else readers had seen before. It also called upon maximum ingenuity from the comic's creators to provide a workable segue from the usual nonsense into nominal adventure story 'Fangs of Fear' – which they did by having our man retire to bed to read a spooky book and then advising us, 'And this is what Cheeky read...'

Endlessly impressive, the title even managed to pull off the old trick of knocking out a reprint to pad out a page with tremendous élan, as the eponymous lad rummaged in his dad's loft to discover a 1949 copy of *Knockout Comic* (Amalgamated Press/Fleetway Publications, 1939-63). 'Ask your mum and dad if they remember this lad?' was the exhortation as the low-concept adventures of 'Mike' were dusted down for another outing.

A year into the title's run, the parameters were now being more clearly defined, and despite the paper still bringing us the lowdown on 'Cheeky's Week', there was less ambling from one strip to another for the perambulating character. Instead, the likes of Calculator Kid (he had a talking calculator, if you must know), Paddywack (who essayed gags sent in by readers) and Tub ('Coo! Mum's slipping! Fancy leaving a big bowl of fruit like that unguarded!') were left to get on with their antics unmolested, with those essential seven days instead appearing in between other items, almost by way of punctuation.

Although the change robbed the paper of some of its charm, the individual strips were still lots of fun and proved strong enough to secure *Cheeky* life beyond the closure of its parent comic in 1978. As if that wasn't kudos enough, the title then went on to outlast *Plug* by a clear year. A definite result for the grinning goon who'd declared, '"Laugh at Life", that's my motto.'

Here's hoping he was still smiling when, in February 1980, his own title folded and he had to settle for a sixteen-page pull-out in the centre of *Whoopee!* instead.

Comic Relief Comic
(Fleetway Publications, 1991)

Granted, this one may not tick all the boxes for inclusion in our book but, hey, it's for a good cause, right?

Still smarting from the failure of *Revolver* and beginning to suspect that *Crisis* was also destined for a fast exit via that same dumper, the execs at Fleetway Publications nonetheless agreed to fire up the printing presses and lay on a special publication in conjunction with the charity which, lest we forget, had launched itself onto the world in 1985 as part of Noel Edmonds' *Live Live Christmas Breakfast Show* on BBC1.

By 1991, the endeavour was gearing up to return to British TV screens for its third telethon, to be titled *Comic Relief: The Stonker*, and – alongside a novelty record headlined by Hale and Pace – a comic was deemed a suitable way to raise some much needed funds. With a characteristic intro by Lenny Henry ('Every single person involved has contributed the megastonkingest utmost of their sponditious skills for free'), this truly was a unique publication. Where else were you going to find 'Roger Mellie: The Man on the Telly' (albeit with all profanity outlawed) rubbing shoulders with Superman, Doctor Who and The X-Men?

Perhaps (or more likely, perhaps not) taking its cue from *Cheeky*, the publication featured stalwarts Henry ('Well crucial or what!!'), Jonathan Ross ('Twenty million people are going to be admiring this suit tonight') and Griff Rhys Jones ('Oh, I only did what any other handsome, debonair and heroic guy would do in the circumstances') navigating their way through various strips as they ostensibly hosted a traditional *Comic Relief* show.

The end result defies criticism, of course, what with it all being for charity, but as it happened there was a lot of above average stuff on offer here anyway, the then movers and shakers of the British comic industry all contributing a page here and there (although, it has to be said, no one but no one could capture Rhys Jones' features).

Highlights included a 'who's got the biggest chin in comics' competition which pitted Judge Dredd, Dan Dare, Captain Britain and Desperate Dan against each other, but was won by an interloping...'Bruce Forsyth??' ('certainly *is*, my loves!'); a postmodern argument over whether those pizza-obsessed turtles were 'ninjas' or 'heroes'; a bizarre cameo from the Hoffmeister Bear; the evil Mekon being strong-armed out of a fiver; and

Desperate Dan throwing Noel Edmond's car into a swimming pool.

Less successful were the irregular punctuations in tone, when things suddenly got on-message. A young wheelchair-bound girl lecturing Edmund Blackadder about her problems ('We have rights, the same right to work as anyone else') and an elderly couple debating the merits of charity ('They help the likes of us, all over the country, get *involved* in decisions that affect us') just didn't sit well with the antics of Johnny Fartpants *et al*. However, that's an imbalance that always troubled the telethons over the years too, so you couldn't really blame the publication for that.

All in all, the *Comic Relief Comic* was a fine effort; entertaining enough on its own merits, and a real treat for diehard comic fans who got a kick out of seeing so many disparate characters coming together. With all profits going to charity, it certainly wasn't a bad way to blow £1.50 – and besides, it was loads better than doing 'the stonk, to the rhythm of the honky tonk', right?

Commando
(DC Thomson, 1961-ongoing, monthly)

1961 was a good year for war. It wasn't just thanks to the failed Bay of Pigs invasion of Cuba, a military coup in South Korea or even the onset of the US' campaign in Vietnam. Nope, war ruled OK thanks to the arrival first of DC Thomson's *Victor* and then this gung ho title.

Every month, *Commando* would bring us sixty-eight pages of 'pocket library'-sized stories detailing men fighting other men. Emboldened by one of the most macho logos in the business (which featured a Fairburn Sykes knife lunging through the 'C'), the format proved to be an instant winner.

On the outside were lurid but beautifully painted panoramic front covers traditionally sporting either pictures of teeth-clenching 'Tommies' letting off a few rounds, screaming Messerschmitts (with jaggedy teeth painted on the side) descending upon some innocents, or a moody head and shoulders hovering artistically above a scene of carnage. Emblazoned across this in the most exciting font possible was the title of that issue's story which memorably included such thrillers as 'Jap Killer', 'This Man is Dangerous', 'Massacre by Moonlight', 'Hot on the Trail!' and 'Hun in a Hurri'.

The template for such winning packaging was all but established by Ken Barr. He was the man who designed the logo and painted most of the publication's first two hundred covers. However, following his departure to the world of (whisper it!) US comics, there were plenty of equally talented artists who followed in his footsteps.

Commando – © DC Thomson & Co., Ltd

The first edition sported a Nazi officer giving a piggy-back to an injured but gun-wielding Brit in some inhospitable desert while a plume of black smoke curled up into the sky. The story's title? 'Walk – or Die!' Inside, the skillfully illustrated strip told the tale of happy-go-lucky Corporal Tom Gerrard of the Royal Armoured Corps who, somewhere in the Western Desert, bumped into evil German tank commander Colonel Karl Oberth. What followed was an epic battle of pluck versus panzers.

Over the years the title branched out to include more than just Second World War encounters, embracing futuristic space battles, time-travelling escapades, the Korean War and even the conflict in the Gulf. Anywhere, in short, where men were liable to train deadly implements on each other, and meet their maker with the requisite cry of 'AAAGHHH!' But despite all the experimentation, it was the Jerry-bashing that remained the back bone of the comic, as exclamations of '*Himmel*!', '*Achtung, Englander*!' and '*Schweinhund*!' fast entered the lexicon of boys who devoured the stuff.

Make no mistake, although *Commando* might have had simplistic ways, scribes for the comic carefully trod a fine line between genuine der-ring-do and parody. Latter day writing *wunderkind* Grant Morrison admits that back in the Seventies he just didn't have what it takes to come up with stories for the title that didn't fall into self-mockery. His ideas – one featuring a trio of soldiers made up of an Englishman, Irishman and a Scotsman heading off to 'batter Hitler' – never getting past the DC Thomson editors. Along the way similar efforts such as Fleetway Publications' *Battle Picture Library* (1961-84) fell by the wayside proving *Commando* had that additional something which secured its longevity.

Incredible as it may seem, at the time of writing the comic is still going strong, and putting out a prolific eight issues a month; six brand new stories and two reprints.

Cor!!
(IPC Magazines Ltd, 1970-1974, every Monday)

Not just one exclamation mark, mind, but two accompanied the title of IPC's first humour magazine of the Seventies.

Former company employee and **Whizzer and Chips** editor Dez Skinn well remembers his surprise when he heard the name of the paper – which had been codenamed 'JNP32' in pre-production. This wasn't so long after an era when the phrase 'cor blimey' had been considered too risqué for British weeklies, for fear that the blasphemous slang term for 'God Blind Me' would offend parents. But now we were being treated to a publication that – to all intents and purposes – was trading under the banner of 'God!!'

And, without labouring the point, turning a comic into a glass of fruit drink certainly seemed like a miraculous proposition. But that's exactly what *Cor!!* did with its first issue, advising readers to 'have a drink on us!', thanks to a sachet of Gulp appended to the paper.

Kicking off proceedings was Gus Gorilla who, to be fair, was never IPC's most imaginative character – a walking talking simian, clad in shirt, tie, braces and cap who would go on to have the slightest of slight adven-tures on the front page, usually ending up with a moustachioed chap pro-claiming, 'You can't make a monkey out of Gus!' Nevertheless, he did at

least provide the title with an ace logo, the goggley eyed chimp screaming the comic's name across the cover every week.

Inside we were introduced to an impressive fleet of strips boasting
varying degrees of inventiveness in their conception. At the simplistic
end of the scale we had 'Whacky' ('He's always getting whacked!' ran the
subtitle, in this tale of perhaps comicdom's unluckiest lad, who'd exit
each week's strip with a sore arse), 'Tomboy' (a girl who acted like a boy,
unsurprisingly), 'Ivor Lott and Tony Broke' (the title says it all, really,
but here began IPC's obsession with pitching the rich against the poor),
'Spoilsport' (a singularly evil child dedicated to ruining everyone else's
fun), 'Football Madd' (starring Mickey Madd) and 'Eddie: He's Always
Bored!' (bracketed explanation not required).

Rather more fanciful were the likes of 'Hire a Horror' (which predat-
ed BBC1's *Rentaghost* in its use of ghouls as odd-job labourers); 'Freddie
Fang: The Werewolf Cub' (a pre-*Teen Wolf*, if you will, helping to stoke
up the horror content in this pre-*Shiver and Shake* age); 'Andy's Ants' (a
boy who commanded a legion of creepy-crawlies); 'Tricky Dicky' ('I can
get out of anything,' boasted the Roger the Doger-esque lad before
pulling off another scam); 'Barney's Brain Box (a young chap whose day-
dreams regularly became confused with reality); and 'Kid Chameleon'
(the 'serious', lushly illustrated adventures of an 'English boy' who'd been
reared by reptiles in the Kalahari desert which, obviously, meant he was
able to change hue at will – and ensured he always nabbed the colour centre page spread every week, clever fella).

For a first night line-up, *Cor!!* hadn't fared too badly, but things would
really come together over the ensuing weeks as other strips debuted. 'The
Slimms' was great fun, son Sammy trying to prevent his morbidly obese
parents from filling up at the tuck shop ('Quick, let's get home and eat it
before Sammy sees us!'). Meanwhile, 'Swopper Stan' obsessed about
exchanging as many items as possible, 'Jasper the Grasper' did the miserly thing to great effect ('*Bah!* My shoes are nearly worn through! I'm not
spending good money to 'ave 'em repaired!'), 'Wonder Worm' (from
Buster) was an invincible invertebrate who – for some reason – went about
in an early John Lennon-style peaked cap, and 'Chalky' used his artistic
talents to teach bullies a lesson pretty much every week.

However, arguably the two best ever features to grace *Cor!!*'s pages
were also its most idiosyncratic. In 1970, Bill Oddie, Tim Brooke Taylor
and Graeme Garden launched their slapstick comedy series, *The Goodies*,

on BBC1, and, despite protestations that their show wasn't just kids' stuff, began turning up within the publication for two pages of comic-strip action every week. Nicely drawn fare that remained faithful to the show and was apparently rubber-stamped by the 'Super Chaps Three' themselves, it also had the rather desirable side-effect of prompting Bill to ditch *The Beano* as his choice of reading on screen, and reach for some Gus Gorilla-helmed antics instead (check out the 1973 episodes 'For Those in Peril on the Sea' and 'Camelot' for proof).

Cor!! – © Egmont UK Ltd

Alongside their 'do anything anytime' antics, we also had the spooky 'Rat-Trap'. This strip told of The British Institute For Foiling Felonies' (BIFFF) efforts to capture cunning king of crime Doctor Ratty Rat (a disturbing fusion of man and rodent) who lived in a sewer below the streets.

Cor!! notched up a pretty impressive four-year run, but, for almost every comic comes a time when that 'exciting news for all readers inside' strap-line becomes unavoidable. With a cavalcade of characters trooping out on the front of the 15 June 1974 issue, the news was out that next week, the title would be engulfed by *Buster*.

Countdown
(Polystyle Publications Ltd, 1971-1972, weekly)

A handsome brute indeed, *Countdown* was Polystyle's attempt to revisit the splendour of *TV21*'s glory years, for a new decade. Helmed by Dennis Hooper, who'd been the original art editor on that publication (which was now hurtling fast towards a degrading merger with **Valiant**), its intention was to cash in on an apparent new sci-fi boom which was being spearheaded by Jon Pertwee (who'd recently donned the satins and velvets as the third incarnation of Doctor Who) and Gerry Anderson's continuing franchises (the live action *UFO* had been launched the previous year).

Indeed, the latter's programmes were to be the key here, as the publishers negotiated the comic-strip rights to his shows in another effort to repeat what was once the winning *TV21* template. However, as Hooper soon discovered, he was only able to use the Anderson-related stuff for a proportion of the comic's content – and thus had to look around for other material to fill out its twenty-four pages. With public interest in America's Apollo space missions still relatively high, he opted to include regular scientific features ('Lasers – death ray or miracle machines?' ran issue eighteen's front cover) before persuading **TV Comic**'s editor Dick Millington to let him pinch *Doctor Who* from the paper, arguing the TV show was now too mature for that publication's readership.

Issue one hit the news-stands on 20 February 1971. Sporting a larger-than-normal paper size, it was a glossy affair with eight pages in full photogravure colour. That this title was intended for a slightly older audience was indicated by the front cover – a magazine-like photograph of a spaceship orbiting the Earth.

Inside, sharp-eyed readers would have spotted one of the comic's many neat features – the pages were numbered in reverse, meaning as you progressed through it the digits literally counted down.

'Doctor Who' started off proceedings nicely in a story entitled 'Gemini Plan', which was beautifully illustrated by Harry Lindfield. It was followed by the factoid-spouting 'Think Tank!' (more computer fontery afoot here), one-page silliness courtesy of 'Hanna-Barbera's Dastardly and Muttley', a much-trumpeted 'Do Flying Saucers Exist?' thinkpiece, and then a black and white adaptation of *UFO* (which would go full colour the following week).

This was followed by a *Thunderbirds* strip, which was notable for being illustrated by Don Harley, a graduate from Frank Hampson's 'Dan Dare' school of artists on *Eagle* mk I and was thus another superbly drawn item. Bringing up the rear we had 'Captain Scarlet' and then something which unexpectedly turned out to be one of the highlights of the whole venture.

Running low on proper TV-related stock, Hooper created 'Countdown', the paper's title strip which was only tangentially linked to the world of screen sci-fi. Detailing the exploits of the eponymous spaceship (one of the Discovery series of vessels featured in the film *2001: A Space Odyssey*) and its crew, the story was dynamically illustrated by John Burns. A superior slice of sciffy indeed.

The following week, another bit of Anderson-related whimsy arrived in the form of 'The Secret Service', an adaptation of the little-watched part-live action, part-supermarionation espionage thriller starring Stanley Unwin as an ecclesiastical, crime-busting, incredibly shrinking version of himself...which for some reason didn't catch on with TV audiences. Alongside him, another bespectacled and bookish secret agent put in a debut appearance, as *Joe 90* also turned up in comic-strip form.

More puppets jumped on board over the following editions, the hoary old aquatic antics of *Stingray* in issue three and Lady Penelope from *Thunderbirds* – who'd previously starred in her own self-titled comic from 1966 to 1967 – with issue four. Meanwhile, 'Doctor Who' was going from strength to strength, as the dandified time traveller set up home in his own quaint cottage, and tore around the countryside in his souped-up vintage roadster 'Betsey' (sic).

Issue twenty-one saw the Doc embroiled in a tangle with the Vogans – yet another comic race of baddies obviously inspired by Dan Dare's nemesis the Mekon – while *Countdown* opted to pull an old 'Fireball XL5' strip from out of the *TV21* archives to be reprinted sideways across two half pages. Other old features soon followed, and the reliance on non-TV related stuff began to increase. Clearly, money was starting to run out – and so was the interest in sci-fi.

When those outrageously coiffured crime-fighters 'The Persuaders!' arrived in September, it was clear the wind of change was blowing up a storm, and *Countdown* had grossly over-estimated the public's interest in spaceships and jump-suits. What the audience was into now was straightforward action, sans glitter, chromakey and laser beams. Even Gerry Anderson was baling-out of the genre. As *UFO* proved something of a flop, he turned his attention to the power trio of Robert Vaughn, Tony Anholt and Nyree Dawn Porter and their relatively down-to-Earth sleuthing in *The Protectors*.

On 1 April 1972, the comic got a complete overhaul as the garish shirts of *Persuaders* Roger Moore and Tony Curtis were complimented by the even louder apparel of Jack Lord for a *Hawalii-Five-O* adaptation. Now renamed *TV Action in Countdown* the focus on straight-ahead heroics would buy it another year and a half's worth of shelf life.

Cracker
(DC Thomson, 1975-1976, every Monday)

'What do you call a twenty-foot gorilla?' asks Sammy in the clutches of said simian. 'Sir!' replies his faithful mutt, Flash, whilst also being mauled by the junior King Kong.

This was how *Cracker* would sign off after just twenty months on the shelves and eighty-seven issues – but it was a fitting epitaph; a silly throwaway joke for a title that carved out a niche for itself by being ever-so-slightly wackier than its rivals.

Rewinding back to issue one, we discover that the paper launched itself onto the world with a similar sense of humour. Arriving with a free 'Squeeze 'n' Squeak' balloon, it offered up two potential serving suggestions for the item: you could either hide behind a bin and emit a noise when a policeman peddled by on his bike (thereby making him think he needs to oil the machine), or cause an elephant to jump in terror onto a chair, exclaiming, as pachyderms invariably do, 'Eek! A mouse!'

Inside, Sammy wheeled into action on his wind-powered go-kart, commendably cutting to the chase with little promotional puffery. 'See your newsagent now and place a regular order for this great new comic.' He'd pop up throughout the rest of the paper too, scene-setting when required ('Hi mates! Meet Mr Branny, our janitor!'), filling in with jokes when the strips ran short ('Hey! Talkin' of ghosts, did you hear about the ghost that wore a red coat?! It was a fox haunter! Har-har!') and enticing us with all-too-scant details about a forthcoming competition which had prizes to the value of £1000.

A (sort of) highlight of that first edition had to be 'Young Foo: The Kung Fu Kid'. An entrant from the 'It Couldn't Happen Now' file, the

Cracker – © DC Thomson & Co., Ltd

comic-strip billed as 'honourable fun with number one son!' presented us with a stereotypical oriental child who prefixed every second word with 'honourable' and was – get this – pretty smart at martial arts. As if the Commission for Racial Equality wasn't getting twitchy enough, we then had Sammy capping things off by appearing at the foot of the story, giving himself 'slitty' eyes.

Bruce Lee had a lot to answer for.

Thankfully, the other strips were less controversial. 'Simple Spyman' followed the misfortunes of a hapless hirsute secret agent; 'Big-Head Branny: The Strong-Arm Janny' told tales of a bitter old janitor (is there any other kind?); 'Spookie Cookie: He Cooks for the Spooks' mined the hitherto unexploited seam of comedy to be found in the antics of a ghostly chef whose job was providing supper to other – quite demanding – spirits ('Aw! Not corned beef butties again!'); 'Scrapper' obsessed about opportunities for violence; and 'Billy the Kid' did your generic 'naughty boy' stuff, complete with Dennis the Menace's shaggy hair-do.

Predating *School Fun* by a good eight years, the centre pages were devoted to 'Skooldaze', a collection of scholastic strips set in *Buzz*'s

Skookum Upper School, while the rear pages brought us comment in the 'Sammy Says...' section (*'Private!* Not to be read by mums and dads – and that goes for big sisters, too!'), and more comic-strip craziness, best exemplified by the wonderfully on-the-nose 'The Nutters': three squirrels waging war on septic sea dog Percy Potters.

Finally, on the back cover we were presented with a series of spoof adverts (or 'Mad Ads') for hilarious items such as 'High 'n' Dry' swimming gear (a hot air balloon strapped to a pair of trunks), steam-driven football boots, and 'Toothy' toothpaste, a quick appliance of which would bring on the sudden growth of Dracula fangs.

Always nothing less than an amiable read and forever obsessed with jokes (the 'Jest a Minute' page netted readers two quid if their gag was printed), *Cracker* still paled in comparison to the new wave of humour comics that were coming through, particularly from IPC. By the time it was forced into a merger with *The Beezer* in September 1976, the likes of *Whoopee!* and *Whizzer and Chips* were really hitting their stride, while *Monster Fun* had arrived on the scene and the seminal 'stupid' comic, *Krazy*, was just a year away.

Sorry, Sammy, no matter how mad you thought your title was, it didn't occur to you to spell it with a 'K', did it?

Crisis
(Fleetway Publications, 1988-1991, fortnightly)

In the 17 September 1988 issue of *2000 AD*, alien editor Tharg was going nuts. 'This is the week!' he exclaimed. 'In a few short days the first issue of *Crisis* will be on sale and comics will never be the same again.'

Intended to be the sister publication to the 'Galaxy's Greatest Comic', the new venture was aimed at older readers and represented the country's first real news-stand adult comic, but not its last (see *Deadline* and *Revolver*).

Although the trend for grown-up publications had arguably kicked off with *Warrior* (which never really made it into WH Smith's), it had been the US companies who'd hastened its growth, things going thermonuclear when former *2000 AD* scribe Alan Moore wrote the – and here comes that horrible term – graphic novel *Watchmen* for DC comics; a gritty, 'realistic' tale of super-heroics which treated the brightly clad crime fighters with undue respect. It sold by the bucket-load, popularised the smiley face badge so much it became an acid house icon and even made its way into the pages of the broadsheets who, in unison, declared, 'comics aren't just for kids anymore'.

Crisis – © Egmont UK Ltd

It seemed the appetite was there for more complicated stories, and – aside from anything else – John Sanders, the managing director of the company's Youth Group, was keen for a spin-off title from *2000 AD* which could be specifically repackaged for the States. The plan was quickly cooked up to produce a fortnightly full colour title that featured two stories at fourteen pages each, meaning every month they had a couple of twenty-eight-page strips that could be distributed across the US through an American-based company, SQP Productions – thereby overcoming prejudice against non-Yank content from the buyers, who assumed the titles had originated in their country.

So who could lead the new project?

2000 AD's founding father, Pat Mills, had been involved in more comic launches than most, and was one creator who'd been flirting successfully with those slack-wearing men across the pond. In 1986, he'd written *Metalzoic* for DC (which had then been serialised in *2000 AD*) and was now mulling over a project for Marvel's Epic line (which would result in the super-hero-hating character Marshal Law, who would later turn up in *Toxic!*). He was awarded *Crisis'* lead story, 'Third World War'.

Set twelve years in the future, the portents weren't great; the tale commencing with a lengthy quote from Luis Silva, the Brazilian Labour Leader. You could check your guffaws at the door right now.

Telling of a time when multinationals had formed a kind of peace-keeping force to help maintain the equilibrium (and cheap crops) within so-called third world countries, it followed the travails of Eve, who'd been conscribed into the FreeAid corps against her will. Being black and female may have marked the character out as something fresh for British comics in the eyes of many, but, hang on – what about Ebony from *The Crunch* ten years before?

As she inevitably learned more about the horrors of the company, it became clear she was operating in a world where even fizzy drinks were morally reprehensible ('They put six teaspoonfuls of *sugar* in every can to give it "positive mouth feel"'). When an evil-looking pig clad in a business suit, wielding a fat cigar and festooned with dollar bills appeared on the front of issue seven, it was safe to say we'd all got the idea.

The title's other story was, on the surface, a bit closer to Sanders' original vision for the comic, which was intended to cash in more overtly on the renewed interest in superheroes post-*Watchmen*. Absolutely the second stringer here, and never getting so much as a whiff of front cover action, 'New Statesmen' (a look at the possible future consequences of genetic engineering) by *2000 AD* bright young thing John Smith was wilfully confusing and much too slow for any-one to follow, despite delivering more than 'Third World War' on the action front.

Utterly po-faced, *Crisis'* design was similarly unappealing; all army fatigues and sensible fonts, with just two main colours on the cover for its first five editions.

As the editorial team (or, uggh!, '*Crisis* Cru') went on tour around the country's comic shops, it felt as though Fleetway Publications finally had the credible publication it wanted, one that had no time for jokes, thought balloons or WASPs. The Press loved it too, this was right-on stuff and, yet again, comics weren't just for kids anymore. Sales of issue one also seemed to confirm the new effort was a hit, with 80,000 copies snapped up by *2000 AD* devotees impressed by the good word from Tharg.

Things continued, the comic ditching the camouflage look, and 'New Statesmen' winding down with a series of seemingly endless epilogues. However, the initial good vibe had been quick to fade away and circulation plunged to just 25,000. In an effort to combat this, on 1 April 1989, the paper debuted a new line-up as rubbish sitcom 'Sticky Fingers' ('Stand by for a total shakedown – in Camden Town!') and actually rather good treatise on 'The Troubles', 'Troubled Souls', arrived. A more agreeable, and less claustrophobic line-up, at least there was now some contrast to Pat Mills' tub-thumping. By issue twenty-nine, things really were looking up, and 'True Faith' began its run, telling the tale of a schoolboy who was forced into assisting a demented widower on his quest to 'kill God'.

Despite the title's efforts to sock it to The Man, real controversy didn't arrive until it elected to run Brendan McCarthy and Pete Milligan's story, 'Skin', about thalidomide skinheads growing up in the Seventies. Deemed edgy stuff, its scheduled appearance in issue thirty never happened. 'The reproduction company who make our printing film refused to handle the strip because of the content,' explained an awkward editorial in that issue. 'We are currently taking legal advice, trying to find another repro house and placating the understandably miffed creators.' In the event, the story didn't ever appear in *Crisis*, and was published by US outfit Tundra instead, in 1992.

Various other strips came and went, making points about hot topics such as homosexuality and prisons, while 'Third World War' remained a constant. Issue thirty-nine joined forces with Amnesty International to popularise the organisation's work, while the following fortnight a comedy sequel to 'Troubled Souls' showed up in the shape of 'For a Few Troubles More...'

Then, more outrage as *Crisis* reprinted Grant Morrison's 'The New Adventures of Hitler' from the small Scottish magazine, *Cut*. One of that title's columnists, Pat Kane (of Hue and Cry infamy), had objected on principle to the publication of a comic-strip serialisation of the early years of the *Führer* and walked off in protest, whipping up something of a media storm. That the actual strip was really rather good was an added bonus, and Morrison would return to the publication later with his musings on serial killer Bible John.

Despite the fact the comic was now in danger of becoming not a half-bad read, falling sales and the abandonment of its original US strategy forced it to adopt a monthly schedule, albeit with an increased page count. When its sister title *Revolver* bit the dust in 1991, the writing was on the wall. Absorbing its Dan Dare update, 'Dare', and then – a couple of issues later – 'Happenstance and Kismet' into its own line-up, by this stage it had resorted to running a veritable potpourri of odds and sods, including European erotica in the form of a reprint of 'Trip to Tulum'.

And so, after sixty-three issues, it was all over. Despite its campaigning ways, and frequent rails against big business, at the end of the day it had been Fleetway Publications' own men in suits who'd brought *Crisis* into life. And it was they, now, who snuffed it out while Tharg just stood by and watched it all happen. Comics were officially just for kids again, now.

The Crunch
(DC Thomson, 1979-1980, every Monday)

Interpreted by many to be DC Thomson's counterblast to *2000 AD*, *The Crunch* took the company into relatively new territory (bar some exploratory work undertaken by *Warlord*), with its hard-nosed roster of gritty characters, specifically designed to appeal to a modern audience.

'*The Crunch* is now!' declared issue one's editorial. '[It's] a whole new experience in boys' papers! It's for the boy of *today* – packed with never-before told stories with true-life features on the men who have faced the crunch in their lives.' So there it was; the high concept – the title referring to that point were men had to be men and take the tough line. It's also interesting to note that comment about 'never-before told stories', almost is if DC Thomson was trying to distance this new publication from the ranks of its other boys' comics which regularly recycled old strips.

If you were in any way uncertain of the proposed ball-busting nature of the venture, then the front cover would surely have put you straight.

Featuring a fist pounding out of the pages of the comic (sporting the free black band – or bracelet if you were a bit sissy – that came with the issue), this was set to be 'the sensational paper with the most dynamic bunch of stories ever!'

And, to be fair, it pretty much delivered on that. The first strip brought us the adventures of Mark Sabor, a writer who dared to speak out (albeit in pamphlet form) against the injustices he saw in the draconian world of the twenty-first century. As a result, he was put on a sham trial, and then forced to fight to the death every week in 'The Arena'.

Next up was 'a man who faces the crunch every day', apparently: 'The Mantracker'. 'Hated by lawbreakers and despised by society' Bearpaw Jay was a cigar-chomping Indian warrior turned bounty hunter. A typical exchange would have the 'Injun' challenged by a couple of goons as he went about his business. 'Hey! This guy's packing heat!' declared one of the ill-advised boneheads. 'It comes of being a hot property, buster!' was the rejoinder, before Jay let fly with his fists: 'People get singed just touching me!'

By comparison, the footballing-meets-twisted-scientist-with-a-machine-that-clones-people action detailed in 'The Kysler Experiment' and the Second World War rumpus of 'Hitler Lives' looked a little bit ordinary. Nuclear mayhem in Surrey ('The Walking Bombs') and a super-paranoid *Parallax View*-wannabe featuring a traffic cop getting to the bottom of the assassination of a US president ('Who Killed Cassidy?') were much more on the money. But there was more. The first issue bowed out with the promise of 'another great story next week!' ('Clancy and the Man', of which more below) and the declaration that some bloke called Andy (there was a photo of him and everything) would be available to answer any problems you might have. A problem page? In a boys' comic? You'd better believe it, and one that offered up a two quid postal order for every one printed, and a snazzy Sinclair calculator for the letter Andy liked best.

And write in they did, as this supremely grounded grown-up offered strait-laced advice of the 'do what your parents tell you' variety. Poor fourteen-year-old Derek Connoly from Ireland nursed dreams of joining the RAF, but suffered from poor eyesight. Could he get away with wearing contact lenses? 'I'm sorry, but I'm afraid the answer is "no",' came the reply. You could have sugar-coated it a bit, Andy! In another instance, KB from Crewe felt moved to share: 'I have had two halves of my fingers taken off. I can't hold my fork properly and all the other kids laugh at me. Can you help me?' Andy: 'Your disability is slight compared to people who are seriously handicapped... The knowledge that there are people far worse off than you should make you stop feeling sorry for yourself.' Harsh, but fair, and at least KB was awarded one of those slimline calculators for his efforts. Here's hoping he was still sufficiently dexterous to operate it.

But, back to 'Clancy and the Man'. This was *The Crunch*'s own version of your standard odd couple cop drama. In the first story, Detective Joe Clancy went undercover to break up a mob, however things quickly turned nasty and he was overpowered and tied up. At this point a 'Negro' loomed over him with a knife and things weren't looking great until he delivered a boot to his apparent assailant's jaw, quipping, 'have a little "sole" music man!' It was thus inevitable that said assailant was actually his new partner, also staging a covert operation: 'Yeah baby! Manfred's the name! From now on it'll be Clancy and the Man!' Although it's easy (and enjoyable) to make fun of the comic's clunking contribution to race relations, it has to be acknowledged this was fairly progressive stuff, particularly when you consider the mainly square-jawed Anglo-Saxon characters that were dominating the industry at the time. It should also be noted that near the end of 1979, the publication was introducing us to 'Britain's only female secret agent', Ebony. 'Black, beautiful and deadly!', and a good ten years before the arrival of Eve and 'Third World War' in *Crisis*.

So, a cautious tip of the hat for that.

Over the next year, the mix remained pretty much the same, with the comic essaying an above average selection of sci-fi, sport and action. 'Manhunter' and 'Arena' were regular presences within its pages, as was – hooray! – Andy. Other highlights included space opera action from the twenty-sixth century with 'Starhawk', a precursor to *Spike*'s 'The Bleak Street Bunch' in the form of school misery strip 'The Mill Street Mob' ('I told you before about sniffling!' says one child to his weeping peer. 'Shut up or I'll thump you properly!') and the gripping 'Operation Omega' which told the tale of a group of international criminals who held a North Sea oil rig hostage.

But, alas, it wasn't to last as *The Crunch* faced its own crunch decision in light of poor sales. Just fifty-four issues and one year after it had made so many promises, the title merged with the comparatively wimpy and decidedly old-fashioned *Hotspur*.

The Dandy
(DC Thomson, 1937-ongoing, every Friday)

This is the big one and, really, it's here our story starts. Surely there can be no one in the country who hasn't held a copy of Britain's longest-running comic in their hands at least once in their life?

Any way you look at it, *The Dandy* is an incredible publishing success story. Not only was it the first 'real' comic produced in the UK but – unlike ninety per cent of all the other titles referred to in this book – at the time of writing it's still going strong(ish).

It's almost unthinkable to consider a time before the children's comic-strip weekly was formulated, but let's look at that grisly era now. Having established its presence in the story papers market with the likes of *Adventure* (1921-61) and *Wizard* mk I (1922-63), DC Thomson began to dabble in humour. One of the first fruits of this experiment was a pull-out comic supplement, *Fun Section*, which appeared in the company's *Sunday Post* newspaper. It was here legendary strips 'Oor Wullie' and 'The Broons' debuted, and before too long it became obvious there was a real market for funny stuff.

The company's managing director of children's publications, RD Low, took charge of putting together a team to capitalise on this discovery, drafting in colleagues who were, in the main, employed on the story papers and appointing an editor in the form of *Wizard* mk I and *Rover* (DC Thomson, 1922-73) chief sub-editor Albert Barnes. Together they created something that was both anarchic and archaic right from the very beginning.

The Dandy Comic, as it was first called, was lumbered with a name that seemed old fashioned even in the Thirties. Surely not intended as a throwback to the outrageous behaviour of Oscar Wilde, it seemed to be a fumbled effort by DC Thomson to get with the kids' street slang. But it didn't really matter because, as with the equally cluelessly named *The Beano*, the moniker was immaterial. In fact, for the majority of the audience, it didn't actually mean anything – it was just a name.

Besides, there were far more notable things going on here. Unlike other children's titles, *The Dandy Comic* was half-tabloid in size (the norm at that time was for something akin to broadsheet) and shockingly colourful. Not only that, aping the American titles, it was vulgar enough to use speech balloons in a significant number of its stories, eschewing the traditional pictures and caption arrangement.

Issue one was dated 4 December 1937, and even back then, it was *de rigeur* for new launches to be accompanied with a free gift. *The Dandy's* wasn't half bad; an 'express whistler' which, according to the pre-publicity, provided 'eight different [steam] engine whistles in one'. On that historic front cover we found 'Korky the Cat' (he'd remain in residence for nigh-on fifty years) who came up with a clever wheeze to steal a plump fish being worked on by a chef (he swapped if for one from a display case). Owing more than a little to American cartoon character Felix the Cat (created at the start of the century), poor old Korky would barely utter a word until 1942.

Inside, readers found a mixture of 'proper' comic-strips, picture stories with captions and text-only tales. Here, they were also introduced to another legend-in-the-making (and the man who'd eventually unseat that feline from the cover in 1984), Desperate Dan. 'He's the toughest of the tough – watch our Danny do his stuff' ran the tagline as we were introduced to a Wild West varmint who seemed rather handier with his fists ('Aw gee, Dan! You wouldn't beat me up, would you?') than the lovable great lummox we'd take to our hearts.

Other strips included the permanently snacking 'Hungry Horace' ('Now for that pie!'); junior Red Indian braves 'Wig and Wam'; the tale of one lad and his 'queer-looking' pet, 'Jimmy and his Grockle'; 'Freddy the Fearless Fly'; naughty juvenile 'Podge' (who, to be honest, was not overly corpulent, despite the name); perpetual peeping tom 'Keyhole Kate'; and 'Mugg Muggins: The Crazy Inventor'.

It was a strong opener and one in the eye for rivals Amalgamated Press whose titles – which included *Comic Cuts* (1890-1953) and the relatively new *Jolly Comic* (1935-9) – suddenly looked painfully old-fashioned.

No sooner had *The Dandy* established itself, than the entire publication was placed in jeopardy with the outbreak of war. Although paper rationing quickly became a fact of life, the comic wasn't truly affected until 1941, the 6 September edition declaring across the front: '*The Dandy* now appears every second Tuesday', while below, Korky concerned himself with getting one over on a Mexican pie thief. The page count reduced to sixteen, and for the next eight years the publication would alternate weeks with *The Beano*, while dispatching Desperate Dan to ape Lord Kitchener's famous recruitment poster, advising kids '*You* can help Britain by collecting waste-paper'. In addition, the burly cowpoke also contributed more directly to frontline efforts, in one instalment allowing his over-grown chest hair to be turned into bayonets, in another, enlisting with the Navy and using a frigate's anti-aircraft gun to compete in a fairground shooting range.

Meanwhile, the young scamps who populated 'Our Gang' constructed their own tank, Korky laid on catering for the RAF, Hungry Horace used his gas mask case as a handy place to store cakes (while Keyhole Kate diligently took her equipment to be examined and tested), Podge helped the AFs put out a fire and Freddy the Fearless Fly pilfered from a food salvage container – which wasn't really observing the spirit of things.

Determined to keep the nation's morale buoyant, the publication also introduced us to 'Addy and Hemmy'; Hitler and pal being generally crap Nazis, speaking in tortured Teutonic tones ('Der search is over! Soon now we eat! Three heils for me, Hermy!') whose nefarious schemes always ended up with the pair of them getting a black eye.

Aside from the propaganda, the war years also bequeathed *The Dandy* with an iconic character in the shape of champion sheepdog Black Bob, who arrived in 1944 (regularly returning to the comic until 1982, making him God knows how old in canine years come retirement). With his master, the be-capped, shepherd's-crook-wielding Andrew Glen, '*The Dandy* wonder dog' would rescue children stranded at the bottom of deep gorges, tangle with evil birds of prey, care for the blind and, more than anything else, foil the schemes of poachers, spies, smugglers and crooks everywhere.

A less successful innovation from those years was 'The Amazing Mr X'. 'What is he? What is the Secret of his Amazing Strength?' ran the breathless prose. 'Every boy and girl will be speaking about the Mysterious Mr X!' A blatant rip-off of Superman (who'd been created eleven years previously) alas, few found themselves chatting about the bespectacled 'private enquiry agent' Len Manners, who transformed himself into a black-clad superhero to go off and do daring things. His first mission involved saving the crew of a sinking ship before rescuing a boy from some falling logs on his way back home. He'd only have another thirteen such sorties until the strip was axed; hastily drafted in replacement 'Danny Longlegs: He's ten feet tall and up to the ears in trouble!' being much more the sort of thing readers wanted to see.

Following the war years and into the Fifties, *The Dandy Comic* became just plain old *The Dandy* and, with paper rationing easing off, its page count gradually began to increase. Highlights from this decade included the introduction of Dennis the Menace wannabe, 'The Smasher', rubbish handyman 'Screwy Driver' and 'Willie Willikin's Pobble' (something of a sequel to 'Jimmy and his Grockle' in that it too featured a lad and his weird looking pet, this one in the habit of saying 'pobble-pobble-pobble').

Into the Sixties, and it was here the bellboy was finally given his cards as the comic embraced a bold new look. Corporal Clott now signed on for duty inside (long after hostilities were over, it has to be said), whereupon he set about continually annoying his poor superior officer (*'Aargh!* You nitwit, Clott!') and quickly found himself billeted across the centre pages.

January 1961 saw the comic celebrate its thousandth issue, with Korky demanding a present from the editor to mark the fact he'd appeared in every one of them so far. Also arriving around this time was 'The World's Wiliest Wangler', schoolboy Winker Watson who seemed to attend a version of public school that harked from the nineteenth century. There, he tangled with Greytowers School's most feared housemaster, the cane-happy Mr Creep.

Then, in December 1964, another highly successful scholastic-based hero arrived, in the shape of robot pupil Brassneck. With flesh and blood chum Charley Brand, he got up to all manner of hi-jinks – the public at large being unconcerned about the walking-talking automaton within their midst. A less whimsical partnership were Bully Beef and Chips. The former was a malevolent, burly lad with a pudding basin haircut (the inspiration for *Viz*'s 'Biffa Bacon' strip) who'd regularly visit violence on the comparatively small Chips ('Ooh! You rotter!'), until the latter employed his superior intellect to outwit him at the story's end. It didn't take long for their constant feuding to spill out onto the back cover.

With other strips including 'Young Dandy', sci-fi kid 'Jack Silver', 'Sir Coward de Custard' and 'Monkey Bizness' keeping things ticking over nicely, the comic sailed on into the Seventies to enjoy something of a makeover halfway through the decade. With an influx of new characters suddenly invading the comic, the most notable of the lot had to be the feuding 'The Jocks and The Geordies', all-out gang warfare as the representatives of neighbouring regions (one side decked out in tartan bonnets, the others in school uniform) inflicted maximum damage on each other.

Others, such as the poverty-line dwelling Izzy Skint ('You bet he is!'), 'Tom Tin and Buster Brass' (*Tom and Jerry* cartoons translated into two battling robots) and a canine cowboy, 'Desperate Dawg', kept things ticking over as the decade drew on.

In 1978, the title invited readers to demonstrate their allegiance by joining 'The Desperate Dan Pie-Eaters Club' where – for a measly postal order – you would receive a 'hand painted 3D plastic badge' depicting the cowboy's mug, a 'brightly coloured metal badge' emblazoned with the titular pastry-encased foodstuff, a set of six stickers (including 'I'm a Hee-Hee He-Man' and 'I Love School...' and then in tiny letters: 'closed'), a membership card, club passwords and 'secrets of Dan's muscle-building exercises' all in one themed wallet. Arriving two years after *The Beano* had pulled the same stunt with its 'Dennis the Menace Fan Club', the secrecy with which kids would guard this paraphernalia would turn siblings against each other all over the country.

Celebrating its 2000th edition in 1980 (Korky barbecuing a huge fish over birthday cake candles), *The Dandy* was sailing into uncertain waters as comics began falling by the wayside left, right and centre. Of particular relevance was the failure of *Nutty*, which became the subject of the title's first takeover bid in 1985. As mentioned above, by now Dan was on the front cover, but incoming star Bananaman certainly gave him a run for his money. The following year, the same thing happened again, but this time it was *Hoot*, a short-lived humour title helmed by *Nutty*'s tearaway toddler, Cuddles, who quickly formed a double act with *Dandy*'s own Dimples to ensure his longevity in his new abode.

Into the Nineties the comic increased its page size and embraced full colour, while Winker Watson returned for one last hurrah and Beryl the Peril – now homeless following the fall of *The Topper* in 1990 – joined the line-up, albeit sporting a heavy makeover. Although the paper was gradually embracing modernity (Beryl now adding various slang phrases to her vocabulary), cameos from old hands such as *Sparky*'s Puss 'n' Boots, *The Beano*'s Jonah and the comics' own Keyhole Kate made sure the shock of the new was sufficiently mild so as not to aver the old-timers still looking in (and now doubtlessly pressing the paper onto their own kids to read).

In 1999, there was something to celebrate as the publication clocked up its 3007th issue, officially making it the longest running comic ever (that accolade was previously held by Harmsworths/Amalgamated Press' *Comic Cuts* which had produced 3006 editions between 1890 and 1953).

But storm clouds were gathering.

By the start of the twenty-first century, the coveted front page spot seemed to be up for grabs. Sometimes Dan was in the spotlight, some-times Cuddles and Dimples, and sometimes Bananaman (who'd devel-oped a rather broad steak of vanity: 'Aren't I fabulous?', indeed). However, despite the innovation, it was becoming increasingly obvi-ous *The Dandy* was in trouble. As rumours circulated it was heading for merger-death with *The Beano*, the likes of skateboarder Ollie Fliptrik ('Mean old Mum – dude!'), a surprisingly faithful Corporal Clott revival and Timmy Mallet lookalike Blinky plied their wares regardless.

In October 2004, it was obvious big things were afoot, particularly when a laconic-looking handyman showed up on the cover, systematical-ly dissembling the comic's logo. 'What's going on?' ran the strap line. 'Huge news about us.' Inside, the enigmatic advert ran: *'The Dandy's* changing...can you handle it?'

The full revelation took place on 16 October that year, as a completely revamped, ultra-glossy *Dandy* arrived on the news-stands. Sporting the 'grossest free gift ever!' (a fake tongue) it introduced us to a new faux editor character (the skin-headed Dermot) who told us: 'We're bigger, better and (most important) funnier than ever!' Thankfully, a host of old favourites had survived the changeover (not Korky, though, who'd now fallen out of favour) albeit, in some cases, in a slightly revamped form (Dan was now looking a little less rugged and no longer kept firearms about his person). New characters included Rastafarian detective Dreadlock Holmes and the 'Office Hours' gang (a fictionalised look at the people – and simian – who were now producing the publication), while tousle-haired young ruffian Zak took over as the main draw.

Loosely themed to appear like a TV show (each story's title appearing inside a television set), this was the old *Dandy* ethos filtered through Japanese animé and *The Simpsons*. Explaining the reasons behind the change the (real-life) editor, Morris Heggie, confessed that lately the comic had been 'fun for traditionalists – those children whose parents and grandparents had read it – but it wasn't fun for new readers.' This version was the result of months of consumer research into what kids wanted and it seemed to work – circulation rose by around fifty per cent.

Alongside that, DC Thomson relaunched the comic's website, running polls on favourite characters and inviting readers' comments on the publication. All in all it seemed a credible, if slightly soulless, reinvention of a definitive children's brand. As for whether it'll be enough to secure it another sixty-plus years of weekly mayhem – that remains to be seen.

One thing's for sure, if it does manage to maintain an increased circulation, it will have pulled off something as revolutionary as running those speech balloons back in issue one.

Deadline
(Cardrest Limited/Deadline Publications Ltd, 1988-1995, almost monthly)

October 1988 was an important month for British comics, as two adult-orientated titles slipped onto the shelves at WH Smiths. But, while *Crisis* would pain to bring credibility to comics, *Deadline* was more interested in just plain old street cred.

'I think *Deadline* will be innovative,' explained co-creator Brett Ewins just before launch, 'and that's why it'll be trendy. It's all street level, in that all the fashions are right.' Published by Ewins and fellow *2000 AD* alumni Steve Dillion (the company name would change from Cardrest Limited to Deadline Publications Ltd with issue two), the title set out with no particular mandate other than to look cool and allow an in-crowd of writers and artists to enjoy themselves.

A fusion of pop culture, the first issue (there'd, irritatingly, be eleven published every year making it not quite monthly) declared itself to be a cocktail of 'comics, media, music and *more*'. Thus the, line-up as promoted on the cover was an eclectic one to say the least: Tank Girl, Dave Allen, Jah Wobble, Danny John Jules, House of Love and Brian Bolland. The fact the skinheaded ex-tank pilot who trained for a war that never happened was the only strip to be promoted speaks volumes about its status in the comic.

Created by new boys Jamie Hewlett (who'd go on to visualise Damon Albarn's twenty-first-century take on *The Banana Splits*, the Gorrillaz) and Alan Martin, it was anarchic stuff indeed; all killings ('Let's kick off with a bit of violence!' began the first strip), talking marsupials, pop cultural riffs (which would take in diverse sources, such as *The Gumball Rally* and the Choices pension adverts) and snogging. Relentlessly cool, in other words.

Still, the character was an undisputed hit, a kind of Minnie the Minx for clubbers, who lurched from one bizarre adventure ('The fridge is full of spunk!') to the next with nary a thought for plot while the strip's creators jotted down details of what they'd been listening to that month in the margins ('Soundtrack – The Senseless Things').

Less effortlessly hip was Steve Dillon's futuristic 'Sharp', detailing the life of a video reporter who worked for a small TV station in a North London, er, garage. All rolled-up sleeves and big hair, it was like the comic's own take on Wham! 'I was a Sex Slave Secretary, Starring Beryl the Bitch!' also tried just a little too hard to really convince, subverting the accepted gender norms for a story about sexual harassment in the office in a slight story too easy to ignore.

A bit more like it was 'Wired World', the fun adventures of Pippa and Elizabeth and their Citroën 2CV. Low key, silly and nicely drawn by Phillip Bond, it would be the nearest thing Tank Girl got to a rival. By contrast to everything else in *Deadline*, Brett Ewin's big-hitter 'Johnny Nemo' was much more traditional fare; a sci-fi story about a private investigator working out of New London. Hardboiled stuff ('New London's dangerous, decadent and disgustingly violent – but that's why

I like it') the macho tone sat uneasily alongside the publication's mostly female-led stories and, coupled with the unattractive boxy art was another strip all too easy to skip past.

Augmenting these stories were the features. Future *Channel Four Daily* presenter Garry Rice spoke to stand-up Dave Allen ('If you started censoring yourself you'd close your head off, close your mind down'), Jim McCarthy chatted with lapsed punk Jah Wobble ('Since leaving PiL I've come to realise what a very conservative industry it is'), Ra Khan checked out the thoughts of *Red Dwarf* star Danny John-Jules ('I was a cat in *Cats* as well, so I seem to get a lot of pussy work, as they say') and Brett Ewins caught up with House of Love ('Our music came out of the area we live in').

Future interviewees would include the likes of Susan Tully from *EastEnders* ('The nation's most famous single parent'), 'cult figure in English dance' (it says here) Michael Clark, Buster Bloodvessel, Cud and Gaye Bykers on Acid.

It all added up to a ramshackle publication, a fanzine with everyone doing their own thing. But it kind of worked. More importantly, the mix of pop and comics made for a title that could be considered in its own way, very much its own sort of a style guide, one that would happily sit on that black ash coffee table alongside the likes of *The Face* and *i-D*.

Strips came and went, while 'Tank Girl', 'Wired World' and 'Johnny Nemo' remained a fairly consistent presence for the first year or so, until creators got bored and moved onto other things; Hewlett and Martin dropping Tank Girl as the personality began advertising Wrangler jeans, to follow supporting characters Jet Girl, Sub Girl and talking Kangaroo Booga into their own increasingly rudely named tales before coming up with the *Wacky Races*-alike 'Fireball'.

Nick Abadiz jumped on board with the navel-gazing 'Hugo Tate' strips ('Dear Diary – What am I doing here?'), while Phillip Bond jettisoned 'Wired World' for the more overtly bizarre 'Cheeky Wee Budgie Boy' (a leather jacket-clad, man-budgie hybrid).

By the time fellow adult comic *Crisis* had bit the dust (and let's not forget Fleetway Publications' own take on *Deadline*, **Revolver**, which came and went in the blink of an eye), founding fathers Ewins and Dillion were nowhere to be seen, but the title continued to bloom.

1991 brought a US edition, published by Dark Horse, which repackaged old strips, while Tank Girl – who'd still show up in the British publication from time to time – went on to bag her own title. All in all, it looked like *Deadline* was going to do more than just survive; it seemed to be taking on the world. However, it was the expansion across the pond that would seal the title's fate.

When execs at MGM came across the *Tank Girl* comic, they contacted Hewlett and Martin about making a feature film adaptation. Despite their misgivings ('They were all full of shit,' recalled Hewlett. 'Really patronising. They'd say things like "Hollywood is like a Pizza. Everyone puts on different toppings and if you get it right you get a good movie!"') they signed the rights away and the result was…a crap film in 1995. To make matters worse, another American Tank Girl comic spun off from this, and suddenly it wasn't fun anymore.

With the movie failing to gross the sort of money expected, the party was over for *Deadline*, which bowed out with an extra-large 'summer special' issue sixty-nine – rather fitting considering its sense of humour. Just as the comic had arrived, so it went with the character who'd made it and then broken it – Tank Girl – wreaking her own brand of mayhem on the front cover.

Debbie
(DC Thomson, 1973-1983, every Saturday)

OK. So you wanted reliable, unthreatening comic-strip fun, in the main themed around stories of ballet, school and horses, and you wanted all this to be helmed by a precocious young lady with a soft spot for small furry animals. Where were you going to go? Well, loads of places to be honest, as back in the day this seemed to be the template for virtually every girls' comic on the market.

However, that's not knocking the format, which proved to be hugely successful while it lasted. In fact, it's a testament to its durability that **Bunty**, **Judy**, **Mandy**, **June** and *Debbie* could sit alongside each other on the newsagent's rack, pretty much offering the same thing as each other, but still expect to find their own audience.

Out of this particular five it would probably be fair to say the latter was the least distinguished. It wasn't as though there was anything especially wrong with *Debbie*, it's just that the comic never really ventured much past mediocre – but that was OK. In the cruel and competitive cliques frequented by prepubescent girls, there was a lot to be said for being one of the crowd, and this tactic bought the comic a decent ten-year run.

Issue one arrived on 17 February 1973, getting all het-up about its 'special free gift for trendy girls!' The exciting item came in the form of 'a lovely cameo Beauty Brooch', which was plastered all over the front cover, and sported a Grecian-looking woman in profile, just what all trendies were looking for to brighten up their lapels.

Debbie – © DC Thomson & Co., Ltd

Inside, it was bog-standard stuff – 'Daisy Dean: The Little Beauty Queen', 'Superstitious Cindy', 'A Horse for Hattie', 'Jane Green's Schooldays' *et al.* contained few surprises but did the job admirably well. Other strips of note during the early years included 'The Circus Slave' (young Lucy Lester duped into performing dangerous stunts in the big top under the misapprehension she was raising money to aid her sick mother), 'The Rival O'Rileys' (feuding sisters Chris and Anne, both of whom wanted careers in show business), 'Lisa The Lonely Ballerina' (a partial retread of Mandy's similarly named 'Lonely Ballerina', only rather than the lead character being sent to Moscow, here Lisa was duped by her evil ballet-hating Aunt Edith into flying to a harsh Welsh retreat instead of the school in Vienna she had set her heart on), the superbly named 'We'll Show Those Boys!' (three girls attend the famous Adventure School for boys) and 'The Dark Days of Dorcas' (the tale of 'a little London waif' who was forced to work for a chimney sweep by the cruel Mrs Greems).

Supplementing the strips were a slew of breezy features. 'Debbie's Bright Spot' had our hostess challenging us with an array of brainteasers ('Look closely at this beach scene and see how many things you can spot beginning with the letter "S"'), the pretty useless 'Bright Spot Star Cut-Out' (a quarter-page black and white illustration of a Bobby Crush-value celeb), the short-lived 'Poets' Corner' (verse sent in by readers) and the bustling mailbag that was 'Penny's Post' ('Super prizes to be won! Cameras, watches, hockey sticks, postal orders, record tokens' etc. etc.).

In January 1978, it incorporated the mystery paper *Spellbound*, meaning a slight tinge of the occult fell over proceedings (the ghostly 'Cat's Eye Cottage' in 1979, for one), but all in all the likes of the calamitous Maisie – who'd by now taken over the front cover – and the cute 'Superpets' feature ('This little papillon dog weighs less than two pounds!') kept everything sufficiently saccharine.

Alas, come the Eighties, even a last-minute flirtation with photo-strip action ('The Randell Road Girls') couldn't stem the drop-off in readers, and after 513 issues, on 22 January 1983, *Debbie* was swallowed up by big sister *Mandy*. Suddenly, your options for reliable, unthreatening comic-strip fun themed around stories of ballet, school and horses were looking a tad limited.

Diana
(DC Thomson, 1963-1976, every Monday)

It was perhaps a bit late in the day to launch a counterblast to *Girl* mk I, but that's exactly what *Diana for Girls* appeared to be. A large format, photogravure publication, sporting a red masthead, it was classy stuff, imbued with a suspiciously Fifties brand of edifying edutainment.

Hence, alongside the typical female fodder of plucky orphans ('Topspin Terry'), talented-but-mystery-shrouded-dancers ('Paula with the White Mask'), fashion conscious young sprites ('Jane: Model Miss') and go-getting bright sparks ('The Sea Stars'), readers also ran slap-bang into – ulp! – actual lessons. This all came courtesy of 'Diana's Special Getting-to-Know Section' which could contain any, or all, of the following: A feature on joining a pony club, a comic-strip biography of Queen Victoria, an adaptation of a Shakespeare play, nifty ideas for summer hats (or, 'gay ways for sunny days'), secrets for successful decorating and some kind of sub-*National Geographic* page telling you about various animals.

Cut, then, to 1976. By now the title had swallowed up old timer *Romeo* and, rather than bringing us the life story of some dusty old monarch, the paper's centre pages were dedicated to 'a super pop cube'. Yep, by taking a pair of round-tipped scissors to the publication's guts and following the instructions provided, you could fold and stick your way to owning an insanely flimsy six-sided shape, decked out with images of Showaddywaddy, the Sweet and Hello.

Fashion was less make and do, and more gawping at photos of girls with back-combed hair modelling a 'Sloppy Joe' velour tracksuit ('£9.50 from Top Shop'). Elsewhere, 'Pop Around' revealed the likes of David Essex were now reading the paper, while features mined the 'readers' true life experience's vein rather than the textbooks.

Comic-strips were still an important part of the mix, although these were less concerned with cruel guardians and more intent on detailing the travails of a Bay City Rollers fan and her quest for love ('I could kiss you and kiss you and...'), or the girl-next-door-type adventures of 'Jo and Co', the heroine of which did her thing decked out in requisite tank top and flared trousers.

Still glossy – although now dedicating its colour pages to photo pin-ups – and still printed in a larger-than-A4 format, *Diana* had proved it could move with the times. Despite that, it had the indignity of being swallowed up by its little sister title *Jackie* in 1976. Blimey the rows that must have gone on when those two siblings were forced into a bedroom share betwixt the same cover...

Doctor Who Weekly
(Marvel Comics Ltd, 1979-1980, every Thursday)

'Fully authorised by the BBC'! 'Top quality full colour glossy covers!' 'Free gifts of transfers with first four issues'! These were just some of the

selling points of Marvel UK's new publication, a tie-in with the then phe-
nomenally popular BBC series which, three days after the paper's launch,
enjoyed its best ever viewing figure of 16.1 million. Although the impressive figure was helped by the fact ITV was on strike, *Doctor Who* was still
a potentially hugely yielding cash cow for any plucky publisher to milk.

It was former ***Whizzer and Chips*** editor Dez Skinn who was first to
really get his hands on those teats. Although the Time Lord's adventures
had been appearing in strip form since 1964 in the pages of *TV Comic*,
the character had only ever been afforded a couple of pages a week. Now,
with Marvel overlord Stan Lee demanding the UK arm bumped up its
portfolio, Skinn approached the BBC about licensing the Doctor for his
own publication.

The result was *Doctor Who Weekly* (thusly named because the editor
couldn't decide if it was supposed to be a comic or a magazine), which
was launched nationwide via a series of personal appearances by Tom
Baker (then playing the Time Lord onscreen), who didn't even get paid
for his efforts.

That 'fantastic first issue' (dated 17 October 1979) had it all: 'Comic-
strips! Features! Pin-ups!' and came free with a set of transfers depicting
the Doc running away from some pterodactyls. Meanwhile, looming out
at us from the cover was a photo of our mildly euphoric-looking hero,
molesting a Dalek.

Things kicked off in style inside, with the first part of the comic-strip
'Doctor Who and the Iron Legion', the creation of *2000 AD*'s Pat Mills
and John Wagner who'd previously submitted the idea to the television
series as a potential story. Illustrated by fellow Tharg moonlighter and
former *Tornado* pin-up Dave 'Big E' Gibbons, it was action-packed stuff,
sufficiently faithful to the TV series' own brand of whimsy ('I don't sup-
pose you accept Zaggan pound notes...? They're a little on the slimy
side, but absolutely inflation proof!') it also made good use of the bud-
getless restraints of the form, providing our hero with an epic-scale
adventure a long way from the relative dimensions in time and Surrey
seen on TV.

Next came another excitement – 'A Letter from the Doctor'. Dated
'Paztenmber 42st, 1845', it welcomed us all to his paper and, most
importantly of all, bid us 'Happy times and places'. To cap it all, he'd
even signed the thing, thereby proving it surely must have come from
the Time Lord's own hand. Er, although obviously it didn't – Skinn

wrote the piece himself when Baker explained he wouldn't have time to pen a weekly missive.

A feature on the history of the Daleks followed, before things took a bit of a nose dive. Here a reprint of a 1976 Marvel strip, 'War of the Worlds' was plugged into the publication to pad out four and a half pages. A head and shoulders of the Doctor was dropped into the start of the thing to make it appear as though he was 'presenting' the story (actually, he was just quoting the opening passage from HG Wells' book), and thus stressing its relevancy to proceedings.

We were back into features again with 'The Story of Dr Who', and a crazy caption competition – a photo of Tom Baker, metallic mutt K-9 and assorted alien nasties lining up for immigrant visas (in reality, a press shoot designed to promote the series' launch in America, but a political hot potato in this day and age, surely?).

As things drew to a close, we were then face-to-face with an unflattering photograph of William Hartnell for a 'Doctor Who Photo-File' ('William Hartnell's favourite role, in his long and highly successful acting career, was as Doctor Who') and finally, more comic-strip action. This was a bit more like it. Although the Doc was again drafted in to provide another scene-setting intro, the story, 'The Return of the Daleks' had actually been created especially for the paper. Telling of a time when the 'preposterous pepperpots' (© every magazine article ever) were seemingly long since extinct, it followed the fortunes of 'hologram-movie' mogul Glax who'd fallen on hard times. Despite the fact his starlets 'do have the cutest antennae on the planet', box office receipts were down. Deciding to produce a feature about the 'metal meanies' (see copyright details, above) he coincidentally became embroiled in the species' sudden return to infamy. 'Ex-ter-min-ate!' and all that; although it should be noted that, at this stage, in their naïvety Marvel Comics had just assumed the BBC owned the rights to the alien critters and gone ahead and put them in the *Weekly* without checking out what permissions were required. In fact, they were actually the property of writer Terry Nation. Thankfully it seems he wasn't sufficiently vexed by the unauthorised use of his characters to do anything about it.

The paper continued in pretty much this vein for the next few months. Doctor Who Appreciation Society bod Jeremy Bentham providing the facts (and, once the publication's initial stock of 300 photos supplied by the Beeb ran out, pictures too) while the comic-strips went about their business in fine style (well, barring that 'War of the Worlds' reprint) with familiar monsters such as Cybermen and Sontarans appearing in the back page stories, plus solo outings for K-9 and the Time Lords.

Although some readers seemed quite taken with the venture – 'I enjoy reading *Doctor Who Weekly* because it is so different, and I was getting bored with all the other comics,' wrote Philip Sadler from Raglan in issue eight's letters page – things were getting tough for the publication. Faced with dwindling sales and an AWOL editor (Skinn jetted off to the US and then quit), it looked as though the Doc's number was up.

April 1980 brought something of a relaunch, amping up the juvenile content. Aside from a greater prominence of comic-strip and new text story fodder, there was also 'Fantastic Facts' culled from *Fortean Times* ('The planet Mars has two tiny moons which orbit in opposite directions') and – better yet – the 'UNIT Club Page'. Devoted to the governments killing aliens division, it enlisted readers to sign-up and help protect Earth from alien invasion, in much the same way **Starlord** had recruited a junior taskforce for a similar purpose. A weekly fix of paranoia, it regularly featured blurry photos of supposed flying saucers, and pumped out coded messages which could only be deciphered by those who'd joined up (shades of **Warlord**'s 'Calling All Warlord Agents!' shenanigans).

With covers increasingly being devoted to the Doctor's comic-strip alter ego, it all proved something of a turn-off for the readership who were in fact older than the editorial team had realised. As the circulation continued to fall, photo frontages crept back in again and Marvel swiftly backed out of that blind alley. But the damage had been done. With sales too low to remain sustainable, it seemed this time it really was the end.

But then *Doctor Who Weekly* regenerated. In August 1980, the titular Time Lord sat down with quill in hand to advise us, 'Big news folks! My friends at Marvel inform me that as of next week *Dr Who Weekly* will become a monthly comic.' The decision had come when the new editor, Paul Neary, had realised the best way to stretch his budget was to print less regularly. This, and increased sales thanks to the title's longer shelf life, secured the publication's existence. Taking note of the readership's preference, the comic-strip content was reduced to just one story a month and instead the magazine concentrated on documenting every imaginable detail about the television series. Now a 'Marvel Monthly', the paper was a comic no more.

Since those times, the title has prospered, surviving the cancellation of the series in 1989 and the all-but demise of Marvel UK in the Nineties. Now published by Panini and given a fresh impetus by the series' return to our screens in 2005, it remains a publishing success story, bringing delight to Whovians everywhere; particularly when it killed off annoying TV companion Ace in a 1996 comic-strip. You definitely 'did good' that time, fellas.

Eagle mk I
(Hulton Press Ltd/Longacre Press/Odhams Press Ltd/IPC Magazines Ltd, 1950-1969, every Friday)

Who would have thought the most celebrated British weekly ever could have arisen from a concerted effort to provide a morally wholesome alternative to the irresponsible and violent comics shipping in from America? Sounds like an unpromising starting point, doesn't it? When you also consider its genesis can be traced back to a failing parish magazine and a man of the cloth who would guide the paper through its glory years, the whole thing sounds like a humungous *Look and Learn*-style exercise in No Fun.

But that was *Eagle* mk I, a glorious product of the Brylcreem and Meccano era which enflamed the imaginations of all who read it. It was the comic that brought the world Dan Dare and Captain Pugwash, set dizzying standards in terms of art (which have never been equalled), published the work of a tyro David Hockney and Gerald Scarfe (who sent in their etchings to the letters page), prompted a young Stephen Hawking to look to the stars and enflamed the imagination of Queen axe-man Brian May – but don't hold that against it.

And yet, despite it lasting nigh-on twenty years, in actual fact it's only the first ten that could be described as truly glorious, because the *Eagle* history is one of two halves: The rise to the top, and then the slow ignominious tumble into merger-death with a comic not even fit to share its staples. Its one of the bitterest tales from the once-competitive world of British comics.

In 1946, rakish Southport-based Reverend Marcus Morris – a self-confessed carouser, drinker, womaniser and clubber – overhauled the St James' parish magazine into a lively publication that owed more than a little to *Picture Post*. Renaming this venture *The Anvil*, circulation quickly rose into the thousands. The discovery of gifted local artist Frank Hampson, who contributed top quality illustrations and strips, was an added bonus.

A success it may have been, but the title quickly fell into debt, the Rev holding numerous jumble sales and the like in a desperate effort to keep his baby afloat.

Trying to raise more money as a jobbing writer, he knocked-up a piece for the *Sunday Despatch* entitled 'Comics that bring Horror into the Nursery' about the recent influx of US publications. Declaring the stuff to be morally reprehensible, it put the notion in his head to come up with something to combat the 'nastily over-violent and obscene' stories that were proving so popular.

The initial idea was to create a strip with Hampson for the *Sunday Empire*. To be entitled 'Lex Christian', the unpromising concept followed the adventures of a tough parson in London's east end slums. However, following the death of the paper's editor in a gliding accident, the duo were prompted to rethink their efforts and decided they should go for broke by producing a whole comic instead.

Assembling a team of Southport-based artists and writers (including Rev Chad Varah who'd go on to found the Samaritans), a dummy was knocked up which the would-be editor hawked around London. Named *Eagle* (although not yet sporting the famous bird emblem, which would be designed by Hampson's wife Dorothy and based on Morris' ornamental brass inkwell), its main attraction was 'Chaplain Dan Dare of the Inter-Planet Patrol' – a character created by Hampson. Sans those famous lightening-strike eyebrows and decked out in a cape and dog collar, this wasn't quite the full Dan, but it showed plenty of promise.

Initially, reaction proved frosty until Hulton Press – who at that time had no stake in the juvenile market and were better known for the aforementioned *Picture Post* – snapped it up. The team were now charged with making the notion a reality and consulted youth workers across the country about their ideas for the venture. Was it going to prove suitably edifying for a young audience? As the launch date drew near, the tension grew – particularly when the schedule was brought forward due to fears of a rival spoiler publication. Hampson established a studio of artists in an old bakery to knock out 'Dan Dare' and everyone knuckled down.

When the first edition arrived on 14 April 1950, boys across the country flocked to the newsagent resulting in sales of just less than one million. Tabloid sized and sporting eight beautiful photogravure colour pages (out of twenty, which would then drop to sixteen with issue two), it was certainly a handsome product and one that superbly displayed the top quality work the team were turning out.

Leading the charge was 'Dan Dare: The Pilot of the Future', Hampson's beautifully wrought imagining of an atomic-powered Britain – all snub-nosed rocket ships, gyroscopic cars and plumes of smoke dissolving into blue skies.

That first issue also included an adaptation of the popular police radio series *PC 49*; the mysteries of radar explained by Professor Brittain; an advertorial in the shape of 'Tommy Walls' (which promoted Wall's ice-cream via one young lad's adventures); three-panel humour with 'Chicko'; cowboy action in 'Rob Conway'; marsupial mayhem courtesy of 'Skippy the Kangaroo' (predating the similarly named TV series by over ten years); salty seadog silliness with John Ryan's 'Captain Pugwash' and the life of disciple Paul in 'The Great Adventurer', in what would become the regular back page God/historical slot.

Over the next few weeks, the comic just got better and better, and reached out to readers in way few had ever managed. While Dan Dare met that melon-headed meanie the Mekon on Venus, tens of thousands signed up to the *Eagle* club, readers devoured Morris' editorials, gawped at the innards of planes, trains and automobiles (and, in 1954, a speculative *Eagle* spaceship) courtesy of 'exploded' cross-section illustrations, and then puzzled over the short-lived inclusion of *Tintin* reprints which briefly replaced Skippy's adventures. They also wrote in to nominate do-gooders for the prestigious 'Mug of the Month' slot, where brave youngsters were celebrated for their courageous deeds.

With sales sky-rocketing, Hulton were keen to expand their empire, prompting Morris to formulate companion paper *Girl* **mk I** in 1951, the tots' title *Robin* two years later and finally *Swift* in 1954. Other titles under consideration also included a new newspaper, *The Sunday Star*, adventure title *Wonder* and a junior *Girl* variant, *Wren* – however, none of these came to fruition.

Meanwhile, back in *Eagle*, other strips came along, including superior cowboys 'n' Indians stuff in 'Riders of the Range', desert-based adventure in 'Luck of the Legion' and defective detecting courtesy of Ryan's hapless 'Harris Tweed'.

None of this could hold a candle to 'Dan Dare', though, which thanks to Hampson's strictly run studio was turning out astonishingly good stuff every week. However, the demands paid a heavy toll on the artist who grew increasingly obsessive about maintaining quality on the strip, and also bitter towards both Morris and the character for the demands they were making on him. When he submitted and then withdrew his resignation in 1957, it was just one of many signs it was all becoming too much. The later discovery that his editor was secretly investigating the possibility of a Dare film behind his back did little to improve the mood.

But there were even greater rumbles in the Hulton head offices as, also in 1957, *Picture Post* (which had boasted it was read by eighty per cent of the population during the war years) was forced to close in light of falling sales. The company was in for a rocky ride. Keeping the faith with Morris, he was promoted to chief executive in 1958. However, a few months later they suddenly suggested perhaps it hadn't been such a great idea after all: 'It is unfair to expect you...to devote part of your time to management,' back-tracked Chairman and Managing Director Sir Edward Hulton. With profits falling, the firm was now actively looking around for someone to buy them out, and they didn't want the Rev impeding their progress.

The following year, there was unrest in the publishing world. The Mirror Group acquired the mighty Amalgamated Press (which, at the time, was putting out forty-two weeklies, twenty-three monthlies and twenty annuals), causing unrest at rivals Odhams Press. Keen to bolster their own position, they started looking around for a company they could acquire. Step forward a ready and willing Hulton, which was snapped up by its new owners in March, and renamed Longacre Press (after their premises in Long Acre, London).

Immediately the new whips wanted to streamline the operation. They couldn't see why Hampson needed a studio of artists to produce 'Dan Dare' every week and were keen to see the strip pass into the hands of a sole creator. But, if it looked like the artist had been backed into the corner – this wasn't the case. During that year he was approached by Leonard Matthews who wanted him to helm a new comic the Mirror Group were planning: *Bulldog*. Willing to pay Hampson twice what he'd been earning on *Eagle*, the deal hit a snag because, although he was keen to oversee the project, he just didn't want to draw anymore. Despite Matthews' best efforts, the plan fell apart.

With budget cuts affecting staff morale on *Eagle*, Morris sensed it was time for him to be going – particularly as his new overlords were getting increasingly sniffy about his expense account. On 30 September he left and took up a job with the National Magazine Company (whose logo was an eagle, neatly enough) to oversee their women's titles such as *She* and *Cosmopolitan*. It had been a long road from parish magazines to this. His last letter appeared in the comic on 31 October. 'Good luck to you all,' he said.

Those left on the title were certainly going to need it.

By now, Hampson had dropped 'Dan Dare' to concentrate on a comic-strip version of the life of Christ, entitled 'The Road of Courage' (which, although credited to Morris, was actually written by Rev Guy Daniel). However, some sources claim the Southport artist planned to return to the sci-fi strip after a year's sabbatical. It didn't happen. Clifford Makins came in as editor, and in March 1960, the comic got a new look. Gone was the familiar *Eagle* red box in the top left-hand corner, to be replaced by a more typical banner. By now, legendary artist Frank Bellamy was drawing 'Dan Dare' (albeit with Hampson stalwart Don Harley told to rework his likenesses, much to both men's chagrin) and the page count had been bumped up to twenty.

There was yet more upset in 1961 when Odhams tried to square up to old rivals, the Mirror Group. Making a bid to acquire the company's Fleetway periodicals and magazines, they were suddenly on the back foot when the Fleet Street giants instead moved in to snap them up in a bitter and hostile takeover bid. The transaction was opposed by the unions citing the monopolies commission, but it came to naught. By March, *Eagle* was under new management again – and this lot were even more prickly than the last.

Overseeing the company's new juvenile properties was – that man again – Leonard Matthews. However, if he thought he finally had Hampson under the thumb, he was to be disappointed, the creator bowing out of *Eagle* altogether upon the completion of his religious strip. He wasn't the only one to go: Makins resigned as editor when he was told he'd have to rubber-stamp a new wave of draconian cut-backs and John Ryan pulled up anchor, deciding to concentrate on his *Captain Pugwash* TV series (which started in 1957) when it became clear the new bosses weren't interested in renewing his annual contract.

Old stories were yanked out of the Fleetway archive, and dusted down for a repeat run in *Eagle*, much to the distress of its remaining long time staffers. In particular, 'The Last of the Saxon Kings' appalled with its slap-dash approach to historical accuracy (said Saxon depicted swinging off a chandelier in one episode) and, as sales plummeted, readers' letters arrived asking 'What are you doing to our papers?' while also begging 'Please bring back all those interesting, colourful educational articles we used to have'.

By 1962, circulation had fallen by 150,000 and, in March, *Eagle* got a radical overhaul. Favourites such as 'Storm Nelson', 'Riders of the Range' and 'Harris Tweed' were dropped, while Dan's appearance on the cover was restricted to just one frame, the rest of his story unfolding in black and white inside. A month later, even that frame was no longer appearing regularly. The comic was now decidedly uninspiring-looking, layouts changing on a weekly basis.

The following year, the Pilot of the Future reclaimed his premiere position 'by popular demand' and the title merged with sister paper *Swift*. Then, in 1964, *Girl* was forced to join up with *Princess* mk I (Amalgamated Press/Fleetway, 1960-7), while the short-lived *Boys' World* (Longacre Press, 1963-4) fled for cover under *Eagle*'s wings, bringing with it the dopey super-heroics of 'The Iron Man' – a robot who appeared in human form.

There was some better news in 1965 when Bob Bartholomew took over the editorial reins, vowing to return the comic to greatness. But the tide was well and truly against him. An issue from 1966 reveals a pretty unremarkable line-up, including school jinks in 'Castle Sinister' ('The wretched rotters have rumbled my ruse!'), tasteless sci-fi courtesy of 'The Guinea Pig' (Mike Lane agreeing to allow nutty Professor Dee to test out his latest creations and potions on him) and sub-*Thunderbirds* action courtesy of 'UFO Agents' (Major Grant and 'Boffin' Bailey averting trouble around the globe in their flying saucer).

And then, to make matters worse, the title's last draw, 'Dan Dare', was well and truly emasculated. Spuriously promoting Dan to controller of Space Fleet around Christmas 1967, this cued in a series of 'reminiscences' – or, in other words, re-runs. But these weren't just straightforward reprints; the stories (and therefore Hampson's original artwork) were brutally chopped up as tales like 'Rogue Planet' were streamlined for their new outing.

The final days weren't pretty, with another old strip, 'Mark Question:

The Boy With a Future – But No Past!' being reprinted under the cunning moniker of 'Mark Mystery: The Boy Without a Past'. Meanwhile, 'Wild of the West!' was a poorly drawn yarn about an old time boxer, while 'Speed Mann in H-Bomb Attack!' was witless, high-octane adventure with a pretty unlikable hero and machine gun-touting baddies.

On 26 April 1969, it was all over. With sales pitifully low, *Eagle* faced the indignity of merging with *Lion*, a comparatively low-fi comic that had been set up in 1952 specifically to challenge its supremacy. For the first ten years of *Eagle*'s life, the pretender just didn't have a hope, but now its patient stalking had paid off. IPC – as the company had now become known following a reorganisation of the Mirror's juvenile arms in 1969 – boasted that when the axe fell, they only received six letters of complaint.

From its humble origins in Southport, to its triumphant launch nationwide and its subsequent mauling by Fleet Street hounds, *Eagle*'s journey was an eventful, inspiring but ultimately sad one. Crawling away from the wreckage, Marcus Morris went on to enjoy a long and successful career in publishing while Frank Hampson – heartbroken about what had happened to Dan Dare – would never produce another weekly strip again. Indeed, he spent his last years trying to escape the shadow of his famous creation. 'Although I often wished he would,' he said in 1981, 'Dan Dare refuses to lie down and die. But that's just what I intend to do now.'

Eagle mk II
(IPC Magazines Ltd/ Fleetway Publications, 1982-1993, every Monday)

Dateline: King's Reach Towers, 1982. Behind locked doors, plastered with carefully felt-tipped '*Keep out!*' signs, the top brass at the Boys' Sport and Adventure Department of IPC Magazines were working on 'Operation Eagle'. IPC Group Editor Barrie Tomlinson and David Hunt, the man destined to be the editor of this new paper, were planning to relaunch the famous Fifties comic.

This new *Eagle* would go on to become 'the success story of 1982' (our source: The 1983 *Eagle Annual*).

The first edition hit the news-stands dated 27 March 1982, boasting the 'Return of the Mekon!' in a nice bit of promotional acumen that secured it some modest press coverage, plus a legion of nostalgic dads marching their sons down to the newsagent's. However, from the old guard of original *Eagle* mk I characters it had been decided only Dan Dare (or at least his great, great grandson) was fit to resume service and naturally, his melon-headed nemesis wasn't far behind.

While Dare and fiends were a nod to past glories, everything else about *Eagle* mk II was brand spanking new. Most obviously – and shockingly – four of the paper's stories were photo-strips, a new innovation as far as boys' comics were concerned. Hence, London's shopping precincts and municipal parks were to become the location for a myriad of unconvincingly staged alien invasions, low-rent scuffles, curiously static football matches and scowling rogues getting their comeuppance as plastic-headed alien Doomlord ('Servant of Nox, master life…bringer of death!'), youthful undercover cop Sgt Streetwise, plucky, football-mad twosome Thunderbolt and Smokey! and sub-'Tharg's Future Shocks' peddler, The Collector strutted their stuff for the camera.

But wait, there were still more innovations, as *Eagle* mk II unveiled its final secret weapon, a suite of celebrities happy to either endorse the comic ('The new *Eagle* is definitely *ooookay*!' – thanks for that, Lenny Henry) or actually write for it ('I'm glad to hear that my friend Allan Wells, the Olympic 100 metres champion, is settling in well at his new home in Guildford,' said Daley Thompson in the first of his weekly 'Diary' columns). It even had Radio 1's Breakfast DJ Mike Read on the inside back pages threatening: 'Next week I'll tell you all about my tennis exploits!'

With all that and the ubiquitous 'Space Spinner' (cf. issue one of *2000 AD*) as a free gift, what could possibly go wrong? For a while, not much as 'the adventure paper of the Eighties' plied its photo power for a good eighteen months. But soon financial realities began to bite. For one, it was far more expensive hiring actors and photographers for the creation of photo-strips than employing the talents of some Argentinan artist to sit down and draw the whole thing. Besides, the photo power wasn't going over so well with the readership who were unmoved by the stagy pictures, and unable to get past the format's traditional association with – gulp! – girls' publications. Similarly, the presence of Daley Thomson and Mike Read left most unmoved, and ate into the *Eagle* finances. That, and the expense of printing the whole thing on relatively glossy paper all had a cumulative effect and that phrase which all comic readers feared: 'Next week, we get a new look!' was wheeled out. *Eagle* prepared to downsize.

The issue that hit the news-stands dated 24 September 1983 was a far cry from the expensive looking publication of 1982. Now printed on bog-standard pulp paper and dropping to the favoured four-colour approach of its stablemates, the new-look *Eagle* mk II was packed with comic-strip action, and nothing but. Well, almost. There was still room to splice in 'The Money Page', where readers could win assorted booty; to wit: If you could prove your dad was a '*superdad*!', then stand by for 'a travel-bag full of Brut 33 products by Fabergé'. And for those readers unhappy with the new lo-fi approach, well the free potato gun that came with the issue did much to assuage grumblings.

Despite its shortcomings, this was actually when *Eagle* mk II entered its imperial phase, running ace strips such as 'The Fists of Danny Pyke', a surprisingly visceral Anglicised take on the *Rocky* films superbly drawn by the *Daily Mirror*'s 'Jane' artist, John M Burns and featuring – get this! – a cameo by Harry Carpenter (or a non-copyright threatening lookalike, anyway). 'Dan Dare' still continued in the centre pages, while Doomlord was re-formatted as a skeletal-faced superhero, and press photographer Luke Hackett found himself drawn into danger thanks to 'The Hand' he'd received during a transplant operation, which used to belong to a 'feared contract killer'.

Over the next few years, *Eagle* mk II merrily ploughed its trough, throwing up the odd classic strip along the way. Who can forget 'The Computer Warrior' featuring young Bobby Patterson who'd been flung into a *Tron*-like world where he'd have to battle a real-life version of whatever Spectrum or Commodore 64 game was shifting a huge number of cassettes at the time (in April 1984 he faced a 'Zyklon Attack')? And then there was 'The Hard Men', a knock-off of TV's *The Professionals*, and included here simply to note the titular men were improbably named Clovis and Chowdhary.

During this phase *Eagle* mk II was all-conquering, becoming the comic others would merge with before finally vanishing from the newsagent's shelves forever. Along the way it munched up new kid on the block *Scream!* in June 1984, veteran title *Tiger* in April 1985, *Mask* (IPC Magazines Ltd, 1986-8) in October 1988 and the abortive *Wildcat* in April 1989.

On 26 August 1989, with the comic sporting another new look, the shout went out: 'He's back! The world's number one space hero! The original Dan Dare!' Yes, this was no mere descendant, but the actual Dan McGregor Dare himself, as last spotted sometime in the Sixties and now pressed into service with new adventures illustrated by kosher Dare artist Keith Watson (who'd assisted on the original strips in *Eagle* mk I). As a publicity ploy, it worked, and once again *Eagle* mk II found itself the subject of some modest press attention. And even if the kids didn't know who this new bloke was, the dads loved it, so that was OK.

But the times they were a-changing, and alongside the new-old 'Dan Dare', *Eagle* was now relying more heavily on reprints of old strips first published in other IPC comics. A year on from the relaunch, even Dan was the subject of some nervous tinkering as the four-square hero found himself ditching the Space Fleet blazer and squeezing into a more modern jump-suit. Before long, he was blasting aliens with gay abandon, letting 'em have it with his brand new 'ram gun' (whatever that was) and generally acting as the kind of space lout he himself would have tut-tutted at in the Fifties.

By the start of the Nineties, it was plain *Eagle* mk II was in trouble; the appearance of Michaela Strachan on the front cover of 1990's Christmas issue a worrying sign indeed. Come April 1991, Barrie Tomlinson – now the comic's editor – had a grave announcement for readers, typically dressed up as 'Big news about *Eagle*!' The comic was to become a monthly organ, which despite promises it would contain 'a vast number of pages', was blatantly going to be stuffed full with even more reprints.

The paper carried on in this fashion until it was finally put out of its misery at Christmas 1993. From boasting a circulation of 750,000 *Eagle* mk II had reportedly plummeted to around 20,000 in its last days. Nevertheless, it had enjoyed a respectable eleven-year run, and by the end it was pretty much IPC's lone standard-bearer for the sort of old-fashioned action and adventure comics that had thrilled generations of boys.

Emma
(DC Thomson, 1978-1979, every Monday)

The comic where it was 'all happening for girls!', *Emma* was an empowering thirty-two pages every week which mixed comic-strip fare with celebrity authored pieces. The first issue featured the titular main character dressed up in a majorette's uniform on the front and sported a free gift in the form of 'your very own *initial* brooch (plus a set of super initials)'. Not sure about that? Well, 'it's the *in* thing' advised the blurb at the foot of the page.

Alongside that was probably one of the most appealing billings for any publication ever – 'Inside: Muppets, Keith Chegwin [and] Kid Jensen.' What girl could resist?

So what did *Emma* stand for? If you turned to the inside front page, there it was laid out for you in a simple acronym: 'Emma' is for 'Excitement, Mystery, Marvellous Free Gifts and Action.' The publication had already delivered on the excitement and free gifts – no one could argue with that – but here was where it made good with the action. 'I'm a TV reporter,' explained our hostess, 'and you can read my special "Emma Report" story every week.' She then, perhaps foolishly, declared: 'You name it – I'll do it' before dancing in front of a chunky TV camera in a pair of dungarees with a stern pay off of 'Get the picture, girls?'

Alongside our go-getting editor (who over the coming weeks tried her luck at being a policewoman, hang-gliding, lion-taming and taking part in a sponsored bed-push) we had troublesome student 'Sue Spiker' who proved a dab hand at volleyball; 'Jodie and the Otter', a story about a swimming champ who bales out of an ailing plane to find herself stranded in the North American wilderness with just a water mammal to keep her company ('It's sure nice to have you along! Suddenly I don't feel lonely any more!'); district nurse 'Angie', in a story drawn by regular *Commando* pen-smith Ian Kennedy, and thus featuring armed robbers and plenty of gun-play; a modern day Wild West saga 'Lynne Against Lareno'; and a more traditional girls' comic tale of cruel guardians and impending blindness in 'Blue Eyes'.

In the early days of the publication, each strip was accompanied by its own tickertape strapline ('+ NEWS FLASH + GIRL SURVIVES CRASH IN WILDS OF CANADA + STORY FOLLOWS +') which continued the television theme established by *Emma* upfront (kind of).

But if that wasn't showbiz enough for you, here came the comic's real draw: 'Chegger's Chat'. Then riding high thanks to his stint brandishing the likes of Buckaroo and Girl's World in various rain-sodden parks across the UK for *The Multi-Coloured Swap-Shop*, Keith Chegwin had signed up to provide *Emma* with dispatches from his busy life every week. The first edition kicked-off in fine style, with Cheggers revealing the time Alvin Stardust advised him on how to avoid getting 'hot and twitchy feet' (take a spare pair of cotton socks everywhere you go) and continued in this vein over time as Keith subsequently mused on his experiences falling off a horse at a Guildford riding school ('Luckily I wasn't hurt. But I reckon the instructor nearly broke a couple of ribs with laughing!'), eating shrimps in a lift with singer Tina Charles and just goofing about on the set of *Cheggers Plays Pop* ('After the last show the sound crew gave me a tape of all the mistakes I'd made on it').

Celebs bedecked other pages too: Kid Jensen brought us his 'LP Spot' and Emma herself ventured out of the confines of her strip to meet personalities such as Noel Edmonds (presumably using Keith's 'in', there), Rod Hull and Emu, Leo Sayer, Basil Brush and the Muppets for a series of photo-illustrated interviews.

A *Heat* magazine-in-waiting if ever there was one, *Emma* even did lifestyle in the bonkers 'Disco Talk', a transcript of conversations held between ravers Carol and Jill. A typical dispatch: 'That was a quick dance Jill.' 'Oh, what a giggle, Carol. I got my hair slide caught in his top shirt button and he couldn't get away.'

Across its run, *Emma* pretty much stuck with the same format bringing us entertaining comic-strip adventures from various go-getting girls, evil aliens and Victorian urchins plus loads of *Swap Shop* and Muppets-related features. But for some reason, the readers just weren't having it – and that's despite the free 'supercomb' that came with issue thirty. *Emma* was neither quite comic nor magazine, and learned a harsh lesson in keeping it simple when it was forced to merge with the more traditional *Judy* after just eighty-three issues.

Nowadays, unfairly consigned to the margins of comic history, it wasn't even mentioned in Chegger's subsequent autobiography. Although, to be fair, neither was eating prawns with Tina Charles.

Fast Forward
(BBC Magazines, 1989-1995, weekly)

The first most people knew about *Fast Forward* was that irritating trail that turned up in the junction between *Children's BBC* and *Neighbours* on BBC1.

'Fast! Fast! Forward! Forward! Forward! Forward! Ooooo, *Fast Forward...*', went the catchy jingle before a BBC voice would urgently run through the exciting goings-on in the latest issue of the corporation's *Look-in*-baiting telly comic.

Yes, after years spent fending off ill-advised sorties into its territory from would-be rival publications such as (in chronological order) *Target*, *Tops* and *Beeb*, here was something that really did scare the horses at the 'Junior *TV Times*'. Given full BBC backing, this was an effusively written publication that zeroed in with frightening precision on what kids were interested in. Hence, in the beginning it was back-to-back *Going Live!*, *Bread*, *Grange Hill* and Bros.

Issue one ('Boo! We're new!') arrived in September 1989, flashing the crap newly recast Joey and Aveline from the scouse sitcom *Bread* across the cover. 'Greetings!' came the inevitable strap line. Ambitiously trying to market itself as an all-things-to-all-men compote of *Smash Hits*, *Look-In* and lifestyle, it simultaneously bigged up comic-strip action (which it referred to as 'cartoons') from *The Flintstones*, *Grange Hill* and *'Allo 'Allo*, while also offering songs words, a Madonna poster and a TV guide. Bundled with a free 'handwriting tester' it promised, somewhat disingenuously, 'inside we test the writing of Bros, Andy Crane, Kylie and millions of other megastars'.

Yes, there may have been oodles of pictures of Phillip Schofield here, but the whole thing couldn't help but look a bit on the cheap side. It was probably those aforementioned 'cartoons' that were the main problem, each of which looked lacklustre to say the least. Despite sporting kosher school uniforms and a logo clearly based on the programme's title sequence, the 'Grange Hill' strip was a pretty shoddy proposition all told, not helped by the fact it dwelt on *Hill* makeweights Clarke Trent and Matthew Pearson. But, 'Bread' was even worse, cursed with an artist who couldn't nail down even one likeness in the Boswell household. ''Allo 'Allo' also suffered in the art stakes, although its script was commendably faithful to the source: 'Pisst!! Gruber! It is René, you have dynamite in your trousers,' cautioned the restaurateur as another convoluted plan collapsed around him. 'Ohh! René!!' replied the flattered Nazi, misunderstanding the danger he was in.

'Radio Wonder FM: Dial FM for French Melons' was a little better; a three-panel funny centred upon Phillip Schofield's inability to operate his complicated studio, as was 'Gordon T Gopher', the adventures of the eponymous glove puppet who at least looked something like his TV incarnation.

Aside from the strips, *Blue Peter* got a look in courtesy of a feature about their summer trip to Zimbabwe ('Both John and Yvette managed to avoid the local food delicacy – crocodile tails'), Chris Packham from the *Real Wild Show* wrote about foxes, Margot Wilson from *Hartbeat* talked us through the construction of a cardboard crazy golf putting green and *Doctor Who*'s Sylvester McCoy was one of the 'millions' who agreed to have his handwriting analysed ('He's a powerful and wacky chap who works very very hard' apparently).

So there it was, the BBC's official organ for the Broom Cupboard – effusive, energetic, a little bit annoying and definitely lacking on the comic-strip front. Nowhere near as likeable a production as *Look-In*, later editions would evolve to include 'Television Centre', a strip that took us behind the scenes at the BBC, while the letters page was wittily helmed by…a lettuce.

Mediocre it may have been, but it was enough to sustain the publication as further urgent ads strafed between the Andy Crane-Ramsay Street divide.

Into the Nineties, the publication began to grow up a little, becoming more of a (let's face it) girls' mag than an all-rounder to be enjoyed by both sexes. Growing more concerned with what was going on in the pop charts than events in the *Blue Peter* garden, by the time its rival, *Look-In*, had thrown in the towel in 1994, *Fast Forward* had all but dumped the cartoons. Come 1995, the paper sported just three strips, and two of these weren't based on any ongoing TV series. 'Peabrain' followed the fortunes of the paper's dim-witted alien mascot, while 'The FF Office' showed the editorial team interacting with various pop stars each week – with hi-hi-hilarious consequences. Meanwhile, 'Byker Grove' gave us two breezy pages from the Geordie youth club. But it wasn't only the strips that were downsized – the rest of the mag was increasingly padded out with posters of Ant and Dec, Zig and Zag and MN8. Suddenly it seemed as though all connections with Television Centre were being severed – but why?

Earlier that year, the BBC had launched a new youth publication, *Chatterbox* ('The mag with the chat') which had quickly honed in on *Fast Forward*'s racket ('Win a day with the stars of *Fully Booked*!'). With *FF* given the cold-shoulder treatment, it was therefore inevitable that editor Nicky Smith was called upon to shepherd readers to the new publication as her's ground to a halt.

And that was it for *Fast Forward*. No more pre-*Neighbours* roundelays, no more going nuts over the latest middle-of-the-road sitcom. Ah well, at least there were two consolations: (1) It had been the only publication to successfully square-up to *Look-In* and (2) *Chatterbox* would bite the bullet just months after its launch, having over-estimated its audience's interest in *Sweet Valley High*.

Girl mk I
(Hulton Press Ltd/Longacre Press/Odhams Press Ltd, 1951-1964, every Friday)

A year and a half after *Eagle* **mk I** had launched, dapper reverend-cum-editorial genius Marcus Morris repeated the trick, but this time with a weekly produced especially for girls.

Destined to ply the same mandate of inspirational and educational fare as its feathery brother, the new venture was very much moulded like its sibling, based on the knowledge that *Eagle* already enjoyed a fairly substantial female following who'd apparently be satisfied with similar strips, albeit populated with heroines.

Titled *Girl* because, apparently, the editorial team couldn't come up with a female's name which didn't also lend itself to a character in history who'd been raped, the edict came down from Morris: none of the characters were to be depicted with breasts. Artists were told to curb their 'salacious instincts' and keep everything above board – including their hands when they illustrated the strips.

'The new super-colour weekly for every girl' arrived on 2 November 1951, in a similar tabloid-sized format to *Eagle*, and laying out its stall with its own female version of 'Dan Dare'. Although 'Kitty Hawke and Her All-Girl Air Crew' wasn't set in the future, it did centre on a uniform-clad adventurer of the skies, only this one had a point to prove – that she could fly a plane as well as any of those (here comes the sarcasm) 'glorious males'.

Inside, highlights included 'Anne Mullion' which brought us smugglers and pirates in eighteenth-century Cornwall; a colourful 'Black Beauty' strip; 'Lettice Leefe: The Greenest Girl in School' which came from the pen of Captain Pugwash and Harris Tweed creator John Ryan; 'Captain Starling' who sailed the Seven Seas in search of her long-lost father; and, on the back page (the Morris decreed 'God slot'), 'The Story of Miriam, Daughter of the Nile'. This tale, which followed the travails of Moses' sister, nearly fell foul of the editor when artist John Worsley depicted maidens cavorting in the bulrushes naked. Needless to say, it was returned to him with a note to add more foliage in the foreground.

Like *Eagle*, features also played a strong role here. 'Jacky the Centre Page Girl' saw stage school student Jacky Curtis meet various famous people for the comic's benefit, while the 'Editor's Letter' announced the formation of 'The *Girl* Adventurer's Club' which planned various outings and expeditions for its members, who would soon number in the region of sixteen thousand.

Initially things were looking good and the first print run was half-a-million. However, sales quickly dropped at a perilous rate. Realising they'd misjudged their audience, who wanted more than just *Eagle* in a pinafore, the publication received something of a revamp, becoming more romantic and traditionally feminine. Alas, there could be no place for Kitty Hawke in such a paper, and thus she was ejected in favour of Manor School chums Wendy and Jinx, who began a successful reign on the cover undertaking various Enid Blyton-type adventures.

Other additions included 'Robbie of Red Hall' ('Here's a grand adventure story about the orphaned Scots girl and her friend Duncan') and 'The Adventures of Penny Wise'. Meanwhile, readers were tutored on a range of important topics in 'Mother Tells You How'. In one edition, the matriarch dispensed tips on keeping cool, which included: 'You'll be much cooler, Judy, if you take off that tight belt' and 'Don't overdo the sunbathing, Judy. You'll only peel and look horrid.' Thankfully, by the time Mother got round to telling us 'How to Use Mint', Judy seemed to have smartened up her act ('Oh Judy, these are lovely,' exclaimed the wise one, trying one of the girl's crystallized mint leaves).

Sales picked up again and held firm at 650,000, despite the mild furore accompanying the comic's first photo of – gasp! – a pop star (Tommy Steele), which caused some parental discomfort at the time. A fashion section arrived in 1958, and problem page, 'What's Your Worry?' was helmed by James Hemming who dealt with all nature of queries from what to do if a boy kisses you, to where babies come from.

By 1961 things weren't quite so rosy. Hulton had been bought by Odhams Press, which in turn had been acquired by the Mirror Group in an acrimonious takeover bid. With the new owners unimpressed by the *Eagle* fleet of comics – which by now also included **Robin** and **Swift** – there were grumbles that *Girl*'s circulation had dropped to an unacceptable low. In fact, the comic was still being read by an impressive 360,000 a week, but things had to change and a spate of endless 'new looks' broke out.

The publication went pop star mad ('Introducing...Helen Shapiro'), ditched the comic-strips on the cover for full colour photographs, brought in hipsters Pete and Penny to host their own letters page, majored in fashion pin-ups and a 'weekly review of entertainments' titled 'Look & Listen' rated the current films, books and records on the market. Worst of all, former comic-strip ballerinas 'Belle and Mamie' broke into television (courtesy of the 'Telegang') and Lettice Leefe grew up into a fashion-conscious teenager (or 'teenager' as *Girl* had it).

It wasn't all bad, though. 'Round Table' was actually a very neat idea: a reader's dilemma was converted into a comic-strip, and then a panel of girls, presided over by Margaret Pride, would discuss what they thought the right course of action should be.

It couldn't last though, particularly as the Mirror was positively itching to kill off the weeklies. *Swift* was first to go, merging with *Eagle* in March 1963. Then, on 3 October 1964, *Girl* announced: 'Exciting news for all readers' and revealed it was joining forces with *Princess* mk I (Amalgamated Press/Fleetway, 1960-7) the following week. Thankfully, by now Marcus Morris had long since moved on to pastures new. In fact, he was making rather a splash in the world of women's magazines. Ah, but would he allow breasts there?

Girl mk II
(IPC Magazines Ltd, 1981-1990, every Thursday)

That step up from the ballet and boarding school of girls' comics like *Bunty* and *Penny* to the bangles and boy-talk of *Jackie* and its ilk could be a daunting prospect. A case of too much too young for some readers, what they really needed was an intermediate stage that would gradually wean them onto the hard stuff.

Enter *Girl* mk II – the trainer bra of all weeklies. Predating the arrival of *Eagle* **mk II**, this revival of a classic title was an 'in name only' affair, with no reference made to the posh Fifties comic within the title.

'Your very best friend' was a glossy(ish) mix of photo covers, comic-strips, pet features, make-and-do's and pop. Youngsters 'Kim 'n' Debbie' (who'd later turn into 'Lisa 'n' Debbie') theoretically helmed the title, and would regale us every week from the talking shop pages of 'Come and Join Us!', wherein you'd also find items such as 'The Art Club' ('See how easy it is to draw this cute little dolly'), 'Pic Puzzle', 'Yummies for Your Tummies!' and the pen pal section 'Make-a-Mate!' ('I like disco dancing, clothes and Blondie, but I don't like school!').

A standard issue would contain three photo stories and two comic-strips, alongside a text tale 'for you to enjoy!', a fashion page (which was too stingy to actually provide photos of that 'cotton skirt with pretty matching top' available from all branches of 'Tammy', and went for an artist's impression instead), tips on homemade couture ('Save yourself some money by making your own brooches!'), pop music, those 'If you answered mostly A...'-style questionnaires, a pet pin-up, horoscopes and – every little brother's first port-of-call when snaffling a read – a problem page entitled 'Help Me!'

But back to the strips, and few were as popular as the slow-moving photographic adventures detailed in 'Nine to Four'. Written by *2000 AD*'s Pat Mills, it followed the fortunes of six girls at the John Milton Comprehensive school, 'girls like you, with your kind of problems'. Years later, the writer remembers his script editor on the comic couldn't understand why the serial was so popular because it featured characters 'standing around, complaining and absolutely nothing happens'. However, this was the world of girls' comics, where the readership pre-ferred soap-opera stories, dwelling on emotions and who fancied whom, rather than high drama and action.

Aside from the inevitable adverts for PGL Holidays, the other main source of excitement during *Girl*'s early days was the comic-strip 'Patty's World...' The freckled-faced policeman's daughter, whose domain we were invited into, gleefully brought us up to speed on events in her hec-tic life; which normally involved talking about boys with better-looking best friend Sharon ('Shar'), ending up in trouble thanks to chaotic 'big sis' Carol and cooing over token lad, Johnny Vowden. With a guest cast this strong, it was little wonder the strip turned into one of the publica-tion's staple features.

In 1982, the title absorbed stablemate of small repute, *Dreamer* (IPC Magazines Ltd, 1981-2) to little overall effect. Then, the follow-ing year, it turned into a handy source of extra pocket money for *Grange Hill*'s Alison Bettles (who played the sporty Fay Lucas in the series) who could be spotted eating a Funny Foot on the cover of an August issue. Two months later, colleague Nadia Chambers (the evil Annette Firman) joined her for the first of many appearances out of the GH uniform, seemingly apropos of nothing (their star status never being acknowledged).

By this stage, the comic also boasted a colour photo story across its centre-pages; a luxury surely unheard of in this market?

On 2 June 1984, the comic unveiled a new order as Lisa 'n' Debbie stepped aside for Sally 'n' Kerry. 'We're going to be bringing you lots more info on all your favourite pop stars, facts, pictures and pin-ups – you'll be seeing much more!' Then, at the end of the month, it gobbled up relative old-timer *Tammy*, again with little impact upon its own line-up of strips. However, all this paled in comparison to the changes that occurred in October as *Girl* went new-look.

Ditching the winsome flower from its logo, this was a much more mature *Girl*, laid out like one of your big sister's mags. To celebrate, even Patty got a makeover, shedding her cascading locks for a Lady Di hair-do. The pop content was now promoted far more heavily ('Everything you ever wanted to know about Andrew Ridgely – and more!'), however the mixture of photo and comic-strip stories remained pretty much the same.

And so it continued, as Sally and Kerry (they eventually dropped the 'n') drove the comic onwards, with little alteration to the mix, bar the inevitable changes in pop personalities deemed suitable for the publication ('Shirlie + Pepsi – talking their way to the top!').

During its run, despite the packaging, *Girl* always steered clear of the main thoroughfares frequented by the more mature teen mags. Thankfully, there were no worried readers writing in about 'vaginal discharges' here (although one girl's admission of cruelly pushing an AIDS leaflet through a homosexual's letterbox was perhaps a little bit near-the-knuckle) – concerns were much more centred on pressures at school and how to get rid of blackheads. Meanwhile, the strips only ever dwelt on safe topics, such as school, 'kid sisters' and, occasionally, mild sci-fi (the adventures of the space hopper-alike alien Splat being a real oddity).

All in all, it made for a title any parent would be glad to buy for their daughter, unaware their little darling was by now regularly sneaking a peak at Mum's *Cosmo*.

Hoot
(DC Thomson, 1985-1986, every Saturday)

The party may have been over for the seminal *Nutty*, which had been swallowed up by **The Dandy** in September 1985, but for one of its characters there was a new lease of life in the form of *Hoot*.

Hoot – © DC Thomson & Co., Ltd

Yes, while 'The Wild Rovers', 'Peter Pest' and others (although not 'Bananaman', but that's another story) faced oblivion, *Nutty*'s unitoothed infant in the red sweater and nappies – Cuddles – was heading off to front 'Britain's bubbling new comic!' A curious concoction that somehow seemed more juvenile than its progenitor (of course, having a baby on the front didn't help), *Hoot* arguably never really established a voice of its own. Sure, it had a bucket-load of original characters including Wanta Job Bob, Polar Blair, Piggles and Snackula ('the Prince of Guzzling'), but alongside them it fleshed out the pages with short three or four panel funnies featuring established favourites like 'The Three Bears', 'Bash Street Kids', 'Colonel Blink' and 'Jay R' (so at least another *Nutty* regular was managing to stave off redundancy). Somehow, this served to undermine the rest of the fare on offer, and, worse still, few of these seemed to have been drawn by their 'proper' artists – boy, didn't Lord Snooty look odd?

Nevertheless, there was some fun stuff on offer. The inside cover perennially carried 'The Hoot Squad', an insanely detailed full page scene packed with little hidden gags, a modern-day version of the 'Banana Bunch' spreads from the Fifties *Beezer*. The centre spread was devoted to 'Dogsbody', the tale of Eric Wimp lookalike (and indeed the strip appeared to be drawn by 'Bananaman' artist John Geering) Sid Kettle who, following a bite from an experimental mechanical dog, could turn into a mongrel known as 'Hairy Rusty Kettle'. Another amusing effort was 'Sam's Secret Diary'. Written by 'a badly nagged Sam who thinks it would be better if adults and kids changed places', it presented a load of bizarre scenarios where Mum, Dad and offspring did just that – cue a visit to the restaurant and 'high chairs' for the parents.

However, despite all this there was no real interaction with the reader (wot no letters page, or 'Hoot Club'?) and thus come issue fifty-three it was little surprise when Cuddles jumped onto a hospital bed being wheeled along by Polar Blair declaring, 'We're on the move!' Despite still billing itself as 'Britain's bubbling new comic!', *Hoot* was actually heading off for the pages of the *The Dandy*, where Cuddles would quickly strike up a profitable partnership with Dimples to ensure the continuation of his comic-strip career. You can't keep a good man down.

Hornet
(DC Thomson, 1963-1976, every Tuesday)

Despite clocking up an impressive 648 issues in its time, there's something about *Hornet* that just screamed also-ran. Maybe that's a little unfair, but on first glance it was hard to see what the comic was offering that you couldn't already get in *Victor*, which had started two years previously.

Nonetheless, issue one did its best to gee-up those energy levels depicting an astounded-looking boy doubtlessly overcome with excitement about the balsa wood glider that came free with the publication. However, once inside we'd pretty much seen it all before. There was a text story ('The Miracle Man from Mars'), war ('The Younger VC') and

Westerns ('Slade of the Pony Express') amongst others. Sport was apparently seen as the comic's big draw and placed on the front page more often than not (including footballing fun with 'Gay Gordon of Dundee' in issue six). Here, the comic did at least come up with something more enduring, in the form of Charlie 'Iron' Barr-alike scrap metal merchant-cum goalie Bernard Briggs in 'Bouncing Briggs', who would later go on to become some kind of all-rounder super-athlete. As derivative as it may have been, who could resist a man who'd made a motorbike sidecar out of an old tin bath?

As the issues rolled by we also saw some old DC Thomson characters come out of mothballs. William Wilson was dredged up from the pages of *Wizard* mk I (1922-63) and given his first comic-strip outing to some excitement. That he'd serve the paper faithfully was best indicated by the fact that by the mid-Seventies, it had run so many exposés about the seemingly ageless runner's 'secret' origins, it was now having to title them 'The Further Truth About Wilson'. *Wizard*'s text story, 'V for Vengeance' also enjoyed a fairly successful translation into the speech bubble format, as The Deathless Men continued their campaign of terror against the Nazis.

Hornet – © DC Thomson & Co., Ltd

Come the Seventies, the comic was going all out in its promotion of sport, featuring portraits of football players on the cover, with accompanying biographical strips – as per *Wizard* **mk II**. Nevertheless, it was hats off to *Hornet* for at least covering the PE-related activities often ignored by other comics. Surely it scored a first when it brought us 'Cast Hook and Strike', the exploits of young angler Joe Dodds?

However, it was impossible to escape the fact that by now the comic was looking exceptionally dated, and despite introducing its own insect-themed action hero in the form of 'Captain Hornet' (who travelled around in his patented Hornet-Hoverer), upstarts such as the high-action, all-killing-all-of-the-time *Warlord* made it look dead in the water. On the same day it did the decent thing in 1976 and merged with *Hotspur*, *Action* and *Bullet* both hit the news-stands for the first time. It seems as though the shock of the new had just been too much for the old-before-its time *Hornet*.

Hotspur
(DC Thomson, 1933-1981, every Friday)

For the first thirty years of its run, *Hotspur* wasn't actually a comic. However, unlike *Wizard*, it didn't suffer a break in publication while it ditched the text stories for speech balloon action. So for the sake of simplicity, we're going to ignore accepted wisdom (well, in some quarters) that the title's forty-eight year history actually encapsulated three different publications (the story paper *Hotspur* 1933-59, *New Hotspur* 1959-63 and *Hotspur* 1963-81).

One of DC Thomson's 'Big Five' – the others being *Rover* (1922-73), *Adventure* (1921-61), *Wizard* mk I (1922-63) and *Skipper* (1930-41) – which had provoked a grumpy essay from George Orwell in 1939 in which he bemoaned the papers' paean 'to bully-worship and the cult of violence' – the first issue of *Hotspur* (which came free with a 'black cloth mask') featured a huge imposing eagle on the front, looming down on a clearly-kacking-himself fighter pilot.

Despite introducing such legendary fare as the 'Red Circle' school stories, 'Q-Squadron' and the 'Iron Teacher' during this incarnation, its wall-to-wall text stories means we swiftly jump to 1959, and the arrival of *New Hotspur*. This rebranding was to promote the fact the publication was starting to embrace comic-strip tales – and how better to exemplify that than by offering up a free plastic 'jumping frog'? The first new look issue did deliver on the strip action, but text features – including, bizarrely, 'The Boyhood of Desperate Dan' – were still a major part of the mix. Nevertheless, it was great to now enjoy the exploits of Yank House, Conk House and others from the 'Red Circle' tales in pictorial form.

It wasn't really until that further name-change tweak, back to just good old *Hotspur*, that the weekly properly embraced the ethos of what a boys' comic should be all about. With *Victor* having led the way, the Sixties' *Hotspur* dished out stories of derring-do taken from various conflicts throughout history. Although war featured heavily (didn't it always?), the title differed from its stablemates by also offering up a rather fun array in whimsical characters. For example, when the Brits were out fighting 'bandits in the jungles of Kokaland' they were led by Corporal Fry who, in a rather neat rhyme, was just 'one foot high'. It seems a 'tiff' with a witch-doctor had resulted in the officer being shrunk down to that imperially measured size and future instalments were spent variously bashing natives and trying to undo the curse.

Hotspur – © DC Thomson & Co., Ltd

Sci-fi also got a fair crack of the whip, with 'The Young Aces of Space' and 'The Menace from Moon Crater' (that threat being some sort of giant lobster) rubbing shoulders in one issue. Come the Seventies, *Hotspur* was regularly featuring an almost Justice League-style array of very British super-powered characters within its pages.

Some of the best included *Rover*'s Black Sapper (a former criminal-turned-good guy, who strode about in an all-in-one hooded body suit, and travelled underground in his Earthworm burrowing machine); Red Star Robinson (seventeen-year-old Tom Robinson who, along with robotic man servant Mr Thrice and a host of hi-tech gadgets – including a flying car – fought crime, and marked known baddies with a red star); Nick Jolly (a dandy highwayman inclined to exclaim 'zounds!' who, thanks to an 'amazing time ray', was transported from the eighteenth century to present-day England); the Iron Teacher (freed from the shackles of prose to battle evil-doers, giant bats and the like – but do remarkably little in terms of educating); X-Bow (a gang-busting cross-bow wielding Eddie Kidd-alike); and, best of the lot, King Cobra (not to be confused with the criminal mastermind of the same name who'd appeared in *Lion*).

The latter was the nearest DC Thomson ever came to a successful full-on American-style superhero. When mild-mannered journalist Bill King pulled a hidden rip-cord, his ordinary clothes would transform into a hi-tech suit from which he derived all his powers. With abilities including scaling sheer walls, deflecting bullets, generating electric shocks and gliding through the air (via his unimpressive sounding 'flying-squirrel wings'), he fought a series of criminals, chief amongst them being the evil Diablo who had the ability to alter the weather.

In 1976, *Hotspur* incorporated *Hornet*, and the likes of scrapdealer-cum-Daley Thompson Bernard Briggs joined the roster. More excitingly, four years later it also gave refuge to the short-lived *The Crunch*, providing a new home for 'The Mantracker' and 'Starhawk' and, much more excitingly, the paper's pious agony uncle Andy who continued to helm 'The Crunch Question' within the pages of his new home.

Sadly, hard times were around the corner for *Hotspur* too (that, or maybe Andy was just a jinx) and, despite their colourful cast list (and just genuinely charming stuff, like 'Danny Boyd', the story of a golfer who sung 'Oh Danny Boy' to himself as he took a stroke), its followers quaked at a 'big news for all readers inside!' flash across the cover of its 24 January 1981 edition. After over one thousand issues it was all over. The following week the title was folded into the pages of *Victor*. That wasn't quite the end of the story, though. Throughout the Eighties, right up until 1991, *Hotspur* annuals were still issued every Christmas, allowing a new generation of kids to thrill at the exploits of 'crook catcher' King Cobra and friends.

It's Wicked!
(Marvel Comics Ltd, 1989, weekly)

Nothing to do with the rubbish and deservedly short-lived 1987 BBC1 Saturday morning show of the same name, *It's Wicked!* was a not-quite-so-rubbish comic, formulated to steal readers away from *The Beano* and *The Dandy*, and seemingly inspired by *Monster Fun* and *Shiver and Shake*. That these latter two could hardly be described as publishing success stories was surely not a great portent here, but it didn't stop Marvel UK from having a late-in-the-day crack at the juvenile humour market.

Besides, the whole thing was going to be riding in on the back of a TV tie-in, so surely it couldn't go wrong? With a logo all but filched from *The Dandy* (the 'D' in both titles looking pretty much identical), the comic's cover star was Slimer, the ectoplasm-based character from the US cartoon series *The Real Ghostbusters*. In its first issue he was depicted in the unlikely scenario of opening his own orthodontic practise. 'Howdydoodee, readers!' he exclaimed, 'Slimer is now a tippytop *dentist*! Yup!' Faced with a visit from 'County Draculala' (boy, was this going to get old, quick), he declared: 'Slimer too scaredy cat to take out Draky's teeth! You take them, readers! They're yours!' which was a pretty smart way of segueing into the customary free gift – a pair of false vampiric choppers that were stuck to the cover.

Obviously, the theme here was ghost and ghouls, something that spilled into editor Helen Stone's welcome message on the following page which began: 'Greetings, young horrors of the world' and was festooned with silhouettes of various monsters, bats and skeletons. Thus, what followed was a motley array of demonic creations, some quite good, others bloody awful. Of the former camp we had Gordon Gremlin, a pointy-eared lunk in a romper suit whose efforts at making mischief backfired when he yoinked some wally's wig off his head, only to discover it was actually a rather miffed cat. 'Ghostman Bat and His Black and White Rat' wasn't half-bad either, following a half-man, half-flying-rodent mail-deliverer who popped evil spirits through people's doors. 'That male's making a first class noise!' he chortled after leaving a householder screaming his head off.

Meanwhile, Winnie the Witch Doctor was pretty much Minnie the Minx with an occult twist and 'Ghosthunters' was some kind of unauthorised riff on the Frog brothers concept from *The Lost Boys* film, as Mole brothers Moe and Joe made an inept effort to track down various supernatural nasties. Best of the lot, though, was the punningly named 'Clare Voyant', a gypsy fortune-teller who foresaw the truth – but with a twist. For a bit of fun, readers were invited to see if they could guess what was going to happen before she did, with the first episode centring upon her prediction some punter would be *'showered* with money' while she sensed 'I will also be a great *burden* to you!' Can you see what's coming? While he was swiftly informed his great idea for a 'new type of shower curtain' was going to make him a rich man, the Romany was unexpectedly floored by a falling safe.

Far less impressive were the likes of 'Toad in the Hole' (a poorly drawn sword and sorcery laff-fest) and 'Inspector Spectre: Private Eye' (an *Inspector Gadget*-esque story of a phantom private dick). Nonetheless, as a whole *It's Wicked!* was OK stuff, but one of the most blatantly derivative comics on the stand.

Over the next few weeks Ghostman Bat developed a joke-infused letters page, 'Bat Chat!', while the editorials grew increasingly winsome ('Hello again young fun chums. Welcome to another super doopa issue of *It's Wicked!*'). Otherwise, it was business as usual: Slimer up front attempting to lure readers in with his ker-azy antics (somehow getting lost in the jungle in issue five and sampling a teddy bear's cooking in thirteen). However, it could be argued that the whole thing had been doomed from the start. Over the decades, no one had ever made a success of honing in on *The Dandy* and *The Beano*'s racket and, what with the whole comic industry going into a steep decline by the end of the Eighties, the odds of success now were even longer than before. In short, it was the wrong type of comic launched at completely the wrong time.

Jackie
(DC Thomson, 1964-1993, every Thursday)

The publication for 'go-ahead teens' was thin on comic-strip action, but still merits an entry here by dint of its sheer longevity, if nothing else.

Launched during the dying days of *Girl* **mk I**, the tabloid-sized *Jackie* positively flung itself at the pop faces of the era and quickly became every young woman's hotline to the stars, shamelessly splashing the likes of Elvis, The Kinks and The Beatles across its cover while its doomed rival could only coquettishly flirt with photos of young ladies jiving away to a Cliff long-player while their sensible-looking younger brother shot them daggers.

As such, the front of early issues (sporting a huge logo appended by a grinning groovester presumably enjoying the latest Merseybeat sounds) looked like a billposter for an imaginary best-ever gig. Take issue fifteen, for example, which featured a colour photo of Brian Jones, alongside huge text proclaiming the presence of 'Paul Beatle', The Searchers ('in knockout colour') plus 'Cliff, Gerry and Tommy' inside.

But what of the comic-strips? *Jackie* kept them to a minimum, but what it did churn out mainly focused on light romances betwixt willowy shop assistant and hunky strangers. 'It's a beautiful bracelet, but you hardly know me.' 'A situation I hope you'll let me put right.'

Less than a year after launch, the paper got a slight overhaul as the huge red banner head was dropped for a much more simple and achingly modern black text on white logo. Already well defined as the read of choice for girls who'd recently outgrown *Bunty* but weren't ready for the full-on *Woman's Own* experience, it continued to peddle slight stories of love ('I Wouldn't Date You for the World') and recruitment drives for the WRAC ('If you want an active and exciting life, why don't you find out more...post the coupon today'). Juggling the lounge lizard appeal of Mick Jagger with a breathless gosh-wow article on how great tabards are may have seemed like a daunting prospect, but *Jackie* rose to the challenge with *élan*.

As the end of the Sixties arrived, the title became one big *mélange* of browns, floppy hair and huge-eyed waifs. The comic-strips got a pretty good showing during this era too, as the bio-strips ('The Andy Fairweather-Low Story') jostled alongside romance and...yet more romance. In short, just what the readers wanted. By contrast, the next decade was characterised by hues of startling oranges and greens, as 'delicious' David Essex, Mick Robertson from *Magpie* and some bloke called Midge Ure from the band Slik made their presence felt. Anadin flogged its wares to the readership under the huge headline 'Period Pains?', and the pop stars were booted off the front cover pretty much for good by a series of chuckling out-and-about denim-clad girls making doe-eyes into the camera.

Gradually, the comic-strips were phased out altogether (that's despite merging with *Diana* in 1976) and by the end of the Seventies, it was photo love all the way, with a roster of stagy-looking girls shyly peeping out from under their fringes wondering why Steve in the dark glasses never noticed them, before finally falling for good old reliable Geoff in the rugby sweater.

With its huge reliance on pop culture and the crazes of the day (look, there's Hawk off of *Buck Rogers in the 25th Century* in a 1981 edition!), much like *Look-In*, *Jackie* was mining a profitable seam that ensured its content remained fresh.

But, by the Nineties, no matter how hard you threw New Kids on the Block at them, *Jackie*'s readership were no longer interested in keeping up with ebullient weekly titles – this generation yearned for the hardcore glossy action their older sisters were enjoying in their own magazines. As the likes of *Patches* (DC Thomson, 1979-89) and *Blue Jeans* (DC Thomson, 1977-91) fell by the wayside, *Jackie* too succumbed to the pressure. From nigh-on a million readers in its peak years to just a few thousand in June 1993, this leg of the race was well and truly over, and waiting to pick up the baton were the likes of *Bliss*, *Sugar*, *Cosmogirl* and *Elle*.

Jackpot
(IPC Magazines Ltd, 1979-1982, every Monday)

It's almost impossible to imagine how the meeting went in IPC Towers that resulted in the creation of *Jackpot*. Not that the title was in any way substandard, it's just that it didn't have anything about it that was at all distinctive. Just what had been the editorial impetus that brought yet another 'new comic for girls and boys' to light?

Who knows, but on 5 May 1979, there it was, nestling on the newsagent shelves, arriving free with one of six practical joke kits. '*Beware*,' warned the Editor's letter inside, '...the chances are that your pals have all received different gags and no doubt they will be eager to try them out – on *you!*' History fails to record the extent of the doubtlessly bloody novelty products-based war that must have broken out as a result.

So, to the comic itself, and what we got was pretty sturdy stuff, all

told. 'Richie Wraggs' was all about a bucktoothed yokel who, after stinking out his classroom with a particularly noxious slab of cheese, was
chucked out of school. Ever the optimist, he took this as his cue to go
off and find his fortune, with a cheery 'Har-har! From now on it's goin'
to be Wraggs to riches!'

Jackpot – © Egmont UK Ltd

A smart about-turn of a popular TV series' name bequeathed the paper
with its next strip, 'Angel's (Proper) Charlies' which, comparatively
rarely for a kids' comic, centred on a character with sex appeal (*Cheeky*'s
Lily Pop being another exception to this rule) – a diminutive blonde
bombshell who had the local lads fawning over her.

Another story taking its inspiration from the telly was the rather magnificent 'The Teeny Sweeny'. 'Diminutive' being the watchword here
too, what we got was a kind of junior John Thaw and Dennis Waterman
(complete with feather cut) who staged their own high-speed chases in
go-karts (rather than Ford Capris) and proved equally successful in
bringing wrong-doers to book. An even more blatant TV swipe, however, had to be 'It's a Nice Life' about a suburban family who decided to

throw in the rat race and go self-sufficient. They even came complete with a set of disapproving, posh neighbours!

Elsewhere, 'Jack Pott' centred on the exploits of a supernaturally lucky child, while 'Little Adam and Eva' brought – gasp! – nudity to comics. Thankfully, the couple (who were attempting to live 'apple-ly' in Eden) both possessed featureless torsos, bar for the detailing of a belly button.

This being an IPC comic, it was also contractually bound to offer up its own spin on the company's obsession with the class struggle. Absolutely on-the-nose in this regard was 'Class Wars', which outlined the conflict between 'some posh kids' ('I say, that's jolly sporting of you old bean!') and 'some scruffy kids' ('Argue with me and you'll get a thick ear!'). While the former played croquet and ate muffins for supper, the latter enjoyed football in a mud pit under the shadows of a high rise estate before running home for a tea of mushy peas. Naturally, when the two groups collided it resulted in a tremendous frenzy of flying fists. Thus, when they were billeted into the same school together the teachers quivered: 'You know what this means…it's going to start class wars!'

And then, as if to hammer the point home, the title followed on with the perennial chalk-and-cheese take on the same thing, 'Milly O'Naire and Penny Less', a gender-swapped carbon copy of *Cor!!*'s 'Ivor Lott and Tony Broke'.

Later additions to the *Jackpot* stable included 'The Winners', a family who – whatever the situation – always came out on top ('You should have known we'd win in the end!'), feuding siblings in 'Oh, Brother!', 'Mum's the Word' in which the eponymous matriarch always got one over on 'Dad' and 'Son', and 'Sherlock Jnr: The Clued-Up Kid' which was pretty self-explanatory.

It was all robust, big-hearted fare but, as indicated above, not especially accomplished. Thus, it was no great loss when, at the end of January 1982, the title was forced to merge with behemoth *Buster*. Inevitably, while other strips were ruthlessly cut, 'The Winners' survived the transition.

Jag
(Fleetway Publications/IPC Magazines Ltd, 1968-1969, every Saturday)

The last – and least – in IPC's trilogy of big cat-themed comics (the others being, of course, *Lion* and *Tiger*), *Jag* could at least claim to have had better production values than either of them.

A tabloid-sized action paper, its first issue sported an arresting full-page cover illustration of a vest-clad Tommy giving an unseen enemy what for with a machine gun. Supplementing this was the exciting slap-dash logo, a disembodied (but no less menacing for that) jaguar's head and a free gift in the form of 'Bobby Moore's Book of the FA Cup'.

Inside could be found the familiar mix of gunplay, humour and fascinating facts. Highlights proved to be 'The Indestructible Man', the story of Mark Dangerfield who 'armed with many strange powers' vowed to fight evil wherever he encountered it; 'Snob College' which, unusually for a boys' weekly, positioned kindly teacher Owen Jenkin as the star of the strip; 'The Outlaws' – short and brutal biogs of real-life bad guys, here telling us how Ned Kelly bought the farm; and 'The Daredevils', punchy tales of sporting derring do. Best of the lot, however, was 'The Mouse Patrol', which brought us the Second World War exploits of school boys Blackie Knight, Ginger Nobb, and Cyril North who stole a tank and set off to rescue their fathers from a German prison.

Thanks to its dimensions and preoccupation with real-life characters and facts (it would later launch the 'Astounding! Staggering! Funny! Crazy!' page, which would be full of fascinating snippets such as 'the latest idea from America…a car that steers itself'), over its short run *Jag* couldn't help but look like a poor man's *Eagle* mk I. That said, it did manage to come up with its own lead which, while not quite in the 'Dan Dare' class, was still pretty good. 'Football Family Robinson' was a nicely painted front and back page strip which mixed sport with whimsy as the titular clan tried their best to make struggling fourth division team Thatchem United a success, despite the attention of Max Sharkey, who wanted to replace their stadium with a supermarket ('I'll smash 'em…*so help me, I will!*').

For whatever reason, it just didn't seem to be working, and on 15 February 1969 the paper announced: 'Watch out for the new-look *Jag*'. In a bid to reverse its fortunes, the title was reducing the paper size, and upping the page count to thirty-two. Alongside the regular dose of 'punch-ups with MacTavish and O'Toole' (a Scotsman and an Irishman giving the 'slant-eyed monkeys' what for in Japan circa 1942), new feature 'Story of a Star' was set to debut, bringing us the 'incident-packed' biog of England International Martin Peters. Plus: 'Black Patch: The Wonder Horse' ('The gypsy hack who became a world-beater') and 'The Castaways of Shark Island'.

Alas, it was too little too late and just five weeks after the relaunch came the banner 'Exciting news for all readers – see inside!' Despite their best efforts, the soccer-mad Robinson family were indeed being supplanted from their home, as *Jag* – at the age of just forty-eight issues – was taken over by *Tiger*.

Jinty
(IPC Magazines Ltd, 1974-1981, every Monday)

Another title that felt the hand of *2000 AD* legend Pat Mills in its creation, at first glance *Jinty* looked to be trading in the same stories of disadvantaged orphans and weepy girl outsiders as everyone else in the market. But in fact, this was a comic with spunk.

Issue one hit the stands with a free 'Lovely "Smiley" Wrist Bracelet', and deployed the standard issue ballerinas and pretty dogs on the front.

Inside, the editorial claimed that, in formulating the comic, its creators had asked girls around the country what they liked to read. The result of this focus group included 'Merry at Misery House' (set in the Twenties, cheerful Merry Summers is wrongly sent to a reformatory, but refuses to let it get her down); typical IPC rags versus riches stuff in 'The Snobs and the Scruffs'; student nurse action in 'Angela's Angels'; put-upon ennui courtesy of 'Dora Dogsbody'; 'A Dream for Yvonne', about a girl who – somewhat improbably – ran away from the circus to become a ballerina; and 'Make-Believe Mandy', a lass despised by her family, no less.

It may have seemed run-of-the-mill (and to be fair, at this stage in its life it pretty much was), but it didn't take long for more exciting strips to arrive with an increasingly fantastical, proto-*Misty* bent. 'Wenna the Witch' took the whole misfit thing up to a new level as villagers persecuted a girl they felt had sinister powers; 'Slave of the Mirror' told the tale of Mia Blake who fell under the evil influence of the eponymous reflective device; the magnificent 'Golden Dolly, Death Dust!' pit two girls and their sentient corn mannequin against the evil Miss Marvell; and 'The Green People' featured a haven of fairies under threat from encroaching property developers – a metaphor for our times, surely.

In November 1975, the title incorporated the woefully short-lived *Lindy* (IPC Magazines Ltd, 1975) into the line-up. By now, it had adopted an arresting cover layout which differentiated itself from the rest of the market, breaking the page into angular panels, each presenting a pivotal moment from one of the interior strips accompanied by some suitably adrenalin-soaked text ('Crash! Bang! Wallop! It's clueless Katie again!').

Developing the theme hinted at in 'The Green People', *Jinty* began to cultivate a line in ecological stories; 'Friends of the Forest' told of a girl who was trying to prevent a deer being put into a circus and featured a gypsy nymph whose affinity with wildlife helped them overcome the nefarious schemes of the men in suits; rampant flooding threatened humanity in 'Fran of the Floods' ('The end of the world as we know it? What on Earth do you mean, headmistress?'); and 'sly' village councillor Mr Gresby closed down Old Man Stephenson's beloved steam train forcing everyone to use their cars in 'Save Old Smokey!'

Of course, this being a girls' comic, there was lots of cruelty on hand ('Too Old to Cry', 'Go on, Hate Me!' and, perhaps best of all 'The Slave of Form 3B') and plenty of heroines who were determined to overcome disability in order to excel – 'Miss No-Name' may have been a top athlete, but she had no long-term memory; 'Willa on Wheels' was intent on proving that despite being wheelchair-bound she could still be a top nurse; while 'Clancy on Trial' detailed the travails of a keen swimmer with similar mobility problems.

As the Seventies drew on, the stories grew increasingly far-fetched. 'Sue's Fantastic Fun-Bag!', in which Sue Lawton's amazing handbag Henrietta used its magical powers to pitch its owner into various wacky escapades ('Oh No! I'm back in the Ice Age!'), was agreeable whimsy, but 'The Human Zoo' was all out hardcore sci-fi. One of *Jinty*'s best-ever strips, it dealt in flying-saucers, dome-headed aliens and distant planets, as Shona and Jenny were abducted by ETs to be experimented upon. The subtext about man's thoughtless cruelty towards animals was laid on thickly, as one lizard-faced nasty mused: 'They all look alike to me... Don't forget, they're just animals for us to use as we like.'

In April 1980, the comic consumed the comparatively lacklustre and decidedly twee *Penny*, but thankfully remained relatively unaffected by the sudden dose of sucrose, even finding space to depict a girl being menaced by an evil-looking owl on the cover of that all important merger issue. Despite the loss of spooky sister title *Misty* earlier in the year, it continued to plough its rather fantastical trough, with more witchery in 'A Spell of Trouble', hauntings in 'Spirit of the Lake' and downright surrealism in 'Worlds Apart'.

But, unfortunately, the bell was now tolling for *Jinty* too, as falling sales made their impact. It seems the Eighties were no place for imaginative girls' comics that weren't in the thrall of pop stars and photo love (we're looking at you, *Girl* **mk II**) and so, after seven event-filled years and 393 issues, it was absorbed by *Tammy*.

Judge Dredd: Lawman of the Future
(Fleetway Editions, 1995-1996, fortnightly)

So how come *Judge Dredd: Lawman of the Future* only lasted twenty-three issues? The answer to that could be found in issue one's 'Ten Things You Never Knew About Dredd and his Future World', specifically point three: 'Judge Dredd never kills, except in extreme cases of self defence.'

Judge Dredd: Lawman of the Future – © 2005 Rebellion A/S

Surely that's not right.

Created to cash in on the 1995 Sylvester Stallone *Judge Dredd* movie, the comic was designed to appeal to a younger set of readers than those buying *2000 AD* or *Judge Dredd Megazine*. Set very firmly in Sly's version of Dredd's world, it followed the film's lead in terms of design (the hero ditching the fat-wheeled Lawmaster bike and donning the grey gloves, boots and, er, codpiece seen on screen) and presented Dredd as an all new character shorn of the two decades of continuity he'd amassed in *2000 AD*.

As that opening salvo indicates, it was also much less violent, with the fascistic overtones all but bled out of the character. And yet, these were the elements that had made him a hit in the first place.

Old hand and Dredd co-creator John Wagner checked in to supply the first story and a fresh introduction to the world of Mega-City One, however, even with the master at the helm, the character was sounding rather too much like a bleeding heart liberal. 'Stookie farming is a cruel and sickening practice!' he exclaimed in a particularly pious thought-balloon as he prepared to bust a baddy who was slaughtering cuddly aliens to provide an illegal youth-restoring drug.

Each issue featured three 'Dredd' stories, plus a range of obviously juvenile features ('How to draw Judge Dredd'), schematic illustrations of various bits of Dredd-related hardware (well, it's always handy to know exactly where on his gun the 'voice coded microphone ammunition designator' is located) and dozens and dozens of 'exclusive pix' from the film.

Truly it looked like Judge Dredd was taking over the UK, what with the BBC producing a radio play featuring the character, issue one of the comic selling out and – most exciting of all – Hula Hoops running a poster campaign featuring their famous spherical snack refashioned into the Judge's badge. But despite all that, something just wasn't gelling. With all ties to *2000 AD* severed it felt as though whatever happened to the character within these pages just didn't really count for anything. What with the different Dredd tales running simultaneously within the comic, you knew Old Stoney Face wasn't about to bite the bullet in one of them, because he'd leave the others high and dry.

Although the comic continually threw free gifts at its readers and even roped in Judge Death with issue eight (fatally, sans those carcasses on his uniform), on 31 May 1996, Dredd faced 'the final conflict'. Now that the fuss around the film had subsided – with most concluding it hadn't really been much cop (pun intended) after all – the readers drifted away from this neutered version of comicdom's biggest bastard.

Despite *Judge Dredd: Lawman of the Future*'s many crimes, at least it didn't follow the movie's lead in showing the character with his helmet off. Of course, that might have been because Fleetway didn't want to shell out for the use of Stallone's likeness – but we'll give them the benefit of the doubt on that one. Suspended sentence, creep!

Judge Dredd Megazine
(Fleetway Publications/Fleetway Editions/Rebellion, 1990-ongoing, monthly)

The idea of a comic themed around *2000 AD*'s Judge Dredd was surely a no-brainer, and indeed had been considered in the Eighties. Arguably Britain's most famous comic character still in print, if Roy of the Rovers could get his own title, then – by Grud! – so could Old Stony Face.

As a new wave of optimism momentarily swept across an industry which, at the start of the Nineties, had caught a glimpse of a possible escape route from falling sales in the form of the new 'adult comics' boom (see: *Crisis, Revolver* and *Deadline*), Dredd readied for action. However, while the other publications would turn out to be less than sure-footed when the boom turned to bust, Mega City One's legalised hard man proved he was in it for the long run.

The first issue arrived in October 1990, featuring former *2000 AD* 'Tharg' Steve McManus in the editor's chair, with Dredd co-creator John Wagner and long-time writing partner Alan Grant giving it their all in a consultant role. Thanks to recent revisions in the company's contracts with its creators, the former in particular was rather more enthusiastic about this venture than the meat and potatoes of *2000 AD*, simply because he now had a financial stake in the comic's fortunes. The downside to this, however, was that the adventures of Dredd in his original home were left to other, less inspiring hands, as Wagner all but turned his back on the weekly.

Aiming to be more upmarket than Tharg's rag, *Judge Dredd The Megazine* (as it was originally titled) was a plump, all-colour affair that nestled under one of the biggest logos in the business (it took up half the cover) and had the good fortune of serialising across its first seven issues the best Dredd strip ever written.

'America' was an enflamed and typically skewed take on the American dream, as the eponymous girl born to 'poor dumb' immigrants grew up to discover her parents' idolised notion of the country was sorely mis-placed. 'The Judges, they're like a strait-jacket,' she mused. 'Throw them off and we'll be free again.'

Her life was paralleled by that of her friend Bennet Beeny, who grew up alongside her and carved out a successful career as a comedian. Deeply in love with the girl, he tried to persuade her 'you *could* play it by their rules *and* have a good life', but was unable to prevent her joining up with a pro-democracy terrorist group. In a heart-breaking final reel, he grassed America up to the Judges under the misapprehension he was saving her from herself. But, inevitably, she and her rebellious pals ended up shot dead by Dredd and co.

As if that wasn't depressing enough, we then got the final pay-off as the big-chinned one loomed menacingly across the last page to declare: 'Freedom – power to the people – democracy...*the great American dream.* Don't *kid* yourself' and then: '...America is *dead. This* is the real world.'

This terrifying portrayal of fascism had come from the imagination of Wagner and was well served by Colin McNeil's lavish artwork. Aside from being a fantastic tale, it also served to emphasise the *Megazine* was indeed pitched at an older reader than *2000 AD*.

Other stories in the launch issue couldn't really compare, despite the fact all were well above average. 'Chopper' brought back the rebellious skysurfer from Dredd's run in *2000 AD* for an adventure in the former Australian outback (now known as the 'Radback'), while the lawman's arch enemy, Judge Death, had his early years explored in 'Young Death: "Boyhood of a Superfiend"'. Yet another tangential Dredd character, comic-artist Kenny Who, also made a return, here chasing up some scoundrels who'd reproduced his work without any payment. As the bonnet-wearing scribbler wailed about 'creators' rights', laughter echoed out in the nefarious publisher's bullpen. Obviously Wagner (who wrote this one as well) was still smarting from the previous two decades of poor treatment at the hands of IPC.

In May 1992, the publication jumped to a fortnightly schedule and launched 'Judgement Day' which, taking a leaf from US comics, required readers to buy both the *Megazine* and *2000 AD* if they wanted to follow the story in its entirety.

By 1995, the title was celebrating five years of publication and the arrival of the critically panned *Judge Dredd* film starring Sylvester Stallone. Although this should have brought in more readers, it could be argued Fleetway got just a bit too Dredd happy by launching the rather more juvenile **Judge Dredd: Lawman of the Future** to cash in on the interest, leaving a potential new audience confused about which comic they should be picking up.

The following year, Wagner turned out a long-awaited sequel to 'America' in the form of 'Fading of the Light', but it was back to the monthly routine for the comic and – in a further cost-saving exercise, a load of 2000 AD reprint strips staged an invasion. They've been a constant presence ever since (albeit to varying degrees) as the *Megazine* has continued to evolve in an effort to retain its readership. In recent years the publication has become pleasingly self-obsessed, running a series of fascinating articles about the history of 2000 AD and other titles, while also speaking to some of the industry's hottest talents.

At the time of writing, issues of the *Megazine* are less reliant on archive 'thrill-power', filling up those pesky back pages with a series of reviews tackling comics, films, cult TV and animé under the banner 'Heatseekers'. But most important of all is the fact that if you're looking for proper hardcore Dredd bastardry from the pen of his creator, then no matter what Tharg might tell you, this is still the place to come.

Judy
(DC Thomson, 1960-1991, every Thursday)

'Companion paper to *Bunty*', *Judy* followed on two years after its sister title, offering up pretty much more of the same. Featuring two little kittens on the front (a third would quickly follow), presumably as a counterpart to *Bunty*'s Scottie dog, the first issue of the comic came with a free 'lovely bangle'.

To start with, covers were devoted to a silver-haired little miss clad in a polka-dot blouse and sensible dungarees – the titular Judy herself. Here she got up to various low-powered activities, always accompanied by those three diminutive moggies. Watch Judy hang wallpaper! Check out Judy sipping fruit juice under a parasol! Quiver, as Judy discovers an upended vase of flowers, and those cats cower nervously behind a curtain! However, it was a fair representation of the innocent nature of the material that lay within.

Ballet loomed large on the agenda and, indeed, on the cover of many early issues a sprightly ballerina darted about underneath the price tag, providing the paper with a half-hearted mascot. The first story featured in the publication was tellingly 'Sandra of the Secret Ballet'. The title character would serve *Judy* well over the years, later dancing her way into trouble in tales such as 'Sandra and the Frightened Teacher' (wherein she tangled with a tutor who had unfortunate mob connections), 'Sandra and the Blackmailed Ballet' (the youngster's company is strong-armed into delivering mysterious packages across Europe) and 'Sandra and the Girl Nobody Knows' (our heroine mentors a promising, but mysterious, young dancer).

Horse-related stories were also much loved ('Boomerang: The Horse That Always Comes Back', 'Bobtail the Beach Rescue', 'The Rivals', 'Patience in the Saddle' *et al.*), but where *Judy* really excelled was in its depiction of go-getting role models. Who wouldn't want to be 'Doctor' Katie King, a veritable James Herriot in a gym-slip who tended to all creatures, great and small? Or how about 'Petra: The Party Maker' whose job was laying on a good time for all ('Don't be such an old square... What's wrong with young people enjoying themselves?')? Pat Pride may just have been a school secretary, but she still found time to get herself into plenty of scrapes at Hatton Hall, while 'Publicity' Penny Martin moved Heaven and Earth to promote her father's circus. Elsewhere 'Sally of Studio Seven' dabbled in the exciting world of TV, thanks to her job as Programme Assistant (arguably providing a prototype for *Emma*'s title character) and Nina Barrett from the future year 2009 AD foiled the nefarious plans of Mekon lookalike (he even got about on his own little hoverboard) Yexar.

In terms of pluck, *Judy* had one stand-out character; the freckle faced Bobby Dazzler who was the only girl at Westbury Boarding School, where her mother was matron. Her daily existence was dedicated to showing Mike Norton and the other third formers they were sadly mistaken in their belief boys were superior to girls. So strident was the young feminist that by the middle of the Sixties, she'd made her way onto the paper's front pages – although silly old Mike still wouldn't give her a break ('This is what comes of letting girls go on dormitory raids! Trust Bobby to mess things up!').

The ethos of empowerment didn't quite end there. Every week 'Busy Bea's Page' would encourage readers to make their own fancy dress costumes, talk about hobbies, create brand new party games or just send in photos of their pets.

Judy stuck pretty much to the same format throughout its life, albeit sneaking in the occasional pop and fashion feature as the Eighties drew on. Nevertheless, a comic that, in 1984, was giving away dog food as part of a competition prize could never be seriously accused of slavishly following the zeitgeist. In 1979, it swallowed up the excellent *Emma*, and six years later absorbed the less impressive *Tracy* (DC Thomson, 1979-85) to little obvious effect upon its contents.

By the time the Nineties dawned, it had outlived most of its rivals but couldn't survive any longer in the rapidly diminishing market of girls' weeklies. When the end came in 1991, it wasn't too awful. Joining forces with fellow stalwart *Mandy* it became *Mandy and Judy* which, thanks to a latter 'funky' name change to *M&J*, survived for a further six years until 1997.

June
(Fleetway Publications/IPC Magazines Ltd, 1961-1974, every Tuesday)

'Free gifts for the next four weeks' – what kind of a gravy train was this? Upon its arrival, Fleetway's girls' title was certainly happy to throw the cash around when it came to luring readers away from DC Thomson's *Bunty* and *Judy*, and offered up a floral bracelet as the first instalment on future treasures to come.

Resolutely wholesome, that first number led with the charming comic-strip 'Diana's Diary', half-page funny 'Jenny' and then a text story by Enid Blyton, 'The Mystery of Banshee Towers'. Mixing further funnies ('My Dog Cuddles' and 'Cloris and Claire: The Sporting Pair') with more pages of text ('My Zoo Friends' by Gerald Durrell, for one) and adventure strips ('The Black Pearls of Taboo Island' and 'Kathy at Marvin Grange School'), the comic also struck out for a bit of self-improvement by way of its 'Cookery Nook' column.

Before long, photo covers were jettisoned in favour of pen and ink depictions of the low-concept domestic sitcom lived out by the comic's title character and her naughty dog Jiffy (uh oh, the pooch has scoffed one of its owner's desiccated coconut 'South Sea Islander' cakes again!) with pop-star pin-ups getting all the (black and white) lens action on the back. By 1963, the title was proudly referring to itself as 'the most popular schoolgirls' weekly' while also employing Kathleen Sheridan to bring readers all the up-to-the-minute news on 'delicious fashions'. 'Shirt-waisted dresses are the rage too – and with a shirt-waister in your wardrobe that awful feeling of "I've got nothing suitable to wear for that occasion" just does not exist!'

The title also turned its hand to pop reporting, with its minuscule 'Record Round-Up' column ('Gregory Phillips is a name to watch for'), which couldn't help but be overshadowed by the 'Nature's Wonderland' spread that shared the same page ('Most of the tummy upsets suffered by dogs are caused by overfeeding').

Although, in the main, around this time stories were pretty down-to-earth, *June* would allow itself one dalliance with the fantastical every week as the likes of 'Secret Agent 13' and then 'Vanessa from Venus' graced its pages.

In 1964 it consumed the nine-month-old *Poppet* (Fleetway Publications, 1963-4) before setting its sights on the former million-selling *School Friend* the next year. An impressive scalping indeed, the occasion was celebrated by giving away a copy of – what else? – 'Lulu's Friendship Album'. More notable than that, was the arrival of Bessie Bunter, the guzzler of Cliff House school and not-quite-so-famous sister of Billy.

Then, in 1966, the paper ran a curious twelve-part TV tie-in, 'The Growing-Up of Emma Peel'. 'Week after week you thrill to her adventures in ABC Television's *The Avengers*,' it explained, 'now, for the first time, we're telling the story of Emma as a girl.' What followed were the travails of Emma Knight (as she was known then) who lived with her shipping magnate father John, travelling the world in their yacht. Here she clashed with the evil Sheik Abul of Abul Babul while also learning judo from Chinese chef Mao.

The mixture of fashion advice, laffs, school stories and the odd bit of fantasy steered *June* through into the Seventies, where it made its last merger. This time it was the distinctly babyish *Pixie* (IPC Magazines Ltd, 1972-3) which lost its footing as the now self-proclaimed 'friendly paper with exciting stories' made its move.

During this time strips such as 'Boss of Beadle Street' (a young girl inherits dominion over a suburban enclave), 'Olly Goes to School' (Mary Moore becomes a boarder at Castlemere school, along with her pet otter) and 'Henrietta's Horse' (a tower block-dwelling lass wins a pony) maintained the comic's traditions, while 'Lucky's Living Doll' ('She talks and walks into lots of fun and trouble!') and the magicking 'The Silver Savage' upped the fantasy content a little.

However, despite this slight change in direction, *June* was a comic out of time – good-hearted but painfully twee in comparison to newcomers *Jinty* and *Tammy*. Thus, on 22 June 1974 it was folded into the pages of the latter where Bessie Bunter – formerly 'your plump chump', now 'the funniest girl in the school' – continued her noshing unabated.

Thirteen years? That wasn't a bad run – particularly as the free gifts had all but dried up after week four.

Knockout
(IPC Magazines Ltd, 1971-1973, every Monday)

Not a resurrection of *Knockout Comic* (Amalgamated Press/Fleetway Publications, 1939-63), but yet another IPC funny from the early Seventies – the era when they seemed to be foisting a new humour title on the market every other week.

Knockout – © Egmont UK Ltd

A bit of a minnow in the scheme of things (although notching up over a hundred issues is always commendable) the title was hardly bulging with innovation but did its job with little fuss. Tempting readers to pick up its first issue with the free gift of an 'Arrow' toffee bar ('chew while you view this super comic!') the title's star attraction was undoubtedly 'The Super Seven', a crack squad of kids, each sporting a special skill as indicated by their nicknames: Dead Eye Dick, Thunderball, Wanda Wheels, Stinker, Windy, Booter and Whistler. Patrolling town on their home made go-kart (the Super Sevenmobile, with Wanda steering, natch) they assisted citizens or foiled crimes, using various combinations of their special powers, although you'd be amazed how often a problem could be overcome simply by Windy's huge set of lungs. 'Thanks a lot, Super Seven! Allow us to stand you a big nosh up for that!' declared one grateful client in 1972. 'Sorry, kids, but we've more calls to attend to! So long!' replied the ever-diligent septet.

Although their adventures originally took place on the front of the comic, they were soon shifted to a permanent slot on the centre spread.

IPC's reliance on feuding characters was exercised with two competitive father and son teams in 'Beat Your Neighbour' and the all-out class warfare of 'The Toffs and the Toughs', while rather more imaginative was 'Boney', the exploits of a ghost train escapee skeleton. 'My Bruvver!' was standard sibling squabbling as 'Littl'un' tested the patience of Len, and also prompted readers to write in with tales of their own annoying family members: 'My bruvver, when he was small, emptied the goldfish bowl into his pram and tried to eat the goldfish!' Thanks for that, Andrew Stott from Castleford. Even more generic was the lazily titled 'Joker'. He played practical jokes, and that was it – but incredibly it was enough to propel him onto *Knockout*'s cover, usurping the far more imaginative 'Full House' (which, every week, dished out its comic-strip wares via a cutaway section showing what was going on in every room of the eponymous dwelling) in the process.

Rather better was 'Pete's Pockets' (a boy who kept all manner of items in his voluminous pouches) and 'Fuss Pot' (a snooty madam for whom nothing ever came up to scratch), while 'The Haunted Wood' and 'Barry and Boing' (the semi-serious adventures of orphan Barry Bates and a 'spring-built' robot) were just plain weird.

Never really coalescing into anything more than the sum of its parts, *Knockabout* was only ever average stuff. As such, few tears were shed when that 'great news for all readers' banner hovered into view in 1973 and the title was amalgamated into **Whizzer and Chips** *incorporating Knockout*.

Krazy
(IPC Magazines Ltd, 1976-1978, every Monday, or 'Moanday' over Halloween)

As the name – and indeed spelling – suggested, *Krazy* ('a new comic for kids only' which, cannily admitted, 'we don't mind grown-ups paying for it, though!') was utterly, utterly nuts, imbued with a free-wheeling sense of humour and a fiendish level of creativity. This was perhaps best illustrated by the comic's running gag of printing 'disguised' back covers so that if teacher came along and caught you reading the publication in class, you could quickly flip it over and brandish the rear which, during the comic's run, made it look like anything from a private diary, to a holiday brochure ('Sunny Costa Bomb'), to a half coloured-in paint-by-numbers scene, to a record sleeve (sporting a 95RPM from the '888 Bottom Flops'). Best of the lot, however, had to be the back of the 1 April edition in 1977 which featured...an exact replica of the front, albeit inverted.

But enough about the cover, what actually lay within? To be honest, you couldn't always be sure as the paper seemed to throw a different combination of features and strips at you from week to week, sometimes printed in an almost unreadable shade of pink.

That said, the headline act was undoubtedly 'The Krazy Gang' – Ed, Blue, Liz, Sporty, Brainy, Freaky and future solo artist Cheeky. These good-natured pals lived in a pleasingly parent-free world and went about their business from out of their gang hunt, often clashing with fellow *Krazy* star Pongalongapongo.

Other regulars included rubbish superheroes 'Birdman and Chicken the Boy Blunder', a Batman and Robin-themed twosome who could regularly be found uttering exclamations such as 'sweltering swallows!'; Mickey Mimic, who, in one 1977 episode impersonated Ted Heath in order to secure more time on a boating lake when the stingy owner called him in too soon ('We're both boat owners you know!' he chuckled, as kids everywhere doubtlessly scratched their heads); cut-price *Six Million Dollar Man* '12½p Buytonic Boy' and junior magician, 'Ray Presto'. Yes, even the strips' titles were great.

With stories regularly spilling into each other, and characters popping up all over the place, it really seemed like anything went. But that wasn't *Krazy*'s only killer-app. Determined to appear modern and relevant to its audience, the paper regularly referenced popular television in its 'A *Krazy* Look at TV' strip (this week: Raymond Baxter arses around with a super computer, with hilarious results) and cameo appearances from the likes of Eamonn Andrews and Bruce Forsyth pepped up other features.

By the time the comic reached its first birthday, it was in jubilant mood – 'Who said we wouldn't make it?' it asked across that cake-festooned front cover. Two weeks later, so buoyant was the mood it launched a spin-off publication starring *Cheeky*. However, there weren't going to be any further celebrations.

Perhaps it was the relatively expensive production values, or maybe just good old reader apathy – whatever the reason, the persistently upbeat paper looked oncoming obsolescence in the face in 15 April 1978, exclaiming '*Krazy* stars on the move!' across its last issue as the comic prepared to merge with **Whizzer and Chips**. 'We're all inside!' announced the bulging front cover of *Whizzer and Chips and Krazy* the following week where Mickey Mimic rubbed shoulders with the likes of Sid's Snake.

But, alas, we all knew the truth. Despite the stoic show of unity, the *Krazy* experiment was over all too soon.

Lion
(Amalgamated Press/Fleetway Publications/IPC Magazines Ltd, 1952-1974, every Monday)

Words such as 'redoubtable', 'sturdy' and 'stoic' could have been invented for this redoubtable, sturdy and stoic stalwart of the UK comics scene. The first of what would turn into Fleetway's trio of big cat-themed comics (the other two being *Tiger* and *Jag*[uar]), *Lion* came into existence as a would-be *Eagle* **mk** I-beater which displayed a tenth of the artistry employed in that fine title and a hundredth of the production values, but would still fatally outflank its rival when it came to the kill.

Launched two years after Hulton Press Ltd's smash-hit publication, *Lion* triumphantly referred to itself as 'King of Picture Story Papers', but rather undercut that epithet by slinging out an own-brand version of 'Dan Dare' on its debut front cover. 'Outlaw in Space' by Frank S Pepper (who'd later create 'Roy of the Rovers' for *Tiger*) introduced us to the year 3000 where the world was ruled by a dictator who sent anyone who dared oppose him to 'the uranium mines of distant Titan, one of the moons of Saturn.' Among these dissenters was the Captain, a former ace pilot of 'inter-planet space-lines' who had his mind set on escape, despite the constant presence of the evil Geeks (mindless, whip-wielding over-lords, rather than bespectacled sci-fi enthusiasts). Accompanying him in his efforts was the good-hearted Peter who, in this opening episode, rather improbably mused: 'I wish I'd lived a thousand years ago. In the twentieth century they'd never heard of the mines of Titan, and there was no world dictators. Those were the days.'

Inside the comic (which, unlike *Eagle*, sported just one miserly page of colour – and that was on the front), we met the Jennings-like Sandy Dean who starred in 'Sandy Dean's First Term'. Arriving halfway through the year at Tollgate ('Gosh! This looks a wizard school. I reck-on I'm going to have the time of my life here!') he soon ran into resident plum-in-his-mouth bully Bossy and his cohorts, but quickly got the bet-ter of the rotters much to the delight of his new peer group. 'Three cheers for the new boy who dished Bossy!' exclaimed one. 'Let's take him to the tuckshop,' chipped in another.

Other comic-strip excitement came in the form of 'The Lone Commandos' (Sgt Roy Tempest and Jack Steel setting out to destroy a German radar station) and 'Brett Marlowe: Detective' in 'The Case of the Tailor's Dummy'. A Sexton Blake-baiting 'tec who was chauffeured around by his sidekick Rusty, his cases were always swung on a minor detail. Here that involved a dumb crook who employed limbs from a tai-lor's dummy to pad out the sleeves of his raincoat, leaving his hands free to sneak out from under the voluminous garment and snatch a precious statuette. And he would have gotten away with it too, if he hadn't got one small (well, actually not all that small) detail wrong – he put the left arm on his right side and vice-versa. Hardly a master criminal.

However, the most notable strip on show here had to be 'The Jungle Robot'. It opened with the following intriguing text: 'As the steamer arrived at the African port, Ted Ritchie and his pal, Ken Dale, peered around eagerly. Hidden beneath their bunks was Archie, the secret mem-ber of their expedition.' As it quickly transpired, Archie was a robot cre-ated by Professor Ritchie, designed to assist the lads in their expedition. Controlled by Ted via a small panel he wore around his neck, at this stage of the game it was clear the native-frightening creation ('Him big ju-ju!') was only ever intended as a second banana, but over the years to come he'd gain a mouth and a wicked sense of humour which would catapult him into the big chair in the pantheon of *Lion* characters.

Aside from the comic-strip stuff, the paper also featured three text stories (the best being 'Jingo Jones and His Invisibiliser' which scores points for being the most *Boys' Own*-named tale ever), miscellaneous features such as the 'World-Wide Quiz' ('Is this man paddling a kayak, a cobble or a coracle?') and, best of all, 'The *Lion* Club'. Here readers could ensure the comic would print a salutation for them upon their birthday by mailing in details of when they were born, or send a shilling to receive a special badge.

As the weeks unfurled, *Lion* continued with pretty much the same mix of features. Captain Condor did eventually escape from those pesky mines and went on to fight evil-doers across the galaxy in a series of exciting, if brainless, adventures. But, to be fair, even the Cap's creator would later confess: 'I was producing something purely ephemeral. It was designed to amuse children and be forgotten when next week's instalment came out.' That said, who could possibly fail to remember the giant Crabbleclaw, the tortoise-cum-crab encountered by our hero on the planet Zoltar? Meanwhile, with the first term over, Sandy Dean's strip was sensibly renamed 'Sandy Dean's Schooldays', but despite settling in well at Tollgate, he still found himself locking horns with the odious Bossy on a regular basis, in one edition threatening to administer the bully with 'a punch on your ugly boko'.

Not even a printers' dispute in 1956 could fell the mighty *Lion* which, despite being put out of action for a month, continued churning out the derring-do.

In 1957, Condor had his wings clipped by the smiling Paddy Payne, as the ace trouble-shooter in the RAF with a gay neckerchief supplanted him on the front cover. Two years later, further exciting developments were afoot. The comic got a dynamic makeover as artwork improved throughout and a new masthead made its debut, while Robot Archie was finally bestowed with the power of speech. This was also the year *Lion* made its first acquisition.

Over time, *Sun* (Allen/Amalgamated Press, 1947-59) had metamorphosed from a health magazine into a boys' action paper devoted to cowboy stories and the Swiss Family Robinson. However, by the end of the Fifties, it was looking increasingly pointless. With Fleetway now having taken over Amalgamated Press, the new bosses were keen on streamlining their juvenile output. Thus, *Sun* was merged with *Lion* and Billy the Kid found himself doing his gun-slinging routine in a new paper.

As 1960 came around, 'Captain Condor' got a new lease of life courtesy of Keith Watson who had temporarily defected from *Eagle* where he'd been part of the 'Dan Dare' team since 1957. His version of the cut-price space hero – while still confined to the black and white pages inside – was superb and unsurprisingly Dare-esque. In came modern-looking spacesuits and chunky boots as the Cap finally embraced the future. However, it wasn't to last as Watson was lured back to Dan in 1962 with the promise of drawing the whole thing himself.

Despite that disappointment, the decade would prove a good one for the comic. Nicely rendered Viking butchery in 'Sword of Eingar' begat the highly principled 'Karl the Viking', the pipe-smoking 'Sky-High' Bannion regaled us with glider-related stories from his past and 'ace stuntman investigator' (surely the most exciting job title ever?) 'Rory McDuff: Danger Wanted' tangled with bad guys around the globe.

1965 brought the creation of one of *Lion*'s best characters, The Spider. A villainous Leonard Nimoy lookalike whose complicated backpack and gun allowed him to spin his very own webs, his initial goal in life was to become some sort of king of crime. Ever boastful – 'Puny ants! This nerve-gas...to which *I* am impervious...will paralyse all of you!' – he eventually decided to turn crime fighter; an unsurprising change of career when you realise that for much of his life his scripts were written by Superman co-creator Jerry Siegel. Nevertheless, unlike his US counterparts, this was one superhero who always had the potential to go off the rails again should he fancy a change. 'Another crimeless day...it would seem The Spider has the crooks in this city in fear and trembling!' he mused in the third person in 1969. 'And yet I find this forced inactivity just plain...boring!'

The year after the character's debut brought another merger when the short-lived (just fifteen issues) 'companion paper' to *Valiant*, *Champion* (Fleetway Publications, 1966) was welcomed in as, on the front cover of the first conjoined edition, cowboy Texas Jack laid out some varmint with a punch to the jaw simply to illustrate the fact he thought the news was 'knockout!'

The union brought with it another superhero; The Phantom Viking. When schoolteacher Olaf Larsen donned a helmet he turned into a beskirted magic Norseman with super strength and the power of flight...until the south wind blew. Nothing more than a dopey rip-off of Marvel Comics' Thor, it was enjoyable enough, with our Aryan friend

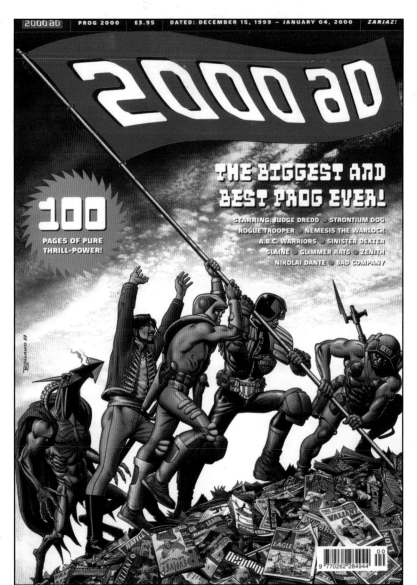

2000 AD celebrates surviving into
the new millennium with style.

IPC's controversial comic hits the news-stands with 'the toughest stories ever'.

Ginger finds himself in another low-concept scrape on the front of an early *Beezer*.

The last boys' comic launched by DC Thomson only manages to notch up twenty months.

DC Thomson's counterblast to *2000 AD*.

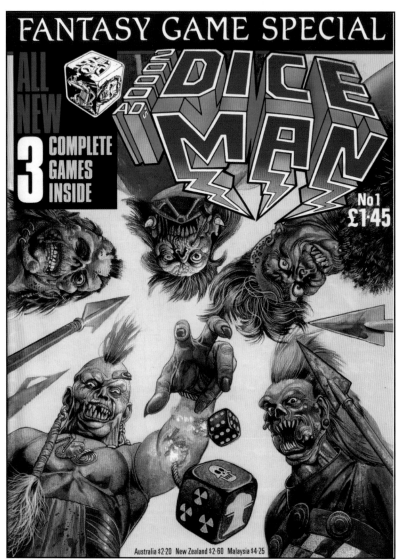

A quintet of nasties launch *2000 AD*'s role-playing spin-off.

Muppets! Keith Chegwin! Kid Jensen!
How can any girl resist?

The legendary *Jinty* goes all sci-fi with the ace
'The Human Zoo'.

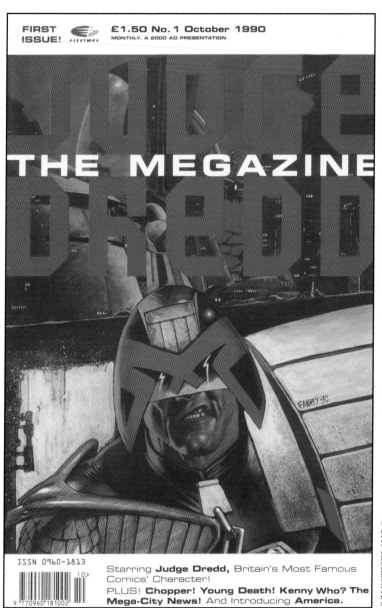

FIRST ISSUE! £1.50 No. 1 October 1990
MONTHLY. A 2000 AD PRESENTATION

THE MEGAZINE

EABRY 90

ISSN 0960-1813

Starring **Judge Dredd,** Britain's Most Famous
Comics' Character!
PLUS! **Chopper! Young Death! Kenny Who? The
Mega-City News!** And Introducing **America.**

2000 AD's future lawman gets his own title
after thirteen years.

Cheeky and the gang go characteristically nuts
for April Fools' Day.

Another typically innocuous *Mandy* cover
hides tales of cruelty within.

A new brand of zaniness for the Eighties from DC Thomson, and the original home of Bananaman.

The Bash Street kid graduate: ... in weekly.

A ghost and an elephant welcome readers to issue one
of IPC's horror-themed comic.

Future *Watchman* co-creator Dave Gibbons dons the
over-sized pants of Big E for *Tornado*.

The only paper that can boast both Rolf Harris and the chance to win a free Bluebird moneybox.

liable to bang on about 'Odin's beard' in times of stress.

Also along for the ride was another ace pilot, Jet Jordan, whose father invented jet planes for a living, and futuristic Second World War retread, 'Return of the Stormtroopers'. Around this time, *Lion* was also going multi-media, running an adaptation of the *Danger Man* TV series.

With the comic becoming increasingly fantastical, the arrival of 'Carson's Cubs' (a footballing strip) supplied a much needed grounding influence and a rare excursion into sport, while in 1968, Archie and friends got their hands on a time-travelling machine and wrought their own brand of mayhem across the ages (well, Tim Kelly had been at it in the pages of *Valiant* for some years now – it was all the rage). One such trip whisked them to a future Britain which had been invaded by evil alien Krulls, who took a severe pasting from the metal men, Ted and Ken. Other outlandish strips from the end of the decade included 'The Day the World Drowned' and 'The Mind Stealers'.

And then, on 3 May 1969, the once unthinkable happened as *Lion* swallowed up the now ailing *Eagle*. Years of takeover bids and disinterested management had taken their toll on the comic which had shed readers as it upped its reliance on reprints and retreads. Dan Dare's thoughts on being forced into Captain Condor's old stomping ground are unrecorded, but it was quite a comedown for the definitive Pilot of the Future, who would eke out a living over the next year or so in butchered black and white reruns of past glories. Also transferring over was 'The Gladiators', the tale of six burly fellas from ancient Rome who'd been transported forward in time to the Second World War where they wasted little time in 'clobbering a dozen Jerry soldiers'.

In the Seventies, whimsy ruled the day. Carson's Cubs found themselves pitted against *Eagle*'s Circus Wanderers on the footie pitch, the result being manager Joe Carson agreeing to let his lads train with the big top-based team in future – 'Your unusual play can help us to score goals!' Meanwhile, 'Stringbean and Hambone' followed the fortunes of two hapless wrestlers (the latter being a Scot, and thus taking to the grappling mat in tartan bonnet and shorts, natch) who'd provoked the ire of the dreaded Chong Tong by inheriting a Chinese junk boat with a magic stone hidden in the ship's lantern; while 'General Johnny' introduced us to schoolboy Johnny Quick who was discovered to be a military genius and quickly received call-up papers from the British Army; and 'Flame O'The Forest' brought ye olde masked crime-fighting action to Saxon England.

1971 brought the last *Lion* takeover as this time it got its claws into *Thunder*. In this case, the fallen title's line-up proved so appealing that, although the oversized feline claimed top billing in the merger, the conglomeration featured more strips from the supporting act as 'Fury's Family', 'Phil the Fluter', 'The Jet-Skaters', 'Adam Eterno' and 'Steel Commando' all made the transfer. Metalheads everywhere were doubtlessly delighted to see the latter now in the same comic as Archie (although, the tin-plated legend was tactfully taking a short leave of absence at the time, presumably to let his new neighbours have a few weeks to bed in).

However, the sword of Damocles was now dangling over *Lion* as IPC execs were pushing for another merger. Before that fateful day, there was just time for another classic character to emerge, as the evil Professor Krait developed the means by which he could turn himself into The Snake. This reptilian reprobate leapt around London formulating a plan to take control over the country with a squad of hypnotised thugs, while issuing distinctively sibilant threats: 'My slaves will rise again – to *ssspread* violence and terror all over Britain!' Later, he joined up with fellow evil scientist (did they have their own union, or something?) the wheelchair-bound Ezra Creech to become 'Masters of Menace'.

In 1974, a fearsome face-off took place, as *Lion* stared down *Valiant*. Compelled to join forces by a management edict, it's said both editorial teams insisted their comic should get top billing, claiming their publication was the more buoyant proposition. Despite the fact *Lion* had convention on its side (in previous years, the two had combined to do the summer special thing under the shared banner of *Lion and Valiant*), it must have blinked first, as the rival title ultimately retained the big font.

After an impressive twenty-two years, the first predator of British comics had finally become someone else's lunch.

Look-In
(Independent Television Publications Ltd/IPC Magazines Ltd, 1971-1994, every Friday)

A legend in juvenile publishing, *Look-In* managed to be both excitingly modern (bags of stuff about current TV and pop favourites) and reassuringly old-fashioned (surely no-one had 'looked in' on television since the

Fifties?). It was to prove a winning formula that many would try to copy, while the paper just carried on about its business, providing households with a junior equivalent to Mum's *TV Times*. Indeed, 'The Junior *TV Times*' was the comic's adopted subtitle for most of its life.

In the planning stages, the publication was a conglomeration of two dummy editions that were floating around: a proposed comic-strip-heavy successor to *TV21* and a feature-based variant of its listings-magazine parent. Originally titled *Magpie*, there was a notion that it would be tied in with Thames TV's kids' show – and certainly the programme and its presenters loomed large during the paper's early years.

The first edition of *Look-In* was dated 9 January 1971, and, on the front, featured a photo of *Magpie*'s Tony Bastable gawping out at readers while carrying a stack of books. This was to promote his weekly column, 'Backchat'. The expected free gift took the form of a flat-pack 'make your own TV studio' cardboard diorama that readers had to assemble themselves ('You will have hours of interest and fun by lining up the model cameras before the presenters,' ran the perhaps over-optimistic instructions inside). However, this wasn't just any old studio. Nope, it was a miniature replica of a certain Teddington-based, ornithologically-named magazine show.

Other items worth shouting about from the front were the *Please Sir!* comic-strip (a photo of John Alderton, looking a little uncertain in a rowing boat)...and a lizard from the dull natural history series *Survival*.

Inside we were presented with a they-don't-make-'em-like-that any-more editorial from the sharp-suited former *TV21* boss Alan Fennell (his picture included alongside his sage words). 'Look through the list of contents and you will see how exciting *Look-In* is,' he said before signing off with: 'And remember, there will always be something new in *Look-In*.'

Even from first glance it was obvious this was something very different for the world of children's weeklies, with the likes of Dickie Davies (here known as Richard), a pre-combover Fred Dinenage, a baffled look-ing Ed 'Stewpot' Stewart and a reassuringly avuncular David Nixon shar-ing the same page.

Even more exciting was the launch of the 'Teletalker!' campaign, which planned to get readers sharing their opinions about TV. First, you had to fill in a coupon and then, every week a computer (Yes! A comput-er!) would select fifty random respondents to fill in a questionnaire about what they liked to watch.

The comic's first strip arrived, 'by arrangement with Leslie Crowther'. The former *Crackerjack* regular appeared here in the succinctly named 'Crowther in Trouble'. Fun stuff indeed, the first edition found Leslie breaking the fourth wall by speaking to us at home ('That boxing sketch we're doing, where I get knocked out of the ring, should be funny') before falling foul of a fellow motorist's poor driving. Discovering the burly chap was actually due to perform in the skit with him later that day, a swift script rewrite saw our man delivering a knockout punch to the hooligan instead. By panel thirteen, it was all over, Les tucked up in bed ruminating on the day just gone, and setting up the great conceit that each of his strips would open and close with him snuggled up under the covers.

Next up, edutainment staged an invasion, with two pages devoted to 'the first of four articles introducing the Arizona desert, by Colin Willock' – a *Survival* tie-in no less, and lavishly illustrated with colour photos of lizards, cacti and birds.

Then, we were onto sports features, which were, naturally, helmed by the aforementioned Mr Davies. 'We will have already met if you watch my *World of Sport* programme on Saturday afternoons,' advised the low-rent Clark Gable lookalike. 'If not, we can get to know each other on this page in *Look-In*.'

Comic-strip action then resumed with an adaptation of the kids' spy series *Freewheelers* (another Southern Television production) while Tony Bastable fulfilled that contractual obligation by showing up on page 15 decked out in boxing gear to bring us his first 'Backchat', reassuring readers that despite his apparel, 'I hope we never come to blows'. That said, he was keen to get some sort of a ruck going with the *Look-In* massif: 'Judging from your letters in the *Magpie* programme's postbag every week, a lot of you are happy to pitch in and have a good old row.'

Away from such inflammatory talk, comedy re-emerged with the paper's 'Please Sir!' strip. A tie-in with the London Weekend Television sitcom, we did indeed get to see poor old Hedges and the shavers of class 5C messing about on the river (so, that hadn't just been a standard library shot of Alderton after all – or maybe the story had been written to order to correspond with whatever stills they had available). This was accompanied by a slender column from David Nixon, who taught us the trick of 'The Vanishing Queen' and how to make an egg balance on its pointed end (although this one presupposed everyone lived in a home that employed tablecloths).

As the end drew near, we came upon the mesmerising *Look-In* programme planner, two whole pages devoted to regionalised TV listings – complete with all the various local stations' logos – which detailed the child-friendly fare on that week (including *The Golden Shot*, *It's Tarbuck* and *This is Your Life*). Bringing up the rear we found a sumptuous colour adaptation of ATV's sci-fi series *Timeslip*, which echoed the publication's debt to *TV21*; another *Magpie*-related feature (following the team's tour of the Far East); and finally, a back page casting call for *Junior Showtime*, notable for featuring a grisly photo of Ken Dodd interacting with a pre-pubescent Black and White Minstrel.

A hearty publication indeed, which really wore its TV association on its sleeve, there was no doubt *Look-In* was going to be a success. As the weeks passed with a succession of *Magpie* cover shoots ('Make Sue's dish-cloth vest: see inside') the paper showed itself adept at jumping on the next big thing (dragooning in Ayshea from *Lift Off* to pen a pop column in issue eighteen for example, and ditching 'Please Sir!' for an adaptation of its sequel: *The Fenn Street Gang*), displaying the capricious tendencies that would ensure it always remained the most up-to-the-minute read kids could get.

After nearly a year of photographic covers, they were dumped in favour of superbly painted montages, more often than not from the brush of film poster artist Arnaldo Putzu. This change had come about when it became clear the team were struggling to find suitably arresting images, and even though the alteration was bemoaned by some who felt the photos gave the paper a pleasing 'magazine' quality, the floating heads and lurid colours quickly became the publication's calling card.

As the Seventies progressed, *Look-In* increased its focus on pop, going nuts over The Bay City Rollers, David Cassidy and the like. Meanwhile, seminal strips like 'The Tomorrow People', 'Follyfoot' and 'Kung Fu' proved its finger remained on the pulse, while adaptations of popular sitcoms such as *On the Buses* and *Bless This House* provided readers with a definitive snapshot of the era.

In 1975, Alan Fennell left the paper, leaving art editor Colin Shelbourn to jump into the big chair for a heroic run that would stretch until *Look-In*'s dog days in the Nineties. Maintaining close links with ITV, he continued the trend of backing emergent crazes, although steered clear of those shows that went out after 9 p.m. no matter how popular they were with the readers (such as *The Sweeney*) – an edict the short-lived rival *Target* attempted to exploit (with its line-up including comic-strip adaptations of *Kojak* and *Target*). That said, there were still ways around the ruling, the paper printing numerous posters of David Soul under the guise of promoting his singing career rather than his role in *Starsky and Hutch*.

By now, the links with *Magpie* had been pretty much dropped (although the show did promote the publication's 'Star Awards'), Abba, Flintlock and *The Six Million Dollar Man* proving far more of a draw than Puff the Pony. Ever adaptable, by the end of the Seventies, *Look-In* was even taking punk in its stride. In October 1979 it featured The Jam, Blondie and Darts on a series of covers. The following month: Cliff Richard, Abba and The Dooleys. All were grist to the mill.

When the Eighties arrived, potentially serious competition showed up in the shape of DC Thomson's *Tops* and the paper went through something of a relaunch, altering the iconic logo, and reverting back to photographic covers. However, despite the slight reaffirmation of its magazine sensibilities, the same mixture of comic-strip action (although less weighted towards sitcom) and pin-ups prevailed. *Tops* quickly folded, but another similar venture emerged in 1985, courtesy of Polystyle Publication's *Beeb*. By now *Look-In* had changed its appearance again, and a mixture of *The A-Team*, *Robin of Sherwood*, *Danger Mouse*, *Super Gran* and *Cannon and Ball* help put paid to the latest pretender.

Now well into the video age, comic-strips were becoming a less important part of the mix. Whereas before they offered kids their only chance to get a second helping of their favourite show, now it was all too simple to sling a cassette into that top-loader and enjoy Hannibal, Face, BA and co. over and over. As such, the panel-by-panel fare was reserved for more obvious 'comic' material, such as *Trapdoor*, *Roger Ramjet* and *Inspector Gadget*. Strips also branched out to bring us 'behind the scenes'-style exploits from famous faces, to wit 'The 5 Star Life' which presented the daily travails of Delroy, Stedman and the rest of the family.

The Eighties ended with *Look-In* weighted more towards photo features and nervously eyeing up the BBC's *Fast Forward*, which – with its wall-to-wall *Bread* and Andy Crane, and constant TV trails before *Neighbours* – presented a serious challenge indeed. Further upset followed in 1991, as IPC bought out *TV Times* and found itself saddled with the junior paper during a time when it had just slimmed down its own kids' catalogue. Shelbourn was made redundant and a disinterested editorial team allowed the publication to slide into irrelevance, shedding something like 30,000 readers up until its eventual closure in 1994.

Now with an exclamation-mark appended to the title, that last issue was at least respectful enough to pay homage to the first, dusting down the image of Tony Bastable from the first premiere edition to run as a tiny insert at the top left-hand side of the cover (all but blotted out by the 'L' of the logo but – well – the thought was there). Demanding us to 'celebrate 25 years of Britain's best TV comic' it had even gone to the trouble of roping in Take That's Mark Owen and a shed-load of teddy bears to give it a proper send-off.

However, it all left a bitter taste in the mouths of *Look-In* devotees who'd seen the comic hurriedly reduced to a generic teen mag, where once it had been the plushest, most handsomely illustrated thing on the shelves. Even the Michael Jackson and Free Willy posters couldn't provide consolation for that. Plus, *Fast Forward* was still going strong. Now, that just wasn't right...

Of course, none of that matters a jot now, as *Look-In* has long since gained a kind of immortality with the generations of square-eyed kids who thrilled to the extra-curricular adventures of their favourite TV stars and treasured the gorgeous annuals that appeared every Christmas. If you want to know what life was like in the Seventies and Eighties – and what children were really going mad about – there's no substitute. Look out for *Look-in*!

Mandy
(DC Thomson, 1967-1991, every Thursday)

DC Thomson had a theory about girls' comics which informed many of their publications. While boys would be willing to follow male characters young or old, girls could only relate to females who were the same age as them. Hence the proliferation of comics helmed by winsome young things such as *Debbie*, *Judy*, *Bunty*, *Twinkle* (DC Thomson, 1968-99) and, in this case, *Mandy*.

If she was supposed to reflect the title's readership, then the country was well-stocked with raven-haired Alice-band wearing self-starters who were not fazed at the notion of painting a fence, cooking Dad's supper, taking little Bobby Jones to the zoo, or dressing up as an overgrown baby to man a doll stall at a grand charity bazaar.

The first issue (bedecked in a startling blue which would quickly be dropped for a more conservative red and yellow colour scheme) induced readers in with a 'lovely rainbow ring', but it was the stories that kept them coming back. Aside from two all-text efforts ('The Sunshine of her Songs' and 'She Owned 4-Hoofed Earthquake') the publication was packed with imaginative comic-strips that spoke of exotica ('Princess of The Golden Dragon'), dynamic career opportunities ('Peggy the Police Girl'), ham fisted humourists ('Blundering Bessie') and fortuitous gads about town ('Wendy the Winner').

While strips would come and go, the eponymous Mandy's antics on the front cover remained a staple feature. Together with Patch the pup she'd set up some kind of premise via a large splash illustration on the front (for example, constructing a guy for 5 November in 1967) and then work it to its conclusion on the back (luring local ragamuffins to fling sticks at her with a leery 'Yah! Nut-case!' before using said items as fuel for her bonfire). It was charming stuff indeed, but soon felt like an incongruous intro into what quickly became a comic brimming with cruelty and malcontent.

Somewhere down the line it seems the writers had twigged that what young girls really like to read about is suffering. Thus, *Mandy*'s roster of never-say-die troubadours were quickly eclipsed by struggling young orphans, beleaguered by a cruel guardian and ostracised by their peers.

There was 'The Tests of Terry' which told the story of Terry Maxwell and her lazy ('this was her day off and she hasn't even dusted the house!!'), fag-smoking Aunt Hilda. Despite being branded 'toffee-nosed' by local tough girls Dusty and Teddie, she nursed an ambition to win a Duke of Edinburgh Bronze Award. However, her plans were badly derailed in one instance when the rough twosome framed her for a 'cigarettes and sweet' robbery, chuckling, 'she'll get an award now, all right – a prison one.'

Then we had 'The Willing Hands of Meg Smith', the titular Meg being a hardworking scamp bringing up her siblings following the death of her widower father and struggling to make ends meet.

In 'The Door to Yesterday', twelve-year-old Kerry Hollis travelled back in time to meet a scullery maid who was being victimised by an evil dignitary, while 'The Riddle of the Lost Heiress' told of innocent Evvy Collins being forced to take on the role of a girl who'd gone missing five years previously so that her despicable guardians could claim the family's fortune.

As if that wasn't enough emotional torture to be going on with, there was also the 'Lonely Ballerina', the tale of Gwen Jones whose scholarship to a Moscow ballet school took her away from all her friends and brought her into conflict with Madame Pruna, the ballet mistress who was out to make her life unbearable. All of this could be found in just one particular issue of the comic in the late Sixties.

However, it wasn't all flogging, tears and chains in the cellar, as *Mandy* countered some of the anguish with lighter stories such as 'Jill – Junior Reporter' who whizzed around town on her moped finding news stories, the clumsy Milly whose various slapstick mishaps had her regularly exclaiming 'I Should Have Stayed in Bed!' and 'The Double Life of Julie-Ellen', which told of a heroine who pretended to be two identical twins so she could date both the boys she fancied. Alongside that, there was the long-running 'Morgyn the Mighty'-style adventures of wonder girl Valda, blessed with immortal youth, the ability to speak to animals and a mighty leap.

A real bastion of what girls' comics should be about, *Mandy* soldiered on into the Eighties pretty much unaffected by what was going on around it – the one real concession being when it absorbed *Debbie* in 1983, incorporating its 'famous' photo-story 'The Randell Road Girls' into the line-up.

But it couldn't last, and with girls' titles dropping like flies by the start of the Nineties, *Mandy* had one last throw of the dice in 1991, merging with fellow ailing publication *Judy*. Together they became *Mandy and Judy* and in strict contravention of the unspoken rules of comics (also see: *Beezer and Topper*, DC Thomson, 1990-3), carried on as equal partners. Reworked to include more pop and fashion pieces, the title continued for another six years whereupon – despite being rebadged as *M&J* – the story finally came to an end.

Well, not quite. Seemingly built to last, *Mandy* annuals still continue to creep into the shops every Christmas even in the twenty-first century. Looks like that lust for cruelty hasn't quite been bred out of the current generation of Alice-band wearing consumers.

Misty
(IPC Magazines Ltd, 1978-1980, every Monday)

Vampire bats, evil cats, haunted houses, inner-city unrest and a doe-eyed goth presiding over the whole thing; *Misty* was a rather different proposition for girls.

Launched in response to *Spellbound* – which, ironically, merged with *Debbie* a month before this new venture hit the streets – this new kid on the block was positively oozing with attitude, in the main thanks to the involvement of *2000 AD*'s founding father, Pat Mills. As an associate editor on this title, he had firm ideas of the direction it should take.

Despite maintaining girls were more interested in good stories than flashy art, he made the decision to apply the 'rules' of *2000 AD* to this venture, and that included bolder and larger visuals. As a result, stories tended to commence with an arresting and highly impressive full or half-page 'splash' – innovative stuff for the girls' market. And, while the likes of *Mandy* may have boasted their fair share of crippled orphans manacled in dank cellars, *Misty* followed *Tammy*'s lead in taking cruel and unusual to new heights, even pushing the envelope a little by paying scant regard to the natural justice that would always eventually step in to nobble whichever cruel guardian was brandishing the whip this week.

So, what had brought about this revolution? Well, it was pretty much down to the fact that Mills had roped in a whole load of blokey IPC all-stars to work on the publication, claiming (perhaps unfairly – you decide) that in the main female comics writers produced stories that were too 'woolly and soft'. He also felt the majority of them were embarrassed about producing strip stories, instead holding out for the comparative glamour of the feature pages.

And so to issue one. Festooned with a picture of two clearly kacking themselves girls holding a candle aloft as they ventured into a cobweb strewn room, it came free with a lucky charm bracelet (a blue fish dangling off the end). Inside, we met the titular Misty, an escapee from a Roman Polanski nightmare with long black hair, lush eyelashes and an impassive expression, who welcomed us to her comic. 'You've arrived just in time,' she said, 'soon the sun will rise, the mist will lift, and I'll have to go.'

The first story laid out the publication's stall in fine style, with 'The Cult of Cat'. A full-page illustration of some kind of Egyptian religious ceremony was accompanied by the chilling subtitle: 'Some people can't stand cats…Some people fear them, others…*worship them!*'

The next strip was more rooted in the real world, commencing with a finely wrought picture of modern Britain: dull tumbledown terrace houses in the shadows of two huge tower blocks, 'punks rule OK?' scrawled on a wall to give it that definitive touch of inner-city squalor. The high-rises were nicknamed 'The Sentinels' and while one housed numerous happy families, the other was a source of mystery and fear – no one wanted to live there, 'not even rent free'. A fine mixture of social commentary (Mum weeping that she and her family hadn't got a place to stay: 'There's a waiting list a mile long') and spookiness ('Do you believe the stories about the place, Jan?… About ghosts, about people disappearing?'), it proved an electrifying read.

Following on, 'Paint it Black' told the tale of a talentless girl who suddenly began turning out accomplished portraits of a startled-looking lass when she got her hands on a nineteenth-century set of artist's brushes, while 'Moodstone' brought us the travails of young Cathy Salmon, who was turned into a homicidal maniac after donning the eponymous item of jewellery which she'd conned from an old woman.

Both 'Nightmare' and 'Beasts' were regular self-contained strips, pitched somewhere between 'Tharg's Future Shocks' and TV's *Thriller* (or, for that matter *Beasts*) anthology series, while 'Moonchild' brought us an abused and friendless girl who had '*the power!*' (telekinesis, to you and me).

A white-knuckle ride from start to finish, characterised by close-ups of terrified teens, infested with creepy-crawlies and sporting some eerily impressive art, from the off *Misty* was a minor classic. But, there was one thing counting against it. As the weeks unfolded, it became apparent the comic didn't actually sport much in the way of continuing characters. Instead a swathe of female leads would show up, hang around for a few weeks to be terrified, and then disappear from the paper for good once the jig was up. There were to be no 'Four Marys' and the like for readers to latch onto.

Over its run, the comic reworked numerous horror archetypes, usually to good effect. A possessed car showed up in 'Journey into Fear', an evil sorceress drew her plans against humanity in the bleak 'The Black Widow', 'The Four Faces of Eve' brought us a confused amnesiac determined to uncover 'the awful truth' about her mysterious past, a young governess encountered ghosts at an old hall in 'Midnight Masquerader' and an imaginary chum-cum-poltergeist terrorised young Myra in 'My Friend George'. When horse-riding strip 'Winner Loses All' (featuring a character called Jocasta, no less) showed up in issue seventy-eight, it was almost a Vs up to other girls' comics; there was to be no sub-*Black Beauty* whimsy here, instead the horsey stuff was subverted for a hard-as-nails story about alcoholism and Satan himself.

Right up to the end, *Misty* never lost faith, billing itself as 'a different world' and 'not to be read at night'. As it notched up one hundred and one issues, our mysterious editor fluttered her eyelashes at us from within the pages of her own publication for the last time. The comic was being taken over by *Tammy* ('The paper with the very best stories for girls like you!'). And thus, on 12 January 1980, that mysterious alluring fog fell upon the news-stands for the last time.

Once ensconced within the pages of its new home, *Misty*'s stories soon fell down the running order, and when *Tammy* went on to swallow up *Jinty* the following year, the last traces of the comic were banished forever.

Pat Mills reckons he knows why the publication never enjoyed the longevity many people felt it deserved, claiming that as it went on it 'had too many stupid adventure stories in with colourful visuals'. But for its legion of readers, it remains one of the best-remembered girls' comics ever and one that still commands a sizeable following to this day. Have you seen how much some people will shell out for issue one?

Monster Fun
(IPC Magazines Ltd, 1975-1976, every Monday)

The experience of *Shiver and Shake* would seem to indicate horror-themed humour comics weren't getting kids to shell out, and yet, just eight months after its demise, IPC brought us more creepy comedy in the shape of *Monster Fun*.

As it happens, the new effort wouldn't even match the run of its predecessor, but it still provided the company with some top characters who'd filter through into the pages of other publications over the years.

'Meet Kid Kong and his freak friends inside in this crazy new comic...' was the advice that came with issue one. Arriving with a free 'Plate Wobbler' (a device that could be slipped under Mum's favourite china and then secretly inflated, bringing about that promised judder), it was a 'monster mirth maker!!' according to the delighted Kong.

Notionally edited by *Shiver and Shake* escapee and now **Whoopee!** regular Frankie Stein, the undoubted highlight here was the pull-out section 'Badtime Bedtime'; four pages of mayhem illustrated by Leo Baxendale which, in this issue, brought us the tale of 'Jack the Nipper's Schooldays' (future editions would be devoted to 'Robinson Gruesome', 'Mister Punch', 'Dr Jackal and Mr Snide' and the like). However, there was other top stuff on offer too.

'Kid Kong' started off as a fairground attraction ('the son of King Kong') but took umbrage when he was described as 'ugly'. At that point, the 'nana obsessed ape left the show to take up residence with the kindly – but slightly mental – Granny Smith. 'X-Ray Specs' introduced us to Ray who came by his eponymous optical equipment when Squint the optician asked him to test drive a pair ('Hey son! Try these!'). Meanwhile, 'Martha's Monster Make-Up' brought us the adventures of the titular girl and her tub of cream that could turn anything beastly, while 'Dough Nut and Rusty' were two competitive robots, the former a superior droid who preceded his dialogue with a 'whirr!', the latter a down-at-heel creation sporting a tin can for a head and a propensity for bleeps.

Other strips included Dracula's green-skinned daughter, the wittily named 'Draculass'; 'Creature Teacher', a genuinely repulsive-looking, Cyclops-like creation who'd thwart class 3X's attempts to get rid of him; cute dragon 'Cinders' who wore pearl earrings and lipstick; and 'Mummy's Boy', the wretched tale of a teenage lad whose mother kept him in baby's clothes and forbade him from almost all activity, declaring it all too dangerous for her 'choochikins' – its themes of psychological torture a rather more subtle contribution to the comic's monster shtick.

It was all good knockabout fun and there was no reason why it should-n't have run and run, particularly when pathetic shark Gums joined the gang in issue thirty-five, pitting himself into a never-ending feud with cheeky diver Bluey for ownership of his formidable set of false teeth, or 'choppers'.

Throughout its life, *Monster Fun* gave away free posters, booklets and wall charts in a bid to keep its readers sweet – who could fail to be moved by issue sixty-seven's spread depicting some angry cavemen advancing on a startled looking dinosaur? Equally as exciting was the 'Master Ugly Mug – Miss Funny Face – Face-pulling contest' which asked readers to send in photographs of themselves gurning.

Monster Fun – © Egmont UK Ltd

With innovations like this – plus a strip detailing the ker-azy antics of a torturer's apprentice ('Tom Thumbscrew') – the paper should have been guaranteed immortality. But it was not to be. Forewarning us that there was 'important news inside', issue seventy-three revealed that, as of next week, it would be under new management. Frankie would just have to step aside as the publication became the seventh title to be consumed by the all-conquering *Buster*.

Nikki
(DC Thomson, 1985-1989, every Monday)

Not the most distinguished girls' comic ever, *Nikki* nonetheless managed to tread water for a pretty impressive four years thanks to a mixture of school stories and magazine-style features.

The first issue came with a free 'Sunshine Comb' (which, rather excitingly, was depicted in 'actual size' on the cover) and bid girls welcome to the comic, exclaiming: 'It's new! It's ace! It's fun!' 'We hope you like *Nikki*,' read the anxious editorial, which sat in the vicinity of a line drawing of Boy George. 'It's been specially created for *you*!'

Nikki – © DC Thomson & Co., Ltd

The headline story here was 'The Comp', the tale of Samantha Greene, whose family had been living in Germany while her father was serving with the army. Now back in the UK, she was starting at Redvale Comp, a school so working class and gritty the strip's logo took the form of an untidy chalk scrawl. There she encountered punks ('Her hair – it's six different colours!'), bullies and – swoon! – boys ('Ooh, those eyes – and that deep voice – and he wanted to walk with *me*! Maybe he'll ask me out…').

Other strips included the period drama 'School for the Forgotten' ('The story of the worst school in the world!'), 'I Won't Share her With Him!' (Lindy Bateman finds it hard to come to grips with best friend Clare Knowles' boyfriend) and 'Reach for the Stars!' (a *Fame* rip-off set in the Dorretta Stage School, complete with leg warmers, spontaneous bursts of song and a bookish music professor).

You couldn't deny *Nikki* was fun – particularly its 'Bike Shed Wall' page wherein readers' messages were turned into graffiti-style daubings for all to see ('Dear Frog Face, sorry I forgot your Valentine card. I'll make it up to you! – Forgetful, Elgin') but it never came close to carving itself a permanent place in the Great British comics library.

While Samantha Greene and chums were all very well, by the mid-Eighties, girls were looking for something a little bit more streetwise, and less prone to pen and ink pictures of Limahl when what they really wanted was a proper, full colour photographic pin-up of the Kajagoogoo dreamboat.

Thus, after four years on the shelves, *Nikki* was forced to decamp to the pages of *Bunty* where its obsession for all things school was given short shrift.

Nipper
(IPC Magazines Ltd, 1987, fortnightly)

Sometimes a comic comes along that truly baffles. *Nipper* is one such publication. Not little enough to be classified as a pocket library book, but still a good deal smaller than its stablemates *Buster* and *Whizzer and Chips*, the thing was printed on glossy paper, sported a hell of a lot of colour pages, came out on a fortnightly basis and featured a strip created by one of the artists from *Viz*. What madness was this?!

A twenty-four page sampler issue put out before the comic's proper launch gave few clues as to what this new venture was actually *for*. It seemed as though the USP was a comic featuring just child characters. The titular Nipper was a shaggy-haired kid prone to the injustices of life (after his big brother frames him for breaking his sister's doll, he's forced to sit in her toy push chair as penance), while 'First-Time Fred' (drawn by *Viz*'s David Law at around the same time that paper was publishing his 'Roger Irrelevant' strips) dwelt upon the scrapes the eponymous lad found himself in when taking on a new task or activity. More sinister was 'Brad Break' – he was a 'snappy little lad' with what seemed to be a brittle bone syndrome, so often were parts of him encased in plaster.

And so it continued, with other forgettable juvenile-centric fare, the nadir being 'My "Dad", Mum', a whimsical look at growing-up in a single parent family, in which mother continually proved herself to be lacking in all the things a father would traditionally excel at.

When that first issue did arrive (clocking in at a fat forty-eight pages) things were little better. One imagines Cosgrove-Hall placing a telephone call to their solicitors when 'Frankie's Flashlight' (freckle-faced

T-shirt-wearing boy has adventures with his torch) and 'James Pond' (crime-fighting toad saving the Earth from the evil machinations of despotically minded rodent – swap the roles around and you've got *Danger Mouse*) first strutted their stuff, while 'Wonder Boy' day-dreamed about chocolate and 'Blaster Bignoise' courted trouble with his shape-changing tape deck. And as for calling a story about magic train-ers simply 'Magic Trainers'...hmm. The mind fails to boggle.

The problem was, none of this stuff was at all memorable. Where was *Nipper*'s Dennis the Menace, Frankie Stein, or Sweeney Toddler? Hell, even a Gus the Gorilla would have been an improvement. As sales res-olutely failed to happen, the comic switched to a more traditional page size with issue six ('*Nipper* comic is growing up'), meaning that even its format was no longer all that distinctive. A mere seven months after it had whimpered its first squeak, *Nipper* slithered into the pages of *Buster*, which fulsomely welcomed the arrival by staging an exciting competition to win some Matchbox Madballs toys.

You see? That's how it should be done.

Nutty
(DC Thomson, 1980-1985, every Saturday)

Arguably the best-ever contender for becoming that elusive third 'big' humour comic alongside DC Thomson's *The Beano* and *The Dandy* warhorses, *Nutty* seemed to have everything going for it – once it got into its stride, that is.

The publication followed roughly the same format and design as its illustrious big brothers, but imbued it all with a distinctive...nuttiness. Fittingly, issue one came free with that classic 'crazy' confectionary product, Space Dust ('it foams and fizzles in your mouth!'), and described itself as: 'Your *fantastic new* fun paper'. On the front was nom-inal cheerleader Doodlebug (he wouldn't maintain that role for long), unimaginatively named wacky inventor, er, Wacky, and his lumbering home-made rocket (labelled: 'Wacky's rocket'). 'See my adventures blast off on page eleven!' he said.

Inside we met a hit-and-miss array of stories; those which ultimately wouldn't quite make the grade ('Mitey Joe', 'Pig Tales', 'The Bar-o Boys' and 'Ethel Red') and those that would provide *Nutty* with a week-in week-out winner for hundreds of issues to come (troublesome little brother action in 'Peter Pest', movie parodies in 'Steevie Star', canine-infused humour on the centre pages with 'The Wild Rovers' and desert-based hi-jinks in 'Dick Turban'). Somewhat incongruously, the publication also contained 'straight' strip 'General Jumbo' (carefully billed as 'new adventures of *The Beano*'s "famous general" with the fabulous mini-army') which didn't really sit comfortably alongside the wild fare on offer around it. Nevertheless the serious story remained a staple feature, at least for the paper's first year.

Issue one put out an appeal for readers' letters to be sent to Doodlebug, but it soon became obvious no one was really interested in the artistically inclined sprite while *Nutty*'s standout creation was there to be found on the back page. Before long it would be this alluring personality who would be soliciting the rubbish drawings, jokes and stories about clueless teachers.

So who was this character? When schoolboy Eric Wimp chomps on a banana, he becomes the dim-witted, muscle-bound Bananaman, a fruit-based superhero with a sketchily defined remit – although a lot of episodes seemed to be spent panicking about missing the school bus, if that helps.

It quickly became obvious Bananaman was *Nutty*'s biggest draw and in a matter of months he'd bagged the front cover (bumping off full page illustrations of 'snap-happy' Scoopy and the like in the process) and, eventually, the centre pages (sorry, Wild Rovers). Genuinely anarchic stuff, the strip went from strength to strength, receiving a few modifications along the way – the big fruit's costume getting a slight redesign, and his alter-ego suddenly sprouting a full head of hair, banishing his bovver-boy skinhead forever.

The 1983 BBC1 cartoon series, voiced by comedy trio The Goodies, bumped up the character's status even more with *Nutty* taking to billing him as 'Bananaman – your TV star!' However, purists (and they do exist) have it that this period also saw some of the strip's more excessive elements toned down, and appearances from the stupidest gallery of baddies ever – including Appleman, Weatherman, Superteech, Clayman, Doctor Gloom, The Heavy Mob, Auntie, Impossible Man and Vicky-Boo – became increasingly rare as regular nemesis, the pith-helmeted General Blight, increasingly took the blame for the week's bit of mischief.

Bananaman also took on a Scrappy-Doo-esque sidekick in the form of a talking crow called, well, Crow, and began to take orders from a Commissioner Gordon figure, the 'Oirish' Police Chief O'Reilly (with blue revolving light on the top of his hat, natch).

But all this was splitting hairs, because the character was still a hugely appealing prospect and remained *Nutty*'s best feature up until the comic's absorption by *The Dandy* in 1985.

In fact, so strong was the Bananaman brand (which included some much sought-after T-shirts) that, bucking the trend, he actually survived the loss of his own paper and went on to become a *Dandy* regular, albeit initially in a much demoted spot – Desperate Dan and Korky presumably having good union representation, back then.

In recent years he could even be found filling out the first six (count 'em!) pages of the paper, including the front cover. He was also one of the lucky few to survive the cull of 2004, and remerged in the new-look *Dandy* up to his usual tomfoolery. Although, that said, it's perhaps not such a notable achievement when we note that *Nutty*'s generic and much less imaginative 'naughty baby' character Cuddles (''At's me!') also managed to pull off the same coup, only he also got to spearhead his own comic – the ill-fated ***Hoot*** – along the way. Steevie Starr, the Wild Rovers and Dick Turban all want to know: where's the justice in that, eh?

Oink!
(IPC Magazines Ltd/Fleetway Publications, 1986-1988, fortnightly)

'Disgusting! Torture and a bare belly-button on the front cover...I dread to think what's inside!!' So exclaimed 'Mary Lighthouse (Critic)' across the preview issue of one of the comic world's strangest publications.

Irreverent, anarchic and maybe a little bit like *Viz*, *Oink!* sprang from the imaginations of Mark Rodgers, Patrick Gallagher and Tony Husband, three comic creatives who were bored with churning out formulaic funnies week after week. They pitched the idea for the publication to IPC editorial bod Bob Paynter, and were surprised when he gave them a budget to put together a dummy. This found favour with the execs and in April 1986, readers of ***Buster*** were treated to a special 'not for sale' preview edition of the comic.

Here they met Uncle Pigg, the paper's porcine editor, who could normally be found mooching at his desk or chomping on doughnuts. The line-up of stories was rather different from the whiter-than-white fare found in other comics. There was 'David Bewwamy' tumbling around in animal faeces in 'Cowpat County', sick jokes courtesy of 'Nasty Laffs and Specs' ('What do you get if you jump out of a plane without a parachute... You get shorter!!'), 'Burp! The Smelly Menace from Outer Space!', 'Master T' (in which ordinary baby Delroy Teabag revealed he could transform into the muscle-bound *A-Team* star) and gormless skinhead 'Tom Thug (What a Mug!)'.

This was little short of a comic revolution, keen on winding-up the establishment with its Whitehouse-like character declaring: 'I'll have to start the *Mary Lighthouse "Stampout Oink"* campaign!!!' and forewarning readers 'the next page contains four letter words!' (which indeed it did, such as 'that', 'this' and 'said'). As if that wasn't shocking enough, the industry's bad boys were also in on the act, as *Viz* creators Chris and Simon Donald contributed a couple of strips. And while we're talking notable names, the bass player in The Fall turned record label promoter, Marc 'Lard' Riley, was also pitching in, starring in the photo-strip 'Snatcher Sam'.

When the first issue proper arrived, he had really pushed the boat out, co-writing both *The Oink Song* and *Oink Rap*, which appeared on the paper's ace free gift of a flexidisc record. 'It's too loud! It's rude! And it makes me dizzy!' moaned Mrs Lighthouse, while the nation's kids wigged out to the demented theme tune, cajoling listeners to declare: 'Poo-poo, tinkle-tinkle, parp-parp, oink!'

That edition brought us more – much more – of the enjoyable nonsense witnessed in the preview number. 'The Wonderful Adventure of Billy Batt and his Magic Hat' was some kind of twisted nursery rhyme about a child being tricked into wearing mystical headgear, before he was then fed to a big green monster ('Moral: never trust an adult'). 'Billy Bang: The Hot-Headed Kid Who Blows up When he's Angry' did just that when he was denied chocolate fudge ice-cream, that noxious alien Burp! pulled his innards out of his body to show a passer-by his stomach was empty, and pig interviewer Terry Wogham met The Invisible Man in a baffling photo-strip.

As the issues rolled by, kids lapped it up, particularly when the pus-laden 'Pete and his Pimple' joined in the fun (the story of one boy and the huge zit on his nose), and come the start of 1988, the comic went weekly. However, just four months later it jumped to a monthly schedule and ditched the chunky old logo for something more stylish – exactly what *Oink!* didn't need.

This rebranding process, which ostensibly made the comic look like a rather more mature publication, was arguably a reaction to foot-stamping from the world's real-life Mary Whitehouses. With parents concerned about the publication's near-the-knuckle content, newsagents remained baffled over where the thing should be displayed. Some weeks they'd stock it alongside *Whizzer and Chips*, on other occasions it would be banished to the top shelves were it looked like just another *Viz* wannabe or, worse still, a porn magazine. As a result, sales fluctuated like mad.

An additional complication was that in 1987, IPC had sold its entire juvenile line of publications to Maxwell Communications, who were now putting the titles out under the Fleetway banner. The new owners had little patience with anything not regularly netting a nice healthy profit and so, despite *Oink!*'s undoubted appeal, ordered its cancellation in October 1988. Thus a rather emasculated Pete (and his Pimple, obviously), Tom Thug and Weedy Willy made their way into the pages of the oh-so-traditional *Buster*, as the long-running comic swallowed up the piggy brand.

Thankfully, the *Oink!* story didn't quite end there. Patrick Gallagher and Tony Husband went on to carve out a career in television, and created the kids' series *Round the Bend* for ITV. A puppet show based around a fictional comic situated in a sewer, it was presided over by Doc Crock, little more than a reptilian reinterpretation of good old Uncle Pigg.

Penny
(IPC Magazines Ltd, 1979-1980, every Thursday)

To launch a new girls' comic on the cusp of the Eighties, with the bottom of the market creaking ominously, was in retrospect a brave – or maybe a silly – decision to make. Nevertheless, that's what IPC did, bringing us 'bright new picture-story paper' *Penny*.

Penny – © DC Thomson & Co., Ltd

In its favour, the venture had something going for it. Rather nicely printed, it majored on photographic covers depicting toothsome, jovial little misses and – on the back – 'Penny's Pet File'; illustrations of cute little animals (issue one's pin-up: a kitten tangling with a ball of wool).

Boasting you could meet the following array of 'wonderful characters': 'Katy-Jane, Ginny and Shep, Tansy of Jubilee Street, Sad Sal and Smiley Sue' (and doesn't that read like the most girls' comic line-up of features ever?), it also sported a strip adaptation of Enid Blyton's *Secret Seven* books and a serialisation of Louisa M Alcott's *Little Women*.

All the yarns were well illustrated, and pushed the requisite buttons. 'Tales of Katy-Jane' did the usual cruelty thing, detailing the torment felt

by a poorly treated doll which – via thought balloons – was able to com-
municate its hardship to readers, moaning: 'I feel so cold, so weak,' after
it'd been chucked into some bushes, for example. Even more heart-rend-
ing was the ballad of 'Ginny and Shep', which went to great lengths to
detail the loving relationship betwixt girl and Border Collie, before having the mutt run over by a car. Although the canine managed to walk
again, it lived under a constant threat of extermination, Ginny's parents
intent on having the thing put down. As the tears flowed, that coming-
up box twisted the screw: 'Next week: Shep gets weaker.'

Thankfully, Tansy's adventures – which followed – were relatively
blubbing free, being little domestic tales of the 'tsk, that always happens,
eh readers?' ilk. Meanwhile, 'The Village Clock' brought us a fantasy
adventure set in the shire of Little Havenne ('Was it all a dream...or did
I really travel back in time?'); the aforementioned 'Sad Sal and Smiley
Sue' did the old chalk-and-cheese thing with two mates, one an optimist,
the other a pessimist; and the 'Waifs of the Waterfall' paired Scots girl
Fiona Craig with a baby deer.

One of the most saccharine titles ever created, it's little wonder *Penny*
lasted just shy of a year before it was absorbed by the streetwise and
spunky *Jinty*.

Plug
(DC Thomson, 1977-79, every Saturday)

Launching a title based around the self-regarding lanky Bash Street Kid with
the impressive overbite never really seemed like the most obvious thing to
do, not when there were other far more prominent movers and shakers in
the pages of *The Beano* who were arguably more deserving of their own
platform ('Biffo Weekly', anyone?). Nevertheless, this is exactly what happened in 1977, when the comparatively plush, colourful and rather expensive (at 9p almost twice the price of its rivals!) *Plug* hit the news-stands.

Reinventing the erstwhile school kid as some sort of athletic journeyman, the first issue proudly introduced a hurdling 'Percival Proudfoot
Plugsley, known as Plug – world championship sporting supergoon.' It
also unveiled a new simian sidekick for our man in the form of Chunkee
the Monkey, making for a kind of comic-strip proto-Keith Harris and
Cuddles partnership.

Launched a year after *Krazy* comic, it followed in its rival's footsteps by bringing its readers twenty pages of the most off-the-wall, outlandish fun ever published by DC Thomson. In comparison to the company's stable of gently anarchic fare, this was outrageous stuff indeed. Hell, even the front cover strapline was nuts: 'It's *funi*, it's *popi*, it's *sporti*, it's *trendi* – it's today's comic.'

Issue one came with a free 'Screamin' Demon' (a screeching balloon in other words) and the title featured an oddball array of characters loosely themed around assorted sporting activities. Hence, there was the titular character experimenting with tennis, diving and even bowls on the back page; 'Tony Jackpot' (who, in one memorable episode tee'd-off with 'Sheik Yerand', and eventually left his Arabic opponent setting up a new home in the sand bunker); 'The Games Gang' ('They're game for anything'); 'Ava Banana – The World's Strongest Girl' (a strip so poorly drawn, it could have appeared in early *Viz*); 'Antchester United' ('The insect football team with all the talent and all the legs'); 'Supporting Life' (a whistle-stop guide to the UK's football teams, including a visit to Partick Thistle's grounds and an unfortunate encounter with the team's floral namesake – 'Arrgh! Now I know why Partick Thistle are nicknamed the "Jags"!'); plus the curiously named 'D'Ye Ken John Squeal and His Hopeless Hounds' (just what the kids had been waiting for, a daft celebration of fox hunting which also parodied an eighteenth-century ballad into the bargain!).

The theme was continued into the standard 'fanclub' page, branded here as 'The Plug Sports and Social Club', with a baseball cap and T-shirt up for grabs each week for whoever wrote in with the best letter detailing their own 'sporting triumphs and disasters', or even those of their pals, teachers or – as unlikely as it may seem – pets.

But it wasn't all PE-related gubbins. *Animal Kwackers*-esque monsters-cum-beat-combo 'The Bandshees' brought their music to Earthlings, 'fresh from their successful tour of Mars'; fame obsessed antelopes hoped to make it big in the fantastically named 'Gnoo Faces'; 'Eebagoom' featured *Asterix*-style shenanigans with ancient Romans (albeit, a couple of Lancastrians – one complete with flat cap – fulfilling the Gauls' roles); while 'Dr Rotcod and Drib' depicted the adventures of the titular animal medic and his preoccupation with reversed names ('Keep a look-out for backward words on this page!' cautioned the strip's subtitle).

However, taking the biscuit for the weirdest thing since Dick Emery's Airfix Club Page in the likes of *Buster*, *Lion*, *Battle* and *Valiant* had to be

'I Wanna Tell You a Boom Boom.' Max Bygraves – yes, Max Bygraves – presiding over what was essentially a readers' jokes page, illustrated by various 'hilariously' doctored photographs. As such, Philip Callan from Co. Dublin found his biscuit-related gag delivered by what looked like a navvy clutching a giant Rich Tea.

It was also on this page that in one edition an infant in oversized spectacles loomed out at the reader to inform us: 'Here is the news, read by Anna Frod. The rush to buy *Plug* is still on. Newsagents report that huge crowds are outside their doors all day long!' Would that were actually the case, because just six weeks later the comic's 24 February 1979 edition announced the title was to be eaten up by *The Beezer* wherein it continued as a pull-out section for a couple more years.

Revolver
(Fleetway Publications, 1990-1991, monthly)

For a minute, it looked like there might be a way for British comics to survive the market's collapse over the late Eighties and early Nineties. The short-lived *Wildcat* had proven the appetite was no longer there for juvenile-orientated derring-do. While a next generation of comic readers was palpably not coming through to pick up the habit, those who'd jumped on board with the likes of *2000 AD* and *Warlord* in the Seventies were still hanging on and looking for something a bit meatier to get their teeth into.

First there was *Crisis*, which dealt out reams of morality alongside its own brand of mayhem. However, what about those readers who still favoured the funny papers, but had no stomach for sermons? Enter *Revolver*.

Achingly modern, painfully hip (it was named after the Beatles album and not the firearm, insisted the editorial team) and lavishly presented, this was comic culture for the rave generation. Following in the footsteps of *Warrior* and *Deadline*, the publication was a smart, well-designed mixture of comedy, rock'n'roll, experimental stuff and tame social comment.

Unleashing the big guns, its headline strip married the dream team of fêted writer Grant Morrison and retro-sleek illustrator Rian Hughes (who also designed the publication) with the legendary *Eagle* **mk I** character Dan Dare. Inevitably, the resultant story was both fanatically faithful to the character's past (Morrison had proven his fanboy credentials in *2000 AD*'s 'Zenith'), and wilfully disrespectful. Thus Jocelyn Peabody was referenced, Digby and Sir Hubert Guest put in an appearance and the Mekon even turned up 'unexpectedly' at the end of part seven ('Good evening, Colonel Dare. I can't believe you're surprised'), while at the same time Mrs Thatcher put in a thinly disguised cameo as Unity party leader Gloria Monday, Digby railed at Dan for butchering Treens, and old Melon Head unleashed a powerful aphrodisiac upon humanity, visualising 'one final orgy of ecstasy as my final gift to mankind' before he subjugated the populace.

Revolver – © Egmont UK Ltd

Despite the iconoclastic elements, it was arguably one of the most respectful reworkings of the Dare legend around (certainly better than *2000 AD*'s effort with that – choke! – super-powered gauntlet), culminating in an unexpected but affecting tribute to the character's creator, Frank Hampson, in the final instalment.

By comparison, nothing else in *Revolver* could quite match up to this. The publication proudly displayed its pop-cultural clout by employing Charles Shaar Murray to pen a strip about the life of Jimmy Hendrix, but the end result was a lumpy essay in bad dialogue ('Next full moon, y'all take your *git-tar* there just 'fo' *midnight...*') and over-portentous myth-making (visions of Red Indian huntresses spouting nonsense such as, 'you fail, gypsy, because your desire is all in your arrows...but my desire is in the tree.' Indeed). 'Happenstance and Kismet' was nicely illustrated, but somehow just too densely written to get into; 'Dire Streets' was twee, painfully right-on and – it has to be said – just that little bit too girly for *Revolver*'s reader-ship (which, let's face it, was mainly male); while Shaky Kane's stab at surre-alism on the centre pages was never anything other than highly disposable.

Nope, the only other feature that appeared as though it may give Dan a run for his money was 'Rogan Gosh', the heavily influenced tale of – well – no one's really sure to be honest, but with its imaginative page lay-outs and top colour artwork, it looked pretty good.

So this was how comics would secure their lineage to the end of the twen-ty-first century. Essential style-guides *Time Out* and *New Musical Express* were impressed, but sadly, readers remained unconvinced and by January of 1991, the comic was bidding 'goodbye, baby, and amen' to the world.

'We have absolutely no regrets about this little magazine, and in hind-sight there's nothing we would change,' vouchsafed the editorial team as the shutters came down on the final issue. 'According to the men with the pocket calculators there just weren't enough of you' was the honest explanation for the title's failure. And because we were in the world of grown-up comics now, there was no effort to sweeten the bitter pill. The Dan Dare strip was set to continue in the next issue of *Crisis* (where 'Happenstance and Kismet' would also later appear), but that was it. There was to be no disingenuous 'exciting news' about the title's future, no merger to placate the readership.

A 'Romance Special' followed a couple of weeks later, but otherwise the party was over. 'Take care of yourselves, OK?' came the payoff as another lifeline was cruelly snatched away from British comics.

Robin
(Hulton Press Ltd/Longacre Press/Odhams Press Ltd/IPC Magazines Ltd, 1953-1969, every Friday)

Following the successful launches of *Eagle* mk I and *Girl* mk I, the boffins at Hulton decided to create another red-topped companion paper, this time aimed at the playpen set.

Robin, 'The happy magazine for boys and girls', was created for the under-eights and soon found an audience of 450,000 readers who were quick to declare 'you don't have much bad things' in the comic. The paper's main selling point had to be its licensing of *Andy Pandy* from the BBC. In something of a coup, he and Teddy were depicted enjoying their feast of cake, jelly and lemonade in full colour on the front, while the TV version had to settle for rubbish old black and white.

Joining the pyjama-wearing one for a new, colourful lease of life off the telly were also 'Flower-pot Men' Bill and Ben, who turned up on the centre pages. They were accompanied here by the '*Robin* Scrapbook' (a miscellany of odds and sods kids could cut out and paste into their own books) and the effusive bullock, Johnny Bull. On the back cover, Richard Lion took part in various Rupert Bear-like adventures set in the village of Gay.

Meanwhile, in black and white territory, the '*Robin* Reading Strip' buffed up kids' literacy skills; monkeys Bingo, Bango and Bongo got up to gentle mischief with Mrs Farmer; Siamese cat Princess Tai-Lu stalked across her half-page with grace; Tom the Tractor worked hard on Farmer Brown's land; and one dog and his girl, Mac and Maggie, wrought their own brand of harmless – and uneventful – whimsy.

Despite such strong competition, one of the most popular strips proved to be 'The Story of Woppit' – tales of a slightly misshapen, overweight teddy-bear. The character was based on the mascot, Mr Woppit, carried around by speedboat daredevil Donald Campbell. The creature had been given to him by Peter Barker, who was then in charge of merchandising on Hulton's junior titles – hence the *Robin* connection. Rather chillingly, the toy was on board with Campbell for his fateful attempt to break his own water speed record (set in 1964) on Lake Coniston in January 1967. It was pretty much the only thing to survive the crash.

As was traditional for the *Eagle* line of comics, the editorial voice in *Robin* was an essential part of the concoction. 'Dear Boys and Girls,' wrote head honcho, the Reverend Marcus Morris, 'here is number one of your new paper...I hope you will like it very much. You will enjoy reading about all the friends we have found for you.' Over the weeks, kids were instructed to join the '*Robin* Birthday Club' ('Every member...who had a birthday this week will get a birthday card!') or write in to Pixie, the letter-reading cat, with general chat about what they liked in the comic or where they were going on holiday.

Another hangover from *Eagle* took hold in the form of the requisite religious slot, here billed as 'Bible Story in Pictures: The Stories Jesus Told', later turning into 'The Animals in the Bible'.

And so things continued, the inside back page reserved for *Robin*'s nearest approximation to an adventure strip (siblings 'Jo and Jessie' eventually paving the way for 'Timi in England' before – rather later on – 'Mark and Mary' brought us thrills from their farm in the mountains of Wales); Andy Pandy and teddy cavorting with lambs, bunny rabbits and kittens on the front; and bizarrely disparate objects presenting themselves for the cut-out-and-keep treatment on the 'Scrapbook' pages (in one issue: an egg whisk, Winchester Cathedral, a commissionaire, an armadillo and a 1956 MG motorcar).

Perhaps appreciating its readership wouldn't handle change particularly well, *Robin* was a model of stability on into the Sixties. Here the comic received a minor overhaul as the recognisable red box logo was swapped for a similar-looking strap and new friends Snip and Snap (a pair of dogs), Dumpy (an elephant) and Dick and Danny (cats) joined in the fun. Clifford Makins stepped in as editor when Morris, aggrieved at the new regime imposed upon him following Odhams' takeover of Hulton, quit the world of comics.

It served to be something of a portent, as the tide was turning fast on *Robin*. With Odhams soon absorbed by the Mirror Group, another new layer of management appeared, one who seemed hell-bent on rationalising its acquired stock of juvenile titles. Reprint strips began to appear with a monotonous regularity and, in 1967, the paper was merged with *Story Time* (Odhams, 1965-7) whereupon the axe fell on Richard Lion. By this stage companion papers *Girl* and *Swift* had also been dispatched, and the clock was ticking for both the red-breasted one, and *Eagle* itself.

Unsurprisingly, out of the two birds, *Robin* was the first to cough and on 25 January 1969, announced: 'Next week, *Robin* and *Playhour* come together' as it was forced to merge with the Mirror's long-running TV-centric toddlers' title.

By definition, the very junior *Eagle* was never in danger of tearing up the rulebook, but while it lasted it provided quality, safe and not too exciting fun for kids just cutting their teeth on the weekly habit.

Romeo
(DC Thomson, 1957-1974, every Tuesday)

From 'Nylons – Nylons – Nylons *to be won!*' to 'Double-page pull-out poster of Marc Bolan inside', *Romeo*'s journey was a long and confusing one, but during its time did it ever throw up a single memorable comic-strip character?

DC Thomson's first attempt to create a publication for what the pipe-smoking bods in its Dundee headquarters doubtlessly referred to as 'the fairer sex' even pre-dated the warhorse that was *Bunty*. As its title suggests, it majored on romance, with almost every story ending in the heroine being swept into the arms of some hunk and tilting her head back for one of those kisses where the respective lips barely met that were apparently so popular in the Fifties.

Hugely influenced by the American romance comics of the day, many of the efforts on display were indeed reprints from across the pond – surely over here we didn't go in for bequiffed Brylcreemed fellas in lumberjack shirts who were liable to exclaim: 'Gosh, that dame's dynamite!' Likewise, the stock-in-trade villain was a reedy shyster who wore a suit and dicky-bow and hid behind a pencil moustache. Yup, this was definitely top Americana for the ladies, and all the more gusty for it. Let's face it, *Bunty* or *Mandy* would have positively blanched at a smooch that was described thusly: 'It was no brotherly kiss. It was the kiss a man gives a woman when he cares for her deeply.'

In the main, the stories were self contained, meaning nightclub cigarette girl Ruth managed to progress from being bothered by amorous customer Ted Masters to meeting and accepting a marriage proposal from the swoonsome Philip, all in the space of six pages. As for Nancy Bates, it only took her two to bag her bloke in 'I'm Going to *Kiss* Every Man I Meet'.

Cut to the Seventies, and *Romeo* was quite a different venture – on first glance at least. Having merged with fellow romance title *Cherie* (DC Thomson, 1960-3) during the Sixties, the US imports were now strictly old news. The heroines were no longer stern-faced girls of some indiscriminate age, which could easily have been anything between fifteen and forty. Instead we had an array of post-Twiggy naiads with large sleepy eyes and exquisitely tangled locks of hair. Thankfully, the chaps were still all square-jawed, although, rather worryingly, they all sported bristling sideburns and shoulder-length mops.

Strips were now far more urbanised and hip, meaning instead of the stiff upper lip of 'Bridesmaids Mustn't Cry' we got the languid *Man About the House*-type antics of 'That Guy Across the Way'. Further modern elements included fashion features such as 'Join the Hair Clinic' ('Be kind to hair!' we were advised), loads of pop features (alas 'The Secret in Cliff's Closet' turned out to be the fact that the singer had kept the same wine-coloured pair of flares with silver buttons up each side in his wardrobe for several years, as 'fashions no longer change so much'), 'Lisa's Letter Bin' ('I'll give quids for every letter I use'), counselling on 'Ann's Page' ('His friends don't like me!') and reader's true life confessions ('I'm not the type who casually waltzes off with another girl's boy...').

Like all the best love affairs, *Romeo*'s run was sweet enough while it lasted, but always destined to end in tragedy. And so it was that on 21 September it collapsed into the pages of *Diana*, all kissed-out after seventeen years of snogging.

Roy of the Rovers
(IPC Magazines Ltd/Fleetway Editions Ltd, 1976-1993, every Monday)

He's the comic world's most famous sporting superstar, a man whose name is still invoked today to sum up an exemplary triumph against the odds on the football pitch. Melchester Rover's leading light has battled through marriage problems, an attempt on his life, managed the England squad, survived a terrorist bombing, signed Martin Kemp and Steve Norman from Spandau Ballet to his team and limped away (but only just) from a terrifying helicopter crash. All of this while sporting a preposterous range of haircuts.

Yep, it's fair to say good old Roy Race (Racey to his mates) saw the lot in a footballing career that spanned fifty years. First starting out in the pages of *Tiger* – where he graduated from schoolboy hopeful to player-manager at the mighty Melchester Rovers – his most exciting years would be spent in the pages of his own spin-off comic, wherein fact and fiction merged to make a terrifically exciting (and sometimes entertainingly stupid) sports title.

Launching on 26 September 1976, the recently married Roy was now modelling an outrageous mullet, which doubtlessly proved inspirational to a young Chris Waddle, as he welcomed us into his brave new world. And, by gum, there was a lot to be excited about. Not only did the comic come with a free 'big football chart', but it also featured an 'exclusive article by HRH The Duke of Edinburgh!' Truly this was a weekly by Royal appointment.

With Roy being afforded the only colour pages inside, the rest of the crew would have to work that little bit harder to impress, particularly as Melchester's player-manager (and now) comic editor had included a little box at the end of each strip wherein readers could mark the story out of ten. Luckily, some of this stuff was particularly imaginative:

'The Football' told its tale from the perspective of the eponymous sphere, while 'You Are the Star' rather magnificently attempted to make the reader the hero in a sports story. Providing a space to insert your name into the speech bubbles (in issue three: 'One of these days, _____, you're going to get a knock, and you'll be *out!*') it had the added problem of always having to keep the lead character's features off-panel, thus resulting in a strip populated with people chatting away to nothing more than a hand, the odd foot and the occasional silhouette of a back of a head. 'Mike's Mini Men' was also pretty impressive, daring to centre itself upon the relatively action-free pastime of Subbuteo.

Rather more traditional was 'The Hard Man', which featured the surly Johnny Dexter, a tough midfield player for Danesfield United who was always getting into trouble thanks to his macho brand of soccer. 'Millionaire Villa' told of struggling Selby Villa who were given a cash injection by David Bradley on the proviso he always made the first team…whereupon he proved to be utterly rubbish at football. 'Tommy's Troubles' followed the fortunes of a soccer-mad schoolboy who was tasked with improving his class grades before he would be allowed to play for the English schoolboys side, while 'Smith and Son' brought us the story of Barry and Danny Smith, who co-managed fourth division side Grandon Town.

A hit from the start, Roy couldn't help but get a little smug as his comic went from strength to strength. 'The stories are excellent, aren't they?' he beamed from behind his typewriter in February 1977. 'Even my wife, Penny, is getting as keen on soccer as I've always been!' He was even prepared to step up to a challenge laid down by Billy 'Billy's Boots' Dane in *Tiger* where the young lad had been mouthing-off about his comic outselling Roy's. 'OK pals,' ordered Roy in the vicinity of a cut-out coupon to be presented to your newsagent asking for a regular copy of the paper, 'let's prove him wrong!'

In the 26 March edition of that year, Roy had something more serious to get off his chest: 'I've scrapped my usual "Talk-In" for this week,' he began, before going on to explain it was time he was given his say about the national side's recent dismal performances on the pitch. 'I'm sick and tired of going to Wembley to see England in action, or watching them play on television, and being embarrassed!' As if to hammer the point home, on the opposite page lay a blank box with just one line of text across the middle: 'This space reserved for a photo of an England goal'. Nuff said.

Thankfully, the year would bring happier tidings for Racey, as Penny gave birth to twins Roy Jr and Melinda – billed as 'a double surprise for Roy!'

In 1978, *Roy of the Rovers* clocked up its hundredth issue. The line-up for the comic had barely changed across its first century. Joining the fun here was 'Tipped for the Top!', a tale about schoolboy Steve Taylor (they missed a trick by not making his surname Tipped) who was – inevitably – football mad despite the sarcastic comments from his teacher: 'Kicking a silly ball around a patch of grass...that's very clever I must say!' However, when a scout from Chelford City showed up to watch him in action, was Steve about to have the last laugh? *Jag* refugees 'Football Family Robinson' had also washed up in the comic's pages by this time, as had 'Simon's Secret' (a soccer-playing bionic boy) and 'The Safest Hand in Soccer' (the fortunes of goalkeeper Gordon Stewart). Of more note was Sheik Ibn Hassan of Basran's efforts to sign up Racey for a cool *'half-a-million pounds!'* Inevitably, Roy knocked back the offer, in the process upsetting Penny who felt she should have been consulted about the decision. Uh oh.

Roy experienced a down-turn in fortunes into the Eighties. Not only were Melchester relegated to Division Two, but he crossed paths with the surly Elton Blake, an actor who was portraying him in a TV drama about the team. Highly strung, in August 1981 the thesp gave Roy an earful following Penny's comments he was unsuitable to play her husband. That said, there was a little bit of light relief when the Races decamped to London to watch the wedding of Charles and Di, the royal carriage wafting past with an: 'Oh look, there's Roy Race!' emanating from its confines. But then, in December the headlines screeched: 'Roy Race shot!' This was serious – not only was Roy's chum Blackie Gray forced to step in as player-manager, but he also had to take over Roy's editorial in the comic. The tributes from real life celebs flooded in, with Mike Read wishing the hero 'a "Racey" recovery', Lawrie McMenemy declaring: 'Everyone at the Dell loves you – get well soon' and Eric Morecambe pleading: 'The game needs you.'

Roy of the Rovers – © Egmont UK Ltd

While Roy was laid out, Alf Ramsay thoughtfully stepped in to manage the team, steering them through an unbeaten run until Racey returned to the squad in April 1982. Meanwhile the would-be assassin was unmasked as…one Elton Blake.

Over the next few years, Roy was blessed with another daughter, Diana, and did the unthinkable by leaving Melchester for a short stint as Walford Rovers' player-manager. Thankfully, he was soon back where he belonged.

1985 proved to be a particularly interesting year in the comic's life. By now, production values had taken a tumble, the luxurious photo pin-ups of famous footballers binned off as we went four-colour and the comic's general appearance plunged down-market. *Tiger* then bit the dust in March via a merger with *Eagle* **mk II**, leaving *Roy of the Rovers* to offer a new home to 'the redskin with the iron grip!' Johnny Cougar and Hot-Shot Hamish, who was teamed up with the paper's own comedy character Kevin 'Mighty' Mouse.

Over in Melchester, some far more bizarre signings were taking place. Roy (now sporting a Bryan Robson-inspired coiffure) had called up Bob Wilson and Emlyn 'Crazy Horse' Hughes for the team, and was now augmenting his side with...Martin Kemp and Steve Norman from Spandau Ballet. Although chairman Geoff Boycott was sceptical about the latter two ('If they flop...you'll be branded a sensation seeker!'), Roy's confidence was repaid when the duo put one each past Brayford. If that wasn't reward enough, that Christmas the boys were happy to rope in Tony Hadley and the others to play at the supporters' club party.

As the end of the decade arrived, the comic clawed back some of its glossiness, and new owners arrived as the Maxwell Group took over IPC's juvenile lines in July 1987.

In 1989, the publication staged its one and only takeover bid, absorbing the short-lived Gary Lineker-helmed *Hot-Shot!* (Fleetway Editions Ltd, 1988-9). The merger made for a terrific cover opportunity, as Roy and Gaz shook hands in 'the soccer event of the year!' As if things weren't sweet enough, by now the gobby Billy Dane had been forced to decamp into Racey's publication when he'd been dropped from the pages of his new home in *Eagle* mk II.

Into the Nineties, further change was on the cards. The TSB began sponsoring Melchester, Roy himself was looking a bit long in the tooth and took to the pitch a little less often, while his son (nicknamed Rocky) followed his old man into the game.

By the comic's last year on the news-stand, it had gone full colour and returned the footy pin-ups to the mix. Meanwhile, the story of fifteen-year-old Andy Steel who played for Millside City was sponsored by Quasersport, and Rocky took over the reformatted letters page, now titled 'Kickaround' (also sponsored by the bank).

Rovers, meanwhile, were under the grip of new boss Ralph 'Flash' Gordon whose 'total support system' of play was proving a total washout. In the comic's final edition dated 20 March 1993 (which sported a suitably sombre black cover that reprinted Roy's first ever appearance from

Tiger issue one in 1954), the players mutinied, abandoning their guvnor's tactics and reverted back to the old 'Melchester Magic' which immediately brought them results. Gordon was furious, accusing Racey of engineering the rebellion, but when he delivered an ultimatum to the board, they wasted little time in offering Roy the management of the club again. The town of Melchester was overjoyed at the news – 'You're back where you belong, Racey!'

Alas, tragedy was in the offing. Deciding to check out a promising new player in the Bexley Homes League, our man took his helicopter to their home ground. Circling over the place, the aircraft developed a technical fault and hurtled to the ground in front of a slew of horrified onlookers. 'Racey didn't stand a chance!'

The comic then cut to a 'Newsflash!', presided over by Trevor McDonald, which provided a nifty guide to the hero's life and times. Following that it was back to the action, the Races arriving at the hospital to check out the damage. With the waiting public exclaiming: 'He's not going to die, is he?' Rocky stepped up to the mark. 'I'll promise you *one* thing! Whatever happens, the name of *Roy Race* will be around for a long time to come!' As he strode off to meet his destiny – the fate of his pop still unknown – a waiting journo summed up events nicely. 'Melchester mourns its greatest son – *but the legend lives on!*'

Indeed, the legend did live on as a monthly title followed, revealing the hero had lost his left foot in the accident. He took up a managing job in Italy, while Rocky became the Rovers' new star striker. The publication – which mainly consisted of reprints – lasted less than twenty issues, but Roy and son didn't stop there. They then jumped over to the BBC's *Match of Day* magazine in May 1997, staying with the title until its closure four years later.

Although Roy's no longer actively involved in football, in September 2004, he was brought back for a one-page strip in the pages of the *Guardian* (of all places), in commemoration of fifty years since his debut. Confused at some of the more recent changes that had taken place in the beautiful game ('Hey…y-you're a *woman*!' he exclaimed, catching sight of the ref), he proved he still had that old Racey magic by putting one past the keeper – 'A good player can score at any time'. When asked to sum up what it was like playing in 2004, he revealed: 'Different! If I'm going to stay around, I think I'll have to shave my head and stop shaving my face!'

School Friend
(Amalgamated Press, 1950-1965, weekly)

A giant of the genre, which reportedly became the best-selling girls' comic ever, clearing an astounding million issues a week (even the mighty *Eagle* **mk I** couldn't match that), *School Friend* was, in many ways, the quintessential weekly.

Its name taken from a pre-war story paper, the comic all but depended on just one strip for its success. Yes, despite offering readers the delights of a free 'Radio Stars Photo Album' with issue one, it was the exploits of 'The Silent Three at St Kits' which would keep them coming back for more. Drawn by Evelyn Flinders, one of the few women strip artists working in the business at the time, it brought readers the adventures of three 'great school-girl friends', Betty Roland, Joan Derwent and Peggy West. The trio had formed a secret society and together would get involved in various escapades – at which point they'd don their faintly sinister cassocks and masks.

In their time, they'd tackle villainous squires, uncover treasure maps and make friends with local dogs. This was truly the realm of 'bullies' and 'rotters', but thankfully the three would always win through, calling in the local plod for the obligatory finger-pointing/bundling the baddy off to face justice denouement at the end of every story. Old-fashioned adventuring it may have been, but commendably empowering for all girls looking in.

Other perennials included the scatter-brained Dilly, a plain-looking girl in big glasses affectionately described as 'our loveable duffer' whose blundering would always come good in the end; the much-loved Princess Anita of Sylvanberg who was forever mixing with peasant girls and gypsies; the guzzler of Cliff House boarding school and less-famous sister of Billy, Bessie Bunter, who'd put her ingenuity to good use when it came to scoring free food; and the Storyteller, a debonair, pipe-smoking chap who bewitched readers with a score of spooky tales.

A trooper in its day, *School Friend* merged with the doughty *Girls Crystal* (Amalgamated Press, 1953-63) in May 1963, at which point it was serialising 'Secret Seven' adventures from the pen of Enid Blyton. Here's hoping the septet didn't take umbrage at the similarly themed Silent Three.

As the mid-Sixties rolled around, *School Friend* was looking increasingly like a comic out of time, despite laying on a bit of espionage-themed excitement with 'Mam'selle X: Special Agent'. Inevitably, sales suffered, leaving this once record-breaking title with no option but to merge with child of the Sixties *June* on 30 January 1965.

Although it was a sad end for such an influential title, the likes of *Bunty* and *Judy* had now picked up the baton, ensuring girls wouldn't have to go short when it came to stories about ballerinas, princesses and, of course, gymslip-wearing crime-busters.

School Fun
(IPC Magazines Ltd, 1983-1984, every Monday)

According to the first issue of IPC's scholastic endeavour, one of the company's last cracks at creating a traditional kids' humour comic went something like this...

Four o'clock in the afternoon at the editor's house, and his recalcitrant son comes storming in declaring, 'I'm fed up with school!' 'School days are happiest days of your life!' counters the loafing pop. 'Says who?' exclaims son. 'Says *me*...and to prove it I'll produce a comic all about school!'

Both excited by the notion, editor and child immediately embark on a brainstorming session, the result being *School Fun*.

And, to be honest, it did very nearly happen like that. IPC comic writer-turned teacher Graham Exton pitched the idea of the publication to the company, after polling a classroom of kids in Cannock about what they'd like to see in such an endeavour. The enthused youngsters even produced their own dummy issues...all of which were promptly ignored by the publishers who instead turned out something Exton would later describe as a **Whoopee!**-like creation.

However, that's underselling *School Fun*, which was definitely above average stuff while it lasted (a measly thirty-three issues, worse luck). Billed as 'the happiest read of your life', issue one came with a free 'Slippy Sticky Snake' which was demonstrated by a picture of two rogues chucking one into teacher's bathroom as he shaved, causing the startled master to 'zz-ip' off half of his plump moustache.

Inside, the issue's contents were listed out in the form of a timetable, with a 'single period' being designated to one-page strips and so on. Highlights included 'Creepy Crawler' the tales of Sebastian Creep who – get this – was a bit of a creep. Meanwhile, smart arse 'Walt Teaser' got off on ripping the piss out of people (spying a female preparing to enter into a beauty salon, he shouts through the door: 'All leave cancelled!'); 'B.(e)Ware Caretaker' followed the fortunes of a grumpy janny; 'Teachers United' lifted the lid on a subterranean squad of educators who banded together to thwart classroom naughtiness; and 'Schoolditz' brought us the hilarious travails of Baker Street School kids taken prisoner in a German school during 1939 ('I'm in charge und efferybody does vot I say or gets punished much!').

School Fun – © Egmont UK Ltd

Even more exciting was the fleet of TV-related strips that bolstered the paper. 'Coronation Street School' is perhaps one of the more unlikely concepts – junior versions of Hilda Ogden, Ken Barlow etc. all attending the same comprehensive – but somehow it worked, as Stan Ogden and Eddie Yates nicked anything that wasn't nailed down, Deirdre swooned over Ken, and Uncle Albert bored for Britain ('Who's for a game of shove ha'penny?'). Even more on-the-nose was 'Grange Hill Juniors' ('© Philip Redmond/BBC') which dwelt upon the comings and goings amongst the famous school's eleven-year-olds. Present and correct were Roland Browning, Jonah Jones, Zammo McGuire, Fay Lucas and the rest. Even educational anti-Christ Gripper Stebson got a look in.

The TV flirtation didn't end there, but now we were into rather more unauthorised territory. 'Young Arfur' was a *Minder* adaptation by stealth, featuring a juvenile wheeler-dealer who, while looking nothing like George Cole, pointedly referred to his mum as 'Er Indoors'. And as for which film 'ETT: Extra Terrestrial Teacher' was drawing inspiration from...

And so the title continued on its merry way, introducing a cut-out-and-keep mini comic with issue two, in which it reprinted old IPC school strips from the last eighty years. Further pullout supplements followed ('A to Z of *School Fun*' for one) but, alas, our happy read proved shortlived.

At the end of May 1984 (just over six months after it launched), the title was forced to merge with *Buster*. School was out forever – well, except for the Grange Hill lot who were already getting set for a new term in the pages of *Beeb*.

Scoop
(DC Thomson, 1978-1981, every Thursday)

What was this? DC Thomson boys' comics going all glossy on us? Well, not quite, but with its slick colour pages, large format (albeit not quite tabloid size) and copious photo features, in production values sports comic *Scoop* was certainly a step up from the majority of the company's fare.

But despite the colour pictures of Brighton and Hove Albion FC, Barry Sheene and personal letters from Kenny Dalglish (he'd signed it and everything) the publication's heart still lay in good old-fashioned comic-strip action.

Issue one got us off to a cracking start, with a fantastic full-painted cover by *Commando* cover-star supremo Ian Kennedy, depicting a bearded footballer heading a ball past a befuddled goalie. Free gift-wise, you couldn't go wrong with 'The Big Event Sports Diary' ('Thirty-six pages packed with facts and pics!').

Then, inside, things kicked off (do you see?) in fine style with 'Stark: Matchwinner For Hire'. Obviously marked out from the very beginning by the comics' creators as the stand-out story, readers couldn't get enough of this dribbling mercenary whose business card read: '£1000 per match, plus £250 per goal. No payment for lost game.' So dedicated to his craft was Jon Stark, that he'd even risk death in order to secure that victory-clinching goal (trotting out onto the pitch against doctor's orders). Future strips saw the inspirational soccer star take an apprentice under his wing from the wrong side of the tracks ('I'm no goody two-shoes,' he advised the former layabout Cosmo Kent, 'but I don't like to see talent wasted.'), battle bankruptcy when a 'mystery double' went around writing cheques in his name, and form a deadly double-act, 'Matchwinners for Hire', with the now reformed Cosmo. What a guy.

Scoop – © DC Thomson & Co., Ltd

But it wasn't all soccer. 'Killer' followed the fortunes of tennis star Kris Kilo who, aside from going on to win Wimbledon, worked undercover for 'a branch of British Intelligence known as The Organisation' and, the old '"hypertronic" man under the control of a malevolent force' shtick (see: 'MACH-1', 'Ticker Tait', 'Wonder Mann', 'Sintek' and others) was wheeled out again as augmented athlete Ben Norton was 'Doomed...to Win!'

But, there was no escaping it. *Scoop*'s heart was in football, as evidenced by the plethora of pin-ups, league ladders, fact features and even suggestions for insults you might want to hurl at the opposition ('Hey, centre-half! Haven't I seen your face on a wanted poster?') all related to the sport. And it looks like the comic's connections with the business weren't half-bad either as the likes of the aforementioned Dalglish, Glenn Hoddle, Paul Mariner, Peter Barnes and Stan 'The Wee Man' Cummins provided the paper with regular signed features.

Always nothing less than a pretty damn credible read for sports fans, *Scoop* certainly asked its followers to dig deep, marketing it at a wallet-busting 15p a week. Its end was a sad one, forced to downsize when it was taken over by *Victor*.

Scorcher
(IPC Magazines Ltd, 1970-1974, every Monday)

With DC Thomson's *Hornet* starting to embrace the beautiful game, IPC trotted out *Scorcher*, a landmark publication in that it represented the company's first effort at a themed comic. Rather than carrying a mixture of war, sci-fi and sports, the title was devoted entirely to football. It was an innovation that would go on to beget the likes of *Battle* (war stories and nothing but), *2000 AD* (sci-fi) and even *School Fun* (with its scholastic-related hi-jinks).

A pretty decent legacy by anyone's standards, the title was also the first to bring us two seminal soccer strips: 'Billy's Boots' and 'Hotshot Hamish'.

Mixing comic-strip with features from the off, that premier issue had a cracking cover depicting a grinning striker putting one past an all-at-sea goalie and came with a free soccer wall chart. Alongside a profile of Jack Charlton, a feature on Derby County's Dave Mackay, football trivia courtesy of bespectacled smart-arse 'Know All', and a page of club badges, the issue debuted its neatly titled letters page, 'Goal-Post', and a football quiz, 'Challenge Your Chum'. A fine selection indeed, so how did the comic-strip action match up to this?

Thankfully, it didn't disappoint on that score (ho! ho!) with the likes of 'Bobby of the Blues' (the varying fortunes of Beatle-wigged Bobby Booth who played for – *ahem* – Everpool City), 'Lags Eleven' (Crunchville Prison's soccer side, led by Brainiac and Peter Sellers look-alike Willie 'Brilliant Genius' Smith) and the legendary 'Billy's Boots' (the tale of Billy Dane and a seemingly magic pair of boots that used to belong to striker 'Dead-Shot' Keen) providing the expected thrills and spills – even though, at this stage, the latter's title character looked more like a member of Franz Ferdinand than the cheery-faced boy-next-door we'd come to admire.

The soccer-themed content proved to be something of an early success and, as a result, eight months after *Scorcher*'s launch, IPC presented another footie title, *Score 'n' Roar* (1970-1). Like **Whizzer and Chips**, this was notionally broken up into two separate publications and its first issue came with a free, insanely fiddly football league table. However, the project proved to be short-lived and merged with *Scorcher* in July 1971, ten months after its inception.

The resultant new title formed by their union was *Scorcher and Score* and while the cover of the first combined issue enthused about the inclusion of 'Lord Rumsey's Rover' (a peer and his employees playing to raise money to save his estate), it was arguably *Score 'n' Roar*'s 'Nipper' that contributed most to the paper. A moodily drawn tale of runaway Nipper Lawrence, it was rendered in heavy, grubby black inks, making it something of a football noir piece – if there is such a thing.

Scorcher – © Egmont UK Ltd

Now featuring 'Top Teams' on the cover, such as Portsmouth and Birmingham City, the title was patently keen to maintain its emphasis on factual features (West Bromwich Albion's Colin Suggett revealing the secret of his success, for example). In fact, so hardcore had it become about football factoids by 1973 that the front page was now being devoted to a weekly stream of middle-aged men in camel coats and combovers as the comic invited us to 'Meet the Manager...' of various teams.

The comic-strip action didn't let up though, even if some of it was becoming increasingly esoteric, such as 'The Forward Who Went Back', the story of Terry Baker who was whisked back in time to 1891 where he had to help his own club's ancestor Mill Town Swifts, win the League championship.

Towards the end of its life, the blond, mulleted caber-tossing Hebridean Hamish Balfour also joined the title in 'Hot Shot Hamish', but with *Scorcher and Score* folding into the pages of *Tiger* in October 1974, he would go on to become more synonymous with his new home.

In the grand scheme of things, *Scorcher* had enjoyed only a modest run, and yet it proved a football-related comic could be done. Roy Race was duly informed.

Scream!
(IPC Magazines Ltd, 1984, every Monday)

'Just when you thought it was safe to sleep in the dark...' IPC launched *Scream!* Destined to only last a measly fifteen issues, the horror title was a near-the-knuckle mixture of gore and black humour that, as rumours have it, upset the horses in the boardroom.

Issue one came free with a set of Dracula fangs, and featured a fierce representation of the Count himself snarling at readers, his eyes a fearsome blood-red. Behind him lurked a decayed chap in armour, the Grim Reaper, a hissing cat and a computer screen. OK, so the latter may not have substantially upped that fear factor (and, come to think of it, the tabby was hardly quakesome either), but the sum of these parts definitely made for a sufficiently creepy concoction.

'Not for the nervous!' flashed the warnings. 'We're waiting for you inside...*join us if you dare!*'

Obviously, a challenge like that was irresistible to boys, who immediately knew this was going to be the most brilliant weekly ever. Inside, we met 'Ghastly McNasty', a cowering skeletal figure clad in a long robe and hood, which hid his features. He was the 'once-human editor of this gruesome publication', natch. 'If you horrors out there want to read something really spooky, you've picked the right paper'.

Behind him loomed a fog-shrouded representation of IPC's home at King's Reach Tower. Advising us that this 'is the place where lots of your comics are produced', we were told that although the building was twenty-nine floors high, Ghastly was situated the same number of storeys beneath it. He then went on to challenge readers to send in a drawing of his face with 'the monstrous sum of £50 – yes *fifty* pounds!' up for grabs, while also soliciting nominations for people to be locked up in the London Dungeon (by way of a demo, it was light entertainment legend Bruce Forsyth who was harshly meted out this treatment here – 'nice to lock him up, to lock him up nice').

'The Dracula File' kicked things off nicely – a dark and moody comic-strip, it opened with the man himself leering at a startled youngster: 'Closer, my child. Your heart is pounding...the *blood* is racing through your veins. But soon, it will be flowing through *mine!*' That this scene had no real relation to what followed wasn't too big a deal as the story that unfurled was pretty good. Set 'behind the Iron Curtain', the eponymous vampire was mistaken for a Russian defector by British soldiers who picked him up after he'd evaded capture by East German guards. Back in Moscow, the KGB were torn over what they should do about the situation: 'I say we must tell them who – *what* – that defector is...' 'No! We never give aid to the West!'

The following story, 'Monster' has latterly become the source of much excitement for comics fans, as it was penned by future 'graphic novel' superstar Alan Moore (of 'knows the score' infamy). An early work for the writer, it was hugely atmospheric and mysterious. Readers were introduced to twelve-year-old Kenneth Corman, who was digging a grave in his garden. Through means of a flashback, we learnt he lived in a Bates Motel-esque house with his cruel, belt-wielding dad ('But "please" never did any good. It didn't stop the terror or the look in his father's eyes, or the whistle of descending leather').

At the top of the house lay a permanently locked room. Kenneth's dad insisted there was only some personal belongings relating to his dead wife behind the door, but when the child heard movement it became clear there was more to it than that.

With the evil patriarch picking up a handy club he addressed a picture of his late missus through a haze of booze, declaring: 'He's got to be dealt with! I'm sorry...I'm going upstairs now...to finish it!' Hearing a scream, Kenneth ran up to find his old man laid out on the landing, keys to the room in his hand.

Deciding to bury the body ('He was a practical boy. He saw to things himself'), our Ken consigned the stiff to the soil, thereby bringing us back to the point where we came in. Now it was time to venture back up the stairs to see for himself what was in the room. And, inevitably, here was where the first instalment ended – a fantastic cliffhanger, and no mistake.

'The Thirteenth Floor' followed. Although it would undoubtedly come to be *Scream!*'s highlight, here it got off to a slow start as super computer Max introduced us to experimental council block Maxwell Tower. At the top it housed a huge server room. 'That's me up in the penthouse,' explained the machine (depicted as a pumpkin lantern-like face on a monitor screen), 'Sorry I can't wave to you. I'd sure like to.' Evidentially a chatty little soul, Max's top priority was the welfare of his tenants. Whisking newcomer Mrs Henderson and her son up to their apartment in his lift, the youngster spotted the floors jumped from twelve to fourteen – neatly highlighting the strip's over-riding conceit. 'Many people consider the number thirteen to be unlucky, Billy' explained the pixellated porter. 'I was built without a thirteenth floor!'

However, when a nasty debt collector showed up, menacing the young mother to hand over the ninety-five quid she'd been lent to bury her husband, Max interceded. As the miscreant took the elevator down to the lower floors, it suddenly stopped. Stepping out into the cobwebby darkness, the rogue realised something was up. 'Thirteenth floor? But this building ain't got a thirteenth floor!' With bats whirling around and the Grim Reaper eagerly fingering his scythe, unfortunately, he was gravely mistaken.

Although it wasn't obvious from this outing, the upcoming weeks would develop the gimmick nicely, as other criminal types were dispatched to the fabled floor for a spate of rough justice, which usually meant a gruesome and oh-so-ironic death themed around the crime they had committed.

As for how Max tackled those on a health-kick who'd rather take the stairs, well, thankfully baddies just didn't do that.

'A Ghastly Tale!' was a one-page strip, with a nice line in *Tales of the Unexpected* twists. In this issue, readers were deftly misled into assuming a sideshow monster was actually a boy wearing a costume. 'I don't know what I'd do without the mask,' beamed the handsome chap to his colleague backstage after scaring another round of punters. And then: 'Time for the next show, better get the mask off,' at which point it was revealed his comely features were actually a plastic façade and behind them he really was that impressively tusked freak.

At this point, humour made an ill-advised foray into the comic in the shape of a reprint of *Cor!!*'s 'Fiends and Neighbours', before we were back with another 'Tharg's Future Shock'-style piece, this time entitled 'Library of Death'. In this one a demanding young tyke got his just deserts after moaning his adopted parents wouldn't take him into the ghost house at the local fairground. 'You never want me to enjoy myself. It's because you're not my real parents!' he whined. However, that night he was visited by a spectral figure who whisked him away to the building, where he had an encounter with a slew of spirits and nasties.

As if that wasn't enough, his poor old parents then arrived, only to be killed on entry ('They met death itself!'). With a cry of 'No! Nooooooo!' the little chap awoke in his own bed to discover it had all been a dream. Or had it? Sneaking through to his mum and dad's room, he discovered the pair had been turned into spectral forms. 'Now you shall live in the ghost house...for ever!' they informed him...before he awoke in his bed again, having played the old dream-within-a-dream card. 'Perhaps ghost houses aren't such fun after all!' he declared, lesson patently learnt.

Scream!'s final tale of terror came with the unprepossessing tagline: 'When the purring stopped, there was no escape from...' and then the title: 'The Terror of the Cats'.

Riffing off Hitchcock's *The Birds*, it followed *Barchester Evening Echo* reporter Allen Woodward's investigation into a spate of feline attacks on humans. However, after all the ghouls and ghosts we'd been bombarded with so far, it has to be said, the sight of Tiddles doing his nut just couldn't compete. That said, page twenty-nine's depiction of our hero dispatching a load of troublesome moggies with a spade had to be some sort of comic first.

All in all, it had been an auspicious debut – the kind of comic that provided near *Action* levels of blood and gore.

And so it continued.

With its regular line-up of freaks and fools, and creeps and ghouls, the comic delivered week after week, however, the powers that be weren't happy and – for some reason – the title was pulled with no warning (nary a 'Great news for readers inside') after fifteen issues. Even Ghastly McNasty hadn't been informed, and went about his business as usual ('If you'd like to see more from Dracula's blood-soaked history...write and tell me'). However, the following week, *Scream!* was consumed by *Eagle* mk II. Ever controlling, Max quickly went on to take up the mantle of token 'editor' in his new home. But for Ghastly, it was time to meet his maker.

As for why the axe fell, rumours still persist to this day. Was the comic just too gruesome for the IPC bigwigs? Or was it yet another victim of the hard financial realities of the Eighties? Whatever; with those fifteen *Scream!* comics now considered collector's items by latter-day fans, it's achieved some sort of life after death – which is entirely appropriate when you think about it.

Shiver and Shake
(IPC Magazines Ltd, 1973-1974, every Monday)

It must have looked so obvious. *Cor!!* had been enjoying some success with strips like 'Hire a Horror', 'Fiends and Neighbours' and 'Freddie Fang: The Werewolf Cub' dwelling on the ghoulish side of life, while 'two-for' comic, *Whizzer and Chips*, had been flying off the shelves. So why not combine both elements into one publication?

That, presumably, was the general thrust of the conversation in IPC Towers that resulted in this short-lived venture which may have ticked all the boxes, but failed to find an audience.

Not named after *Cor!!*'s identically titled comic-strip, which featured an undead pantaloon-wearing cavalier who had a sword through his middle and a ball and chain affixed to his leg – Shiver – pitted against a generic bulbous-nosed ghost – Shake – (although, confusingly, the former would actually appear in the new comic, albeit under a different moniker), *Shiver and Shake* hit the news-stands in March 1974.

Playing up that two-titles-in-one gimmick for all it was worth, the cover was split down the middle as, on one side of the partition, Shiver (another generic bulbous-nosed ghost – getting confused yet?) emerged through his office door to greet a terrified child with the words: 'Helloooo! My comic is haunted!', while, on the other side, Shake (a fat elephant in a schoolboy's uniform...for some reason) smashed through his portal, chuckling: 'Hi! Mine is a real solid scream too!'

Accompanying this was one of four free gift practical jokes, which readers were invited to swap with their pals for even more laughs – a promotional idea that would later be replicated in *Jackpot* and *Wow!*

Inside, we met the monstrous Frankie Stein, a smiley-faced Boris Karlof lookalike who'd first appeared in *Wham!* (Oldhams, 1964-8). Here, the 'big lunk' attended school for the first time but – such is the way of things – ended up demolishing the building by mistake. At least the kids were impressed: '*Wahaah*! No more school for months! You may be ugly, mate...but you're *okay* with us!'

Shiver then stepped out for his own story in 'The Duke's Spook', which pitted him against a dastardly butler who usurped his position as the titular dignitary's servant. Then, 'Webster'. This spider, whose 'webs have everyone in a spin!' pitched out his turf as an arachnid determined to spin his silk wherever he fancied by getting one up on a couple of sentry guards. 'No-one, but no-one gets the better of me!' chuckled the little beast as he scuttled away from the devastation he'd wrought.

'Scream Inn' was a slightly different proposition – a two-page tale rendered in muggy greys which detailed the exploits at a horrific hostelry which would pay out £1 million to anyone with the guts to spend the night in the haunted bedroom. In this first instalment, it looked like a tough boxer was all set to scoop the loot, until he was taunted by a ghost into punching through a wall, and tumbled out of the chamber with just one minute to go until deadline. 'You can count the boxer out, boys and ghouls,' ran the text at the bottom, 'so who could stay a night in Scream Inn?' Although a million quid wasn't up for grabs here, readers could still net a handsome £1 if their suggested guest was used in a story.

Other strips in *Shiver*'s section included 'The Hand' (a disembodied mitt that went around causing mischief or merriment, dependent on the toss of a coin, and a bit of a forerunner to *Whoopee!*'s 'Evil Eye'), 'Soggy the Sea Monster', 'Horronation Street' (detailing the life of the grim residents who lived there) and 'Adrian's Wall' (the imaginative – albeit unlikely – story of a lad haunted by, well, a wall). However, none were a match for Leo Baxendale's 'Sweeny Toddler', the fantastic strip about a uni-toothed baby with a penchant for evil.

By comparison, *Shake*'s section was rather less sure-footed. It was hard to see what the overriding theme was here, the preposterous pachyderm's own story being just general naughty-boy stuff. Nevertheless, there were some laughs to be had. 'Lolly Pop' was about a filthy-rich bloke who refused to spread the wealth with his son ('You can 'ave a penny and lump it!'), 'Gal Capone' brought us the exploits of a muscled-up girl who terrorised the community, 'The Fixer' was a cock-sure young lad who had a knack for making things happen and 'Tough Nut and Softy Centre' did the usual chalk versus cheese thing, as a burly hulk who ate 'fried tree roots and nail sauce' for breakfast tried his best to beat a rarefied pansy who was such a sap, he made his dad carry him down stairs for fear of falling over.

Shake's highlight was reserved for the centre-pages, with the high-concept 'Match of the Week', which pitted two naturally opposing factions against each other on the soccer pitch. For the first issue it was 'Cowboys versus Injuns'. The result? 'Game abandoned – rain (of arrows) stopped play'. A later edition setting explorers against jungle plants was a painful signifier that the concept could only be spun-out so far.

To cap off the whole thing, *Shiver and Shake*'s back cover brought us the first in a series of 'Creepy Creations' – a colour poster of an imaginatively conceived creature (here it was 'The One-Eyed Wonk of Wigan'). Another quid was up for grabs if readers' own suggestions for creations were put into service.

As the weeks progressed the covers played up a 'split-screen' theme, depicting the same situation from both Shiver and Shake's perspective. As per, strips came and went, although few comics could boast a story as weird as 'Charlie Williams', one page of fun about the *Comedians* and *Golden Shot* star whose selling point was that while his family hailed from Barbados, he spoke in a broad Yorkshire accent. Cue plenty of dialogue of the 'hello me old flowers' variety.

For a time *Whizzer and Chips*' 'Oddball' and 'Fuss Pot' put in 'star guest' appearances, while Baxendale came up trumps again with 'Grimly Feendish', the story of a money-grabbing old man which was illustrated in frenetic detail.

The split-screen covers were dropped before the year's end, making way instead for good-natured badinage between the rival editors – Shake making smoke messages with Shiver's head on one occasion. However, despite these token gestures, a real feud between the two was what the paper lacked. While the Whizz-Kids and the Chip-ites regularly ran sabotage missions into each other's section of the comic and invited readers to slag off their opponent's wares, a terse word was seldom exchanged between the phantom and the 'phant.

Just nineteen months and eighty-three issues after launch, the title merged with *Whoopee!* in October 1974, where it would continue for a time as a pull-out section.

Eight months later, the company decided they'd have another bash at the spooky comic format, this time undiluted by two notional editors. In terms of sales, *Monster Fun* would prove to be an even bigger misfire – oh, the horror!

Sparky
(DC Thomson, 1965-1977, every Friday)

'The *big* comic' for boys and girls came along at a time when DC Thomson were ruling the roost in terms of humour titles, but arguably never quite managed to become as fondly regarded as *The Beano*, *The Dandy*, *The Beezer* or *The Topper*.

Sparky – © DC Thomson & Co., Ltd

In its early days, *Sparky* felt rather like the safe option to these comparatively robust cohorts, with a collection of gentle stories that wouldn't scare the horses…unless those nags had half an eye on race relations that is. Looking back on the start of the comic's run, you can't avoid register-ing the jaw-droppingly inappropriate title character whose adventures propped up the cover for the first three or four years.

Sparky was nothing less than a 'comedy' black man, complete with swollen lips, grass skirt and huge hooped earrings. Why his ethnicity was supposed to be intrinsically funny was never properly explained, and indeed, most readers could be forgiven for failing to clock the char-acter's origins, instead just assuming he was someone who looked a bit funny (because, to be fair, he did resemble *The Dandy*'s space alien, Pobble). OK, so there was one episode where the funster ended up hid-ing out in a wildlife museum, brandishing a spear so that it looked like he was part of the display, but otherwise Sparky spoke perfect English, lived in a suburban high street and was happy to help out his neigh-bours ('Oh my back's bad, Sparky. I came over to ask if you would do my gardening for me?').

Whether DC Thomson were starting to feel uncomfortable about the character, or he simply wasn't all that popular, it's interesting to note that by 1969, he'd been punted off the front cover in favour of the exploits of Barney Bulldog (who, bearing in mind his penchant for red vests, tiny black shorts and spiked dog collars was something of a precursor to *Little Britain*'s 'only gay in the village', Daffyd). Although Sparky was still allowed to host the paper's letters page ('Fun-Fare') – wherein he was reduced to simply piling on the pressure for readers to write in ('where are all those letters, then?') – even that privilege would be short-lived. The rise of new strip 'We Are the Sparky People!' (which brought us crazy dispatches from the comic's office) was a clear signal the paper was intent on hanging its name off a different comic-strip from now on and, sometime over the summer of 1971, the character was excised altogether from the publication that bore his name.

But back to those early days, and readers showing up for issue one were handsomely rewarded with a free 'Flying Snorter' (read: balloon) before being reacquainted with *The Dandy* and *The Beano* cast-offs such as 'Freddy the Fearless Fly', 'Keyhole Kate' and 'Pansy Potter: The Strongman's Daughter'. There was also high adventure with the unfortunate Kidd family who starred in 'Kidnapped Kidds' and would later return for another spate of imprisonment in 'The Captive Kidds' ('What's going to happen to us?' asks little Nicky as the clan are led off by Sardian rebels. 'I don't know, but try to look brave and then perhaps they'll respect us,' counsels older brother Pat), and whimsical flights of fancy with the narcolepsy-afflicted 'Dreamy Dave and Dozy Dora'.

Better stuff was to come, when Peter Piper jumped onboard with his magic musical instrument that could bring inanimate objects to life and 'Invisible Dick' foiled bullies and rotters with imaginative use of his amazing torch which shone a black beam, making all items within its glare vanish.

As the Sixties drew to a close, the comic went through a slight re-branding process, aiming less at the nursery end of the market and dropping some of its twee fare for the more knockabout humour of *Inspector Gadget*-alike 'I Spy', the wacky adventures of inept coppers Frederic and Cecil in 'L Cars', the all-out weirdness of 'Mr Bubbles' (the washing-up liquid bottle-dwelling genie) and, perhaps best of all, the all-out warfare of 'Puss and Boots' ('they fight like cat and dog!'). Before long, the latter had secured a regular colour page on the back of *Sparky* where the moggy and mutt continued waging their campaign of *über*-violence (remote-control rockets fitted out with boxing gloves, forklift trucks, sticks of dynamite and even 'airyplanes' were all employed in their ongoing struggle) against each other for a couple of years.

Meanwhile, Barney Bulldog was holding onto his front cover slot, but only just. In 1973, his antics were dropped to make way for full page illustrations (while the cat and dog tag team had now been promoted to the centre spread), as *Sparky* became the fussily titled *The Sparky Comic*. Before long he was binned from the paper altogether.

Nearing the end of its life, the title was becoming more and more anarchic, one issue wasting a front and back cover on a one-shot joke featuring Tommy Cooper (revealing that under his fez he had a fez-shaped head!) while inside the adventures of 'Thingummy Blob' (a rubbery creature created by Professor T Potts, who was now intent on killing it) rubbed shoulders with 'Baron Von Reichs-Pudding' ('The flying Hun from World War One!').

But the wanton craziness wasn't enough to stave off destruction, and in July 1977, 'Peter Piper', 'Thingummyblob', 'L-Cars' and the like were consigned to pull-out ignominy in the centre pages of *The Topper*. Still, twelve years wasn't a bad innings for a comic that seems to have been universally forgotten about today.

Speed
(IPC Magazines Ltd, 1980, every Monday)

Latter day gag-meisters would surely have some fun with that title ('So, this kid, right, goes into a newsagent's and says, "Can I put in a regular order for *Speed*, please?"') but you can't deny it was a boss name for a boys' comic.

Speed – © Egmont UK Ltd, London

Devoted, naturally, to all things that moved at some velocity, it was a tremendously exciting premise for a publication, but sadly, the whole thing ran out of steam all too quickly – perhaps because it didn't really seem to be doing anything you couldn't already get in *Tiger*.

Arriving with a 'Free Speed Plane!' ('It climbs, it swoops, it turns and loops!') the paper – plying its gimmick to the max – advised readers they were in store for 'eight high-speed picture stories to make you gasp!' Early highlights included 'Topps on Two Wheels', which was absolutely the sort of things boys wanted to read – the travails of 'daring young motor-cyclist' Eddie Topps who was dead set on becoming the next Evel Knievel. Naturally that meant a whole host of foolhardy stunts were on the agenda including, in one issue, riding his bike over a roller-coaster track ('My – my goggles! They're going *misty*! Things are all blurring up! *I can't see!*' and then: 'How will Eddie get out of this situation? Read on next week!').

Even better, though, was 'Death Wish' which not only also majored on vehicle-based arsing around, but threw in a hideously disfigured character as the lead, to boot. Blake Edmonds had been 'one of the most handsome stars of British sport' but had suffered horrific injuries to his face following a plane crash. Ever since then he'd donned a grim leather mask and vowed to take in as many dangerous sports as possible ('Speed is all I live for'), without a care for his personal safety. Naturally, he never actually came fatally unstuck – although he would provide a crowd-pleasing moment pretty much ever other week when he'd remove his disguise to reveal the seared flesh behind – and is probably enjoying a fine retirement today, doubtlessly jockeying that Stannah Starlift to maximum revs.

'Quick on the Draw', meanwhile, translated the comic's theme to a gunfighter's supple trigger finger, while 'Journey to the Stars' was – to be honest – a pretty hopeless *Lost in Space* wannabe, following the exploits of the Redford family who journeyed from one intergalactic cock-up to another. Thankfully, 'The Fastest Footballer on Earth!' was rather better, centring on Mudport United's star player Mickey 'Flash' Jordan who – thanks to spending part of his life with the animals in the African jungle – moved like Mercury across the pitch.

It didn't take long for the hard times to arrive at *Speed*. By the summer the comic had been forced to ditch its relatively plush production values for crappy paper and less colour, and come October, even our man Topps seemed to be in on the economy drive, swapping his motorbike for a BMX (or maybe he was just caught up in the new craze). As 'Big news issue! Big news issue!' chimed across the cover, it was obvious what was going to happen next, and, sure enough, *Speed* was absorbed into *Tiger* where, to be honest, the likes of Skid Solo had already been doing the high velocity thing for years.

Spellbound
(DC Thomson, 1976-1978, every Thursday)

An occult-tinged weekly that specialised in spine-tingling tales of terror and featured willowy heroines with a tendency to go heavy on the mascara? Surely that was *Misty*?

In fact, DC Thomson's spooky title was the first to bring a regular dose of witchcraft, sci-fi and twisted tales into the world of British girls' comics. Sporting a free 'mystic sun pendant' upon arrival and an affecting front cover illustration of a Pre-raphaelite teen holding aloft a wax-strewn candle (a riff also later repeated in the first issue of *Misty*), this was certainly a beguiling publication.

Spellbound – © DC Thomson & Co., Ltd

The line-up of stories didn't hold back on the scares. 'When the Mummy Walks' brought us Egyptian-themed terror in a museum in Victorian London as an evil old crone brought the titular undead character to life to embark on a crime spree. Meanwhile, 'The Haunting of Laura Lee' was a tale of possession as young Laura found herself taken over by the spirit of a long dead 'bewitching concert pianist' when she donned her ring; 'I Don't Want to be a Witch!' saw Celia Winters battling the overtures of her Aunt Armida who was trying to turn her on to the black arts; and the Supercats, took us on a space age jaunt in 'Supercats Meet the Sun God'.

The latter strip was terribly exciting, introducing us to the empowered tracksuit-clad quartet – Electra, Helen, Hercula, Fauna and their zippy spaceship Kitten. So popular did they become, they spawned their own readers' club, wherein a 40p postal order would get you a 'colourful sew-on-patch', an exclusive pendant (did DC Thomson have a job lot of these or something?), and a 'denim-look pouch containing your zodiac code'. Each week one of the four would take control of the club's page in the comic and print important messages in code, solicit spooky tales from the readers ('The day I became a Supercat I had a very strange dream...') and hand out top-quality merchandise in the form of an 'up-to-the-minute jeans belt' (the premium prize) or a 'fashion tote bag'.

It was all very impressive – but lacking one crucial factor: bite. Where *Misty* would later succeed with its anything-goes mentality which allowed the cruellest of fates to be meted out to the most innocent of parties, *Spellbound* lacked that element of moral fecklessness (unless you count putting a bloody big picture of Alvin Stardust across the back of issue eleven, just so he could recount a meeting he once had with a gypsy at Scarborough Fair). We always knew that at the end of the day, the baddies would lose, while the virtuous would be duly rewarded. Despite great strap lines above its stories declaring things like: 'A flickering light spells great danger for Polly!', 'Spied on by a mysterious watcher!' and 'A young girl in a house of mystery!', you just knew nothing really bad could happen here.

Nevertheless, *Spellbound* had a pretty decent innings, clocking up sixty-nine issues until it was forced to merge with *Debbie* on 14 January 1978 – just three weeks before the first issue of *Misty* hit the stands. Now, that's spooky...

Spike
(DC Thomson, 1983-1984, every Saturday)

With *Buddy* heading into freefall, DC Thomson thought they'd give the juvenile editor-helmed comic one more roll of the dice with this something-for-everyone (providing that 'everyone' was an audience of boys looking for your usual sports and shooting things-related content) effort which pretty much followed the same template as its soon-to-be-deceased stablemate.

Thus, as the perennially thumbs-aloft hedgehog-headed 'editor' beckoned us into his new comic with the enticement of a 'super swooper glider' (one of those polystyrene self-assembly jobs, apparently it was 'grrreat!'), one of the old reliables prepared to be pressed into service again in the story

'The Man in Black'.

Originally stuck with the moniker, Smith, the world record-breaking barefoot athlete in the black leotard who spent most of his spare time jumping unfeasibly wide brooks in the Yorkshire Moors, was actually trailing a long and distinguished history behind him. It was *Spike*'s readers who first noticed it, writing in to declare that their dads had told them Smith was actually Wilson, who'd originally appeared in *Wizard* mk I (DC Thomson, 1922-63) back in 1943 before moving over to *Hornet*. With the revelation public knowledge, the truth was gradually eked out, Smith confiding in close friend Harry Cobb that he was a descendant of the ebony-clad runner, before finally admitting he was indeed the ageless original, who existed on a diet of wild berries...or something. After that, it was no-holds-barred, with *Spike* blowing the whole gaff by running 'The Truth About Wilson'.

Spike – © DC Thomson & Co., Ltd

Despite the enigmatic athlete, *Spike*'s greatest draw was 'Iron Barr', the tale of scrap dealer-cum-Darbury Rangers goalie Charlie 'Iron' Barr. Cast from the same mould as *Hornet*'s Bernard Briggs, the working-class lad-made-good had no time for the likes of Rolls-driving club director Sir Gregory Slade (who once exclaimed, 'that Barr is an uncouth loudmouth'), and played everything by the book on the pitch. And by God, didn't he let you know about it, providing a running commentary as he continually picked fault in the referee's decisions – 'Hey, ref, you should've checked all the players were back in position before you allowed that kick-off!' Always maintaining he would only ever play as an amateur, he even got the call-up for the England squad, whereupon he was immediately fitted up for the theft of an antique statuette, but luckily still went on to help our boys secure an historic 3-1 victory over Brazil.

In later issues, freed up from his commitments in *Buddy*, Limp-Along Leslie joined the team which, along with a burgeoning love interest in the shape of Slade's niece Kim, gave the strip something of a soap-opera feel. Barr's eventual fate was therefore apt, as by April 1984 word was spreading that United – as featured in *Champ* – were interested in signing him. Despite initially declaring he wasn't interested, the hard-as-nails goalie would eventually see out the rest of his career with the team.

Other strips featured over the comic's lifetime included 'The Bleak Street Bunch' (the extremely working-class antics of a group of pupils from Slagley Comprehensive – a kind of sanitised take on *Action*'s 'Kids Rule OK'); 'Starhawk' (a very DC Thomson sci-fi strip which could have come straight from the pages of *Starblazer*, but in fact originated in *The Crunch*); 'A Ghost in the Cockpit' (generic Second World War action, with a touch of spiritualism thrown in); 'Ticker Tait: The Man With a Time Bomb in his Heart' (*2000 AD*'s 'MACH-1' less the ultra-violence, as augmented secret agent Sinclair Tait ran errands for the 'dirty tricks department' of British Intelligence); and 'The Mantracker' ('The Fall Guy' translated into 'Indian bounty hunter Bearpaw Jay', and another *Crunch* refugee).

So far, so ordinary, but there were other delights, such as the superb back page, 'The Spike Report' (subtitle: 'On mums, dads, teachers and other adults' – with the last word crossed out to be replaced by a hastily scrawled in 'nuisances'). Here, the eponymous red-jumpered kid would field-test various 'dodges' sent in by readers, such as Ian Waugh's scheme to confuse parents by using long words ('Due to an error in predicted trajectory, your glass sustained a fracture as a result of being struck by a spherical projectile in flight'). If said idea proved a success (and Ian's was, until Spike pushed his luck) they'd get a fiver, but even ones that resulted in our pal getting a slippering still merited two quid.

However, despite its charm, seemingly bi-weekly competitions to win Dawes Lightening Racing Bikes and photographs of Barry Took, *Spike*'s time in the limelight was depressingly short. Perhaps it was because the mix of comedy, sport, war, and – gulp! – text stories (the '5 Minute Mystery') confused the readership who couldn't quite work out what the comic was supposed to be about. Thus, when United came knocking for Charlie Barr, it was actually the first sign the party was over. After 67 *grrreat* issues *Spike* was consumed by *Champ* and there was no reader's dodge to get him out of that one.

Starblazer
(DC Thomson, 1979-1991, monthly)

It was the late Seventies, and the future had well and truly arrived as the world was going sci-fi nuts. *Star Wars* had cleaned up at the box office and excitement was growing about the imminent *The Empire Strikes Back*. *2000 AD* had proven a huge success since its launch in 1977, the Beeb's new space opera, *Blake's 7* was bringing snogging and stun guns to the small screen, and *Doctor Who* was poised on the edge of delivering its best ever ratings.

Starblazer – © DC Thomson & Co., Ltd

In Dundee, none of this had gone unnoticed and the time was right for DC Thomson to go…sci-fi! The result was a new 'pocket library'-style publication to accompany the long-running **Commando**. *Starblazer* – 'science fiction adventures in pictures' – brought us space age stories from around the galaxy in a 68 page, black and white format which had already been established by the diminutive war series. Again, we had lurid, full-painted front covers, and again, some of the world's most exciting fonts wheeled out to declare story titles such as 'Pirates of the Ether Sea', 'The Exterminator', 'Doomrock', 'Escape from Devil's Moon' and 'The Final Sanction'. The latter example was particularly notable for the unfortunate choice of lettering; the 'F' straying rather to close to the 'I' and thus forming something that looked like an 'A'. Readers expecting a tale involving trade disagreements with bottoms from outer space were liable to be disappointed.

And so to that first issue. Entitled 'The Omega Experiment', the cover depicted a conical spaceship orbiting a planet as another vessel met its maker. That this scene didn't actually feature inside was neither here nor there. The story followed the exploits of the Luke Skywalker-esque Lute Fireball who, along with his cutesy robot chum Archee, ended up marooned on an alien planet after piloting a new craft which generated its own black hole and dropped through it.

It was certainly fun stuff, featuring some imaginative alien nasties and our goldilocked hero displaying the requisite amount of spunk required when captured by the evil robots (or 'biorobots', even): 'Hello, tin can. My compliments to your tailor – he hasn't done a thing for you.'

During its run, *Starblazer* became notable for giving new writers and artists a chance. Future *Crisis* scribe John Smith got his first break on the comic, as did *2000 AD* hero Grant Morrison. Issue fifteen, entitled 'Algol the Terrible' was his first professional commission in the world of comics, and he would go on to pen a further nine titles. Although this was the anything-goes world of sci-fi, he still had to rein in his avant-garde tendencies, being told there was no place for his interstellar stories about pacifism and frequently cajoled to incorporate more 'space combat' into his work.

As the publication reached issue two hundred, it had pretty much remained fixated on the *Star Wars* template of chunky space-ships and lots of hardware.

There was some deviations from the format, however, notably a couple of *Choose Your Own Adventure*-type issues ('Captain's Choice' and 'Doom World!', the latter being another effort from Morrison). But things were about to change. The comic dropped the 'science fiction in pictures' subtitle for 'fantasy fiction in pictures' and started to embrace new worlds of imagination. Thus, we had 'Demon Sword', a Michael Moorcock-influenced saga about the d'Annemarc dynasty who dabbled in the world of demons, magic swords and mythical quests. Various members of this august clan appeared over several issues.

Becoming more self-referential, and willfully pastiching current cinema trends, the comic remained something of a hidden gem (it was always one of the more difficult titles to find in shops). At one point, there was a suggestion DC Thomson might spin the title off into a full colour large-format publication the likes of which were flying out of Forbidden Planet shops at the time, and four issues of such a publication, *Legend*, were indeed produced. But alas, poor sales finally forced *Starblazer*'s cancellation at the start of 1991 and after 281 issues, the world of the future was consigned to the past.

Starlord
(IPC Magazines Ltd, 1978, every Monday)

A year on from *2000 AD*'s launch, the IPC overlords thought they'd have another crack at the sci-fi whip, this time producing a relatively plush publication (eight pages of full colour, if you can believe it) for the more discerning sciffy fan.

The result was *Starlord*, an expensive (12p!) weekly that advised us to 'watch the stars!' Very obviously marketed as a (slightly posher) companion to the 'Galaxy's Greatest Comic', the title even came with its own eponymous novelty alien editor. Not too dissimilar to a bequiffed Shakin' Stevens who'd swapped his denims for a centurion's outfit, he took to referring to the comic as a 'starzine', and, in that first issue, filled us in on his requisite back story. He'd escaped 'the satanic forces of the *Interstellar Federation*,' you see, 'and was here to bring us a *'dire warning!'* (he certainly liked emphasising his words, did Starlord). A *'cataclysmic catastrophe'* was on the cards, but luckily help was at hand: '*Starlord* is *your* paper...*and* your crash-course in Interstellar Survival!'

The first phase of Earth's counter-attack took the form of a free badge. With a random selection on offer, the one that came with your edition indicated your role within the nascent 'Star-Trooper' squads and would allow you to recognise fellow cohorts on the street to form 'Star-Squads'. Those battalions broke down as follows. You could either be a Pilot, a Time Warden, a Laser Specialist, a member of the Robot Regiment, a common-or-garden Trooper or – surely the best? – a Skateboard Strike Force bod. But beware! '*Do not* place it on your skin, as the badge is made from a special metal mined on Axis 1A and you could develop a skin disorder, putting you out of combat.' Had anyone told Lynn Faulds Wood about this?

So, there was the concept: keep buying the comic, or your planet gets it. Luckily, then, it was no small chore to stick with *Starlord* as, during its time, it pretty much eclipsed anything that was going on in *2000 AD*. Promising that 'a new wild era of sci-fi starts here!' the premier issue led with the mediocre 'Planet of the Damned' (originally intended for *2000 AD*'s launch issue), in which a jet airplane disappeared from the Bermuda

Triangle to land on a generic hostile planet complete with nasty aliens which resembled – there's no getting away from it – wrinkled phalluses. Luckily, a local barbarian was on hand to dispatch the nasties with a right-hook and some of the fruitiest dialogue ever seen in comics: 'Squirm as I grind thy vile head and make ye pay for all your kind's foul deeds!'

The paper's main event, 'Strontium Dog', detailed the comings and goings of mutant bounty hunter Johnny Alpha. Created by the same team who'd brought us Judge Dredd, this was familiar territory, with our hero bedecked in shoulder pads and huge boots, battling an array of wittily conceived baddies in a future world where justice was maintained by force. However, unlike Dredd, Johnny was accompanied by a loyal side-kick, a hammer-wielding Viking who mused, 'a skull to crack mit der happy-stick, und old Wulf is fine! But no skulls can ve see!'

Bringing up the rear was an equally notable piece, 'Ro-Busters'. Set in a future world where robot servants were prolific, two antiquated droids, Ro-Jaws and Hammerstein (a bizarre play on Rodgers and Hammerstein – for some reason) faced being crushed to smithereens because 'the punters don't want second-hand droids no more!', until they were saved at the eleventh hour by a Mr Quartz, who put them into service as part of a mechanised *Thunderbirds*-like rescue team.

Much as *2000 AD* had taken to crediting its artists and writers, so did *Starlord*, revealing those all important names in little 'Starlord Blueprinters' inserts dotted around the comic. It was therefore plain to see that the creative forces behind this comic – including Jack Adrian, the pseudonymous 'TB Grover' (John Wagner), Carlos Ezquerra and Pat Mills – were the ones who'd been making its sister title so great.

With a further thrill, 'Mind Wars' (the story of twins imbued with 'terrifying mind powers' being used as pawns in a space-age war) joining the ranks the following week, it looked like *Starlord* had it made. Indeed, sales were said to exceed even that of *2000 AD* so it remains a subject of some conjecture even now why, just five months later, the publication was merged with Tharg's own organ.

Starlord of course tried to talk up his fast-approaching obscurity. 'Earth is saved!' he claimed. 'The Int. Stell. Fed. have abandoned their plan to attack and destroy us...But, do not despair...bright and wondrous events await you in the future and you can learn about them now in the pages of "*2000 AD* and *Starlord*". Yes, the best of both worlds!' Well, yes and no. 'Strontium Dog' and 'Ro-Busters' would go on to enjoy a long and illustrious run in their new home, but, with the green fella from Betelgeuse already calling the shots, there was no room for two outer-space editors in the one title. Thus, Starlord disappeared forever, telling us he was returning to 'the spaceways, for the Gronks are calling and I cannot let them down...'

Swift
(Hulton Press Ltd/Longcre Press/Odhams Press Ltd, 1954-1963, every Tuesday)

The last and the least red-top to come out of the Hulton stable, even its own editor wasn't overly enthused with the company's efforts to provide a publication to bridge the gap between the toddler-centric fare of *Robin* and the more advanced derring-do comic-strips and technical-drawing related centre-spreads of *Eagle* mk I.

'Frankly I don't think I did very well with *Swift*,' admitted the Reverend Marcus Morris in later life. 'I was a good deal preoccupied...and had lost some of my earlier keenness and enthusiasm. Producing papers for children was getting to be rather a habit and perhaps I was becoming bored.'

In retrospect, the editorial team also felt the seven to ten-year-old age group they were aiming at was too small a target to hit with any degree of accuracy, particularly as they had to ensure they didn't also produce something that would provide competition for their other titles, *Robin*, *Girl* mk I and *Eagle*.

Launched on 20 March 1954, with a fleet of cars sporting models of the titular flying creature on top (much the same rumpus that had been kicked up for *Eagle*, then), apparently the marketing team were regularly accosted by wise guys asking if they were selling birdseed. Tsk!

But, what was lacklustre in the Rev's eyes was still a superior production all told, and one its staff would become increasingly attached to until a series of publishing takeover bids ruined the whole thing.

Enlivened by the same production values that marked out Hulton's children's papers, the first issue introduced us – rather abruptly it has to be said (no scene-setting captions here) – to 'Tarna: Jungle Boy'. A junior Tarzan accompanied by chimpanzee, Toto, the lad shared an affinity with the wildlife around him and here tried to stop 'White Men!' from stealing a hippo's calf. Obviously, his reputation went before him, with one of the scoundrels cautioning his mate against shooting the imp: 'All the jungle animals are his friends. They would kill us if we...'

It was pretty grim stuff and no mistake, Tarna being left for dead by the time we reached the strip's cliffhanger. By welcome contrast, then, was the whimsical 'Mono the Moon Man', a shape-changing alien with a TV aerial in his head who made friends with a young boy called Martin. 'Nicky Nobody' followed, bringing us 'the story of a boy and his dog'. An orphan (hence the 'Nobody' tag), Nicky may have strutted about in a school uniform, but rarely seemed to attend any educational establishment. Half his luck, eh readers?

Meanwhile, 'Educating Archie' ('with Peter Brough') arrived courtesy of the BBC and gave the creepy ventriloquist's vent a new lease of life in strip form where he was free to roam at will. 'Tom Tex and Pinto' brought readers their own junior take on *Eagle*'s 'Riders of the Range' ('Golly! A *real* Indian!'); 'Koko the Bushbaby' was a dispensable, albeit cute, four-panel funny ('see Koko spray himself in the face with a seltzer bottle!'); 'The Fleet Family in Island of Secrets' saw a smug clan move into an aeroplane ('That is our new home. It's a flying caravan,' declared Daddy from behind his ludicrous moustache), which they promptly crashed into an island en route to Australia; and 'Paul English' took to the high seas to bring us the adventures of a wide-eyed cabin boy who becomes a member of a certain famous seaman's crew ('Who is that fine gentleman?' 'That, my boy, is the great Sir Walter Raleigh').

Towards the back of the paper, half-page strips proliferated, bringing us funnies from 'Roddy the Road Scout', 'The Topple Twins' and 'Our Gang', white-bread adventure with 'Sally of Fern Farm', thrills thanks to 'Sammy and his Speedsub' and then two Hulton staples; the real-life strip ('Heroes of Today: No.1 Stirling Moss') and – uh oh – the religious bit ('The Boy David').

Aside from Tarno, *Swift*'s other big-hitters were undoubtedly John Ryan's comical 'Sir Boldasbrass', which enjoyed centre-spread status, and the back page 'The Sign of the Scarlet Ladybird', sponsored by Ladybird children's clothes. This was a bonkers strip where baddies wanted to get their hands on the juvenile heroes' lovely clobber, until – apropos of nothing – 'The Jet-Boy' zoomed in via a rocket to foil their scheme. Product placement at its weirdest, but most direct: 'Ask Mother to buy *you* a Ladybird T-shirt' ran the pay-off at the foot of future instalments.

A pretty good line-up by anyone's standards, and all beautifully illustrated, the comic nonetheless went through a major revamp within a matter of months, 'Sir Boldasbrass' yielding to Ryan's other creation, 'Captain Pugwash', 'The Swiss Family Robinson' brought in to show the Fleet clan how it's done, and the Michael Bentine-produced 'Bumblies' sporting an incredibly exciting 'as seen on TV' flash.

1959 would prove a notable year in the comic's history, as publishing magnates Odhams Press acquired Hulton. Immediately clipping the wings of its new employees, they prompted Marcus Morris to stand down as editor from the whole *Eagle* family of titles. Meanwhile, in the pages of *Swift*, Tarno had been booted off the front by 'Smiley: The Boy from Down Under' ('Bonzer!'), TV's 'Dixon of Dock Green' had arrived for a piece of the comic-strip action, while Sammy had graduated from submarines to 'Freight Rockets' and was well on the way to becoming Dan Dare Jr.

On 10 October, much to the displeasure of many of its readers, *Swift* absorbed the *Walt Disney's Mickey's Weekly* (Willbank/Odhams Press, 1955-7) spin-off *Zip* (Odhams Press, 1958-9), but even greater change was on its way. On 22 March 1961, the Daily Mirror Group now weighed in, with their own successful (albeit hostile) takeover bid, acquiring the Hulton/Odhams line lock, stock and barrel. Now *Swift* and its brethren were swimming in a much larger pond, alongside the rest of the Mirror's Fleetway Publications division titles. As the muscle flexing began, edicts came down that *Swift* had to junk the text stories, limit its use of colour and beef up the advertising. Staff left by their droves.

With the new owners determined to quash the religious overtones of all Hulton's fare, *Swift* became more action-orientated, its bird emblem swapped for a speeding arrow, and front covers devoted to full-page paintings of thrilling things like aeroplanes and sinking ships. Inside, Tarno suddenly aged by ten years and turned into a lout, war stories began appearing and even a certain amount of cod-super-heroics infiltrated the paper (hello, 'Blackbow the Cheyenne').

No one liked the changes, least of all the readers and in March 1963, after 477 issues, *Swift* had pissed off everyone so much, there was nothing else left for it but to merge with *Eagle*. The last of the 'family' to arrive, it was also the first to go – but the others wouldn't be far behind.

Tammy
(IPC Magazines Ltd, 1971-1984, every Monday)

Shhhh. Don't tell the boys, but the gore-strewn, grim and gritty IPC comics they enjoyed in the Seventies actually came about thanks to a freckle-faced, pig-tailed girl and her flower-festooned publication.

Arriving in 1971 clutching a free 'fabulous ring and bracelet', *Tammy* presented a new take on girls' comics. With the market entering a dip, the company had carried out research into what young ladies wanted to read. Surprisingly for them, it turned out that, while enjoying the odd soppy story, their audience also liked sporty, intelligent go-ahead characters and tales packed full of jeopardy.

Writer Pat Mills was tasked with turning this data into reality, and, with sales dipping perilously across the market, came up with a new, less conventional publication that would give the genre a real shake-up.

The result was a weekly that, in addition to laying on the occasional bit of ballet and horsey action, majored in a heightened streak of cruelty that would even make *Mandy* blanche. As the writer himself later revealed, his intention was to create 'hard, gutsy stories that don't have to have a happy ending...that, combined with a strong camp quality, very clever plotting, ingenious ideas and totally over the top but still realistic concepts.' In order to achieve this, fellow young buck John Wagner was also roped in to provide scripts.

At the start, this was only hinted at, with moderately unpleasant goings-on depicted in strips like 'Our Janie' (Janie Greaves struggles to look after her siblings following their mother's death), 'Alison all Alone' (a girl is kept prisoner by her foster parents for no obvious reason) and 'The Shadow in Shona's Life' (Shona Gordon is evicted from her home and saddled with a freeloading travelling companion). However, before long things got really cruel and unusual.

The apotheosis of this had to be 1974's 'Becky Never Saw the Ball'. Playing up both Mills' gusty and camp angles, it told the improbable story of a plucky young tennis player who had one major drawback – she was blind. And, just to hammer the point home, the unfortunate girl advertised the fact by wrapping bandages around her head. Nevertheless, thanks to her superior hearing, she could still work out where that spherical object was and return it with a mighty whack.

Good old-fashioned Victorian squalor was also popular. In 'Sarah in the Shadows' a disadvantaged orphan desperately tried to raise money to get her uncle out of debtors' prison and in one episode found herself set upon by flower-sellers wielding dangerous-looking hat pins, angry she'd encroached upon their turf. The early nineteenth century also had its possibilities for nastiness as revealed in 'Katie on Thin Ice'. Here we travelled back to 1815 to meet Katie Williams, a – you guessed it – orphan lured into a thieves' den and set to work by a wicked Mrs Winter.

Meanwhile, a rather debonair chap decked out in a dinner suit and dicky bow presented one-off eerie twist-in-the-tale strips, subtitled 'The Strange Story', while some form of reassurance was provided by the constant appearance of Molly Mills, a plucky young girl with a nose for adventure, in a long-running series of strips.

The formula proved to be a huge success, sales reaching around 200,0000 a week. Meanwhile readers constantly voted for the cruellest stories as their favourite, validating Mills' vision. As a result, *Tammy* strode across the market guzzling up falling titles as it went. The first victim came just a month after launch, as in March 1971 it merged with *Sally* (IPC Magazines Ltd, 1969-71). Then, eleven months later, *Sandie* (IPC Magazines Ltd, 1972-3) fell in its path, before *June* did likewise in 1974, bringing with it Billy Bunter's sister, the equally rotund Bessie (whose whimsy never really made for a comfortable fit in her new home).

As the middle of the decade arrived, Mills and Wagner had proven their effectiveness in revitalising one line of IPC's juvenile papers, and were now moved on to work the same magic on boys' comics, starting with new title *Battle*. Without their contributions the paper became a little less focused and – oh dear – its heroines were less likely to be beaten up by evil crooks, nasty guardians, or a peer group they desperately wanted to become part of. Nevertheless, the comic was still a pretty strong proposition, one that was bolstered by its merger with the ace *Misty* in 1980.

By now, young gymnast Bella had become the cover star, who was being coaxed into physical perfection by the mysterious Mrs Carne who – hooray! – 'appeared to have a sinister power over her.' The 'Strange Story' was still going great guns ('by popular demand', apparently) but it was now presided over by Misty herself – well, they had to find her something to do, didn't they?

With the industry fast heading into a far more serious depression than the one that had gripped it in the early Seventies, *Tammy* took a formidable scalp in 1981 by swallowing up sister title *Jinty*, which brought with it the sci-fi madness of 'The Human Zoo'. Three years later it then made its last takeover by absorbing the underachieving *Princess* mk II (IPC Magazines Ltd, 1983-4) in a union described as 'the happy get-together'. Although this may have presented 'the best of two papers in one', you couldn't escape the fact that, whether it was due to the constant mergers, or just the loss of its leading lights, *Tammy* wasn't really the feisty property it used to be.

Thus on 23 June, it was perhaps a little bit disingenuous to describe itself as 'the most dazzling paper for girls!', particularly as the following week it was eaten up by the non-threatening, sugary sweet *Girl* mk II.

Target
(Polystyle Publications Ltd, 1978, every Friday)

Taking its name from the absurdly violent BBC police series starring Patrick Mower which had been designed to take the wind out of *The Sweeney*'s sails, *Target* was patently hoping it would lure in that shows' huge audience of boys who would be watching it 'unofficially' every week after Mum declared lights out.

The first issue trumpeted itself as 'your *new* TV action paper!', and promised 'exclusive action-packed picture stories!' However, countering these exciting exclamations was the sad truth that the publication was printed on the most appallingly thin paper ever and – at least at the start – most of the artwork was bloody awful.

Thus, an effort to lay on a classic *Look-In*-style montage of faces on the front cover just couldn't compete, with only three colours to play with, and the scratchiest, most rushed-looking depictions of *Hazell*, *Kojak*, *Charlie's Angels* and *Cannon* ever committed to paper. Uninspiring stuff.

It was, however, representative of the comic's contents, which kicked off with a lurid 'Target' strip, apparently drawn on an Etch-a-Sketch. Here Detective Superintendent Hackett got busy thwarting an attempt to snatch a priceless gold relic, and dished out reliably regular fisticuffs action. Far better by comparison was the adaptation of Thames Television's *Hazell*, with some half-decent artwork and a surprisingly adult story involving infidelity, murder...and a bloke who looked like Ernest Borgnine.

'Kojak' was also passable, although the efforts to lay in his trademark catchphrases didn't always ring true ('I had the shakes myself. Since when did police work come without 'em, koochy koo...?'), while 'Cannon' took 'TV's heavyweight supertec' onto an oil rig to investigate a case of sabotage. But then, oh dear, 'Charlie's Angels'. It was here the artwork really fell apart. Panicked, scrawly and often unrecognisable, never had Cheryl Ladd and friends looked so rough.

After this shoddy effort, the back page carried an exclusive interview with *Hazell* star Nicholas Ball, in which he did his best to insist that, yes, Terry Venables did actually co-write the TV episodes – 'We met after I got the part,' he said, 'and I found him a very bright lad.'

Over the next eighteen issues, the line-up of stories remained exactly the same, possibly indicating Polystyle were unwilling to pay out for the rights to any other TV properties. Whatever, it did mean the 'next issue' blurbs quickly grew repetitive and desperately had to big-up the one-page text features the paper had secured for some variation. Thankfully, though, the artwork improved (although 'Charlie's Angels' always remained the weakest link), but covers continued to be a major disappointment; a yellow-skinned Fonz from *Happy Days* giving it all thumbs-up on the front of issue six being a case in point.

As low rent as low rent can get, it was little surprise that, despite the occasional reference to drug-dealing, a hell of a lot of gunplay and some good old-fashioned coshing – a mere four months after its launch, the shutters came down with an 'exciting news inside' flash on the front cover of issue nineteen. *Target* was to team up with **TV Comic** where Kojak and Charlie's Angels would be rubbing shoulders with the Pink Panther, Bugs Bunny, Popeye and, of course, Mighty Moth.

Thunder
(IPC Magazines Ltd, 1970-1971, every Monday)

'Read it...and you'll be *Thunder*-struck!' claimed this short-lived comic which was over and done with in just twenty-two weeks.

Seemingly the line-up, which it billed as a 'feast of thrills and fun!', just wasn't destined to catch on, but in all fairness this was a pretty credible stab at a boys' all-rounder, mixing humour with some above-average action strips.

The first issue arrived with a pretty unprepossessing cover, in the main promoting the free gift of an 'Amazing Jumping Kangaroo'. A cardboard constructed novelty – rather than an actual marsupial – emblazoned with the likeness of 'Ozzie' (whose adventures we could read all about in 'Fury's Family' inside), we were reliably advised 'He jumps… He leaps… He bounds into the air!'

Inside, things got off to a stirring start with 'The Terrible Trail to Tolmec', a quest story following the progress of Tom Taylor as he made his way to the forbidden city of gold where he believed he'd locate his errant father. Accompanying him was the excitingly named Doctor Wolfgang Stranger, who considered himself the greatest explorer in the world, and his oversized beardo manservant, Troll, who was secretly trying to scupper their progress.

'Black Max' was a First World War yarn, about German flying ace Baron Maximilien Von Korr. Rather than relying on old-fashioned gunplay, he preferred to dispatch British planes by use of a giant bat, which he'd trained to rip enemy aircraft apart.

Rather fantastically, 'Cliff Hanger' happened to be about a chap called – yes! – Captain Cliff Hanger, a go-getting, tight-trousered globe-trotter who shared moments of 'breathless peril' with his Gurkha pal Kukri (whose function was to speak in short-hand English, pointing out the various breathless perils that were befalling them). Meanwhile, 'Fury's Family' was a closely crosshatched story of a boy who took his animal friends and ran away from an unkind circus owner. Shadowy and cruel, the strip didn't really deliver on the promise of gaiety which had been intimated by that grinning Ozzie on the front.

Much more light-hearted was 'Dusty Binns'. No, not the travails of Ted Rogers, The Gentle Secs and a remote-controlled trashcan, instead it featured a rag-and-bone man's son and his love for football. Even more whimsical was 'Phil the Fluter', a colour strip about a boy who discovered an old tin whistle at the bottom of a well which, when blown, caused time to stand still – as depicted by the world around him turning black and white. Naturally, as anyone would, over the weeks Phil used this terrible power to stop footballs smashing into windows, and to teach a particularly obnoxious man a lesson on the Test Your Strength machine at the fairground.

Still keeping it light were 'The Jet-Skaters', a trio of lads unimaginatively known as 'The Gang' who'd been given jet-powered footwear which enabled them to fly through the air. Out and out funnies came courtesy of 'The Spooks of St Lukes' (which, to continue the *3-2-1* theme hinted at above, was later reprinted in the show's 1985 spin-off annual – for some reason) and 'Sam'. The latter was a reprint of 'Biff' from *Wham!* (Odhams Press, 1964-8), renamed for no obvious reason and tasked with not only providing back page laffs, but also helming the letters page.

The title's best strips, however, were a trio of imaginative and quirky adventure stories. In ascending order of greatness, first up was 'Gauntlet of Fate'. This one plied the old 'possessed item of clothing' shtick, as a strange glove which had once belonged to a medieval law-maker brought a solid helping of just deserts to whomever put it on.

Then came 'Steel Commando'. By a strange twist of fate, the laziest soldier in the British Army, Ernie 'Excused Boots' Bates, was the only man who could command the Mark I Indestructible Robot, created by the boffins back at base. Forming a strong bond with 'Ironsides' (as he called him), the relationship proved a double-edged sword. Sure, he had his metallic mate on standby to bale him out of trouble, but as a result of their relationship, he'd be billeted to inhospitable locations whenever the tin-pot trooper was sent on another mission.

But, better than either of these efforts was 'Adam Eterno'. This told of an alchemist's hapless assistant who took a swig from the elixir his master was creating. As a result, he was doomed to live forever (the clue was in his name after all) wandering through the ages battling evil. Forever a fish-out-of water, the long-haired layabout wanted just one thing – to kill himself. Learning that a weapon of pure gold was the only item capable of carrying out the job, he regularly found himself within a gnat's wing of various killing machines wrought from the precious metal, but whilst triumphantly declaring: 'At last! My suffering will soon be over…!' something would happen to put the implement from his reach. 'Have pity old one!' he'd yelp at the sky in the throes of torment as, yet again, he failed to escape the scientist's curse.

With only two dozen issues to play with, it's hardly surprising *Thunder*'s format didn't really vary over its run. From issue four, the comic began presenting 'Famous Firsts' on the front cover, a thinly disguised reason to splash various items of butch military hardware across the page ('The standard British Army tank of today – the Chieftain – bears little resemblance to the first tanks of 1916' etc.), but otherwise things continued as established in that premier number.

And then, five months later the end arrived, as boys were doubtlessly 'thunder-struck' to learn the publication was merging with *Lion* – becoming its next acquisition after snacking on *Eagle* mk I in 1969. The title gave it a good new home, unusually keeping its name on the front cover right up until it was forced into a merger with *Valiant* in 1974. 'Fury's Family', 'Phil the Fluter', 'The Jet-Skaters', 'Steel Commando' and 'Adam Eterno' all made the jump across to their new home.

All in all, it was a respectable legacy for a comic that came and went as quickly as the force of nature it was named after.

Tiger
(Amalgamated Press/Fleetway Publications/IPC Magazines Ltd, 1954-1985, every Tuesday)

A giant in the world of boys' papers, Amalgamated Press' follow-up to *Lion* proved to be an even more durable publication, running for thirty-one years. Not only that – it also bequeathed to the world one of British comics' best-loved heroes…who we'll get to in a moment.

When *Tiger* first hit news-stands in September 1954, it marked itself out from its big brother by appearing in a larger format (somewhere between 'regular' and the tabloid size of *Eagle mk I*) and featuring a healthy proportion of sport-based stories – a genre *Lion* barely touched. In fact, so keen on the PE stuff was the publication, it billed itself as 'The Sport and Adventure Picture Story Weekly'. The first issue came with a free 'space gun novelty' and led in fine style with 'Roy of the Rovers'.

Yep, here was where it all began for soccer legend Roy Race, who stepped out onto the pitch in a tale penned by 'Captain Condor' creator Frank Pepper. As the local cup-tie threatened to end in a goalless draw, Roy thundered up the pitch, wrong-footed the defence and scorched one past the keeper. Unknown to him, Alf Leeds – a talent scout for Melchester Rovers – had been watching the whole thing and offered Roy and his pal Blackie Gray a try-out in the reserves. And from here, a foot-balling career that would span thirty-eight years (longer than *Tiger*'s run, in fact) began. One point of interest: although many suspected that, in the grand tradition of comics, Melchester was a thinly disguised version of Manchester United, in fact Pepper and the comic's first editor, Derek Birnage, based the fictional side on the Arsenal team of the Fifties.

Also debuting here was Len Dyson in 'The Speedster from Bleakmoor', Hurricane Hardy in 'Young Hurricane', and Will Strongbow and Dodger Caine in 'The Lad with a Wheeze up his Sleeve', however none of these would come anywhere near Roy in terms of popularity. Like *Lion* in the early days, *Tiger* also sported its fair share of text stories. Here they were titled 'The Mascot of Bad Luck', 'Tales of Whitestoke School' and 'Captives in the Fort of Doom'.

Just four months after launch the comic jumped on the merger band-wagon and made the first of six takeovers. The story paper *Champion* (Amalgamated Press, 1922-55) was first for the chop, but the token share of the action the paper was dealt probably disappointed readers who hoped their doughty weekly would find some sort of continuation in its new home. Aside from having no real appreciable impact upon its host, its incorporated logo was almost invisible to the naked eye on the cover immediately following merger.

Far more exciting was Roy and Blackie's first team debut for Melchester Rovers in August against Elbury Wanders. OK, it may have ended in a 3-3 draw, but good old Racey was responsible for two of those. The following year the squad began their climb up the first division, becoming league champions in 1958 and prompting Roy's promotion to captain. The boy done good.

In the last throes of the Fifties, the comic pounced again, this time devouring *Comet* (Allen/Amalgamated Press, 1946-59) – again, to little obvious effect, other than to thin out the company's unwieldy stock of juvenile titles now Fleetway had taken over, and to provide the paper with its own sub-Dan Dare sci-fi hero in the form of Jet-Ace Logan.

As the Sixties dawned the publication received a slight makeover following a similar sprucing up of *Lion* – the titular big cat now stalking the front cover from within a fetching blue box. Readers were also thrilled by the news combover king Bobby Charlton had taken over penning Roy's stories. However, despite the picture of him working away at his typewriter, in reality it was Birnage who was guiding the soccer star's fortunes. That mild controversy aside, things were improving for Racey. Not only did Melchester win the FA Cup over the 1960/1 season, but some half-decent characters were finally emerging to bolster the inside pages too.

Chief (no pun intended) among these was Seminole Indian wrestler Johnny Cougar: 'The Man With the Iron Grip!' who, in 1962, met up with wily grapple manager Ed Spiro. After proving his mettle by beating-up a cougar in the Florida Everglades, the hulking figure had retreated to his farm, only to discover the place had been flooded out. As if that wasn't galling enough, a bolt of lightning then razed his barn to the ground. Destitute and with no means of income, the big lad was coaxed into turning pro-wrestler by Spiro, who later sneakily confided in his pal Lou: 'Sure the Indian's raw! We'll build him up so high that when he falls, they'll hear the crash in Alaska!'

Around this time, trivia fans may also like to note a strip called 'Billy's Boots' was doing the rounds. Although this featured the exploits of a football-playing lad who was endowed with special footwear, the William in question was a young Master Jackson who donned a pair of 'super blitz boots' when it was time to strut his stuff on the pitch. Strictly played for laughs, it was a precursor of sorts to the famous strip of the same name that would originate in *Scorcher* before eventually finding its way over to *Tiger*. But more of that anon.

When the comic next did the merger-thing in 1965, it had changed appearance again. Reducing its page size to more traditional dimensions, all signs of the eponymous beast were now removed from the front as what would become the iconic yellow text on a red banner dominated proceedings. After two low-key team-ups, the union with *Hurricane* (Fleetway Publication, 1964-5) – another short-lived 'companion paper' to *Valiant* (cf: *Champion* (Fleetway Publications, 1966)) – was much more exciting, not in the least because the newcomer's logo actually got a fair share of the cover action. But then, no wonder, as it contributed some ace strips in the form of 'Skid Solo' (exciting stories of a daredevil racing driver) and 'Typhoon Tracy'. The latter was a super-strong soldier of fortune with an insanely chirpy demeanour who succeeded in shoving Roy off the cover for a couple of years. However, of the strips that did-n't make it across, few were surprised to see the back of 'Hurry of the Hammers' – which had been a rather shameless rebadged reprint of early 'Roy' strips.

Toward the end of the decade, the paper began rotating its featured cover stars; one week it was bog-standard Tarzan rip-off 'Saber: King of the Jungle', the next it would be wronged hard-nut Don Hunter in 'Hunter's Vengeance' and sometimes even – hooray! – 'Roy of the Rovers'. 'The Great Thespius!' also joined the paper during this era, a fantastic story about a vain former actor-cum-magician, who turned to a life of crime in the city of Chikofa. With the police forever lagging behind, in one episode the thespian was outraged when he saw a TV appeal for his capture – 'That televised news photo is the *worst* ever taken of me!' he roared, as he and his gang made a bee-line for the studio, where he conned his way onto camera. 'Yours to enjoy, enraptured ones!' he declared as his face beamed out from sets around the country. 'The most famed profile in theatrical history!'

As it had done ten years before, *Tiger* marked the end of the decade with another killing. This time it was fellow feline *Jag* that was sacrificed as 'two great papers join forces today!' Transferring over from the rela-tively plush over-sized publication were the colour soccer antics of 'Football Family Robison', battling Scotsman and Irishman in search of a punchline, 'MacTavish and O'Toole', bio-strip 'Custer' and own-brand Black Beauty: 'Black Patch: The Wonder Horse'.

The start of the Seventies brought more England caps for Roy Race and a slew of FA Cup wins, while the paper meddled with the zeitgeist by creating an absolutely-of-its-time character in the shape of 'Splash Gorton'. This super-thin longhaired swimmer sported a huge handlebar moustache and a nose for trouble. Somewhere between Jason King and

Mark Spitz, he was a one-man flower power invasion force into the square-jawed world of boys' comics, liable to spout groovy dialogue such as: 'I don't dig this action'. Even his 'next issue' boxes were loved-up: 'Join our hippy-go-lucky beatnik in a new way-out story next Monday!' Patently not built to last, Splash would later sensibly opt to play second fiddle in Johnny Cougar's strip when his own vehicle ground to a halt.

Meanwhile, as Roy began to wear his hair a little longer, he found himself promoted to player-manager at Melchester, 'Martin's Marvellous Mini' brought us two colour pages of fun in that diminutive car; Gordon Banks filed a weekly footy column; 'The Tigers' brought us tales of a youth club run by Chunky Clark which consisted of just him and his mates Biff and Smithy; Johnny Cougar bounced back after a strange professor carried out some mysterious experiments on him; and Skid Solo vied for glory in the World Motor-Racing Championship. The comic was in good shape as it made its penultimate takeover in October 1974.

The latest victim was sports-themed title *Scorcher*, which brought along a fantastic roster of characters. With the outrageously mulleted Hebridean hard-nut Hot Shot Hamish, down-at-heel but plucky youngster Nipper, and Billy Dane of 'Billy's Boots' fame trooping onto the pitch, the comic was endowed with a trio of undisputed footballing legends to supplement Roy's antics. From cover to cover, *Tiger* was now featuring one of the strongest line-ups around. The fact that Trevor Brooking was also on call with his opinions on the beautiful game (Banks had been sent for an early bath) was the icing on the cake.

In fact, *Tiger* was in such good shape that it even survived the loss of its star player, as Racey was lured away in 1976 for his own comic, **Roy of the Rovers** (although he did continue on at his old haunt for a few months during the crossover period) following his marriage to childhood sweetheart Penny. Where once this transfer would have seen the paper's squad fatally weakened, it now had a host of characters who were more than capable of filling the Roy-shaped gap. Billy Dane, for one, was ready to grab a bigger share of the action, launching his 'Sports School' wherein he'd award a fiver to any reader who sent in a valuable piece of advice. As if that wasn't enough for the boy wonder, within his own strip he shamelessly expanded his portfolio by conveniently discovering another pair of discarded 'Dead-Shot' Keen footwear – this time a couple of cricket boots.

Into the Eighties, the new era was marked by – yep – another merger. Like *Scorcher* before it, **Speed** was a themed paper that just hadn't caught on. In this instance the USP was all things that travelled fast, which – in truth – had resulted in it turning out stuff not dissimilar to *Tiger*'s fare. Joining the show was motorcycle story 'Topps on Two Wheels' and the fantastically fatalistic 'Death Wish' – the tale of handsome sportsman Blake Edwards who was hideously disfigured in an aeroplane crash and had taken to wearing a leather mask to cover his features. With little care for his own life, he threw himself into increasingly dangerous sporting activities, somehow emerging unscathed at every turn.

With the new crew in place, the title ventured on into the Eighties, stopping off in 1981 to put out a special Royal wedding issue. Of the many tributes paid to Charles and Di that year, few could have been quite so bizarre as Blake Edwards taking time out from competing in a competition to raise a glass to the happy couple: 'Your Royal highness, to you and your bride, the warmest greetings from everyone in this round-the-world race!' Although just three panels earlier in the story, the sportsman had been nobbling rival nags in a steeplechase with the fearsome sight of his face, this was still a heartfelt moment and one that surely took pride of place in the couple's wedding album.

By the early Eighties, the publication was benefiting from a pretty decent standard of printing which, while not quite photogravure, was certainly a cut above. But all that was to change as, much like *Eagle* **mk II**, the title had to accept a downgrade in quality.

Out went the full colour, and in came bog-roll paper and a limited palette of inks, while the paper width suddenly sprouted a couple of centimetres. But, while the economising had bought its IPC stablemate a bit of extra time, it didn't help *Tiger* out of its tight corner. With sales falling, February 1985 brought yet another new look – and the comic's worst logo ever. Alongside that came the dumbest story in the paper's history, 'Star Rider', which featured a squid-like one-eyed alien from the planet Cyton with a penchant for…BMX-ing. Using a shape-changing machine to transform into a human boy, he was advised by his father: 'Remember, at least once on every three of the blue planet's days, you must recharge your system in order to remain in the shape of the aliens'.

To compound the ignominy, a whole host of reprints were creeping in, with painfully old 'Johnny Cougar' and 'Nipper' strips stinking the place out. The end was patently nigh.

In the 30 March edition – less than two months after the new look – editor Paul Gettens penned a letter to his readers, in which he broke the news *Tiger* was merging with 'that famous publication' *Eagle*. '*Tiger* has been published for thirty and a half years,' he continued, 'and I'd like to thank everybody who has contributed to it and bought it during that time. Now go out and order the new *Eagle and Tiger* – it promises to be the best paper ever!'

While 'Billy's Boots', 'Death Wish', 'Golden Boy' and 'Star Rider' (how did that one slip through?) were all retained, 'Hot Shot Hamish' and 'Johnny Cougar' dived into the pages of *Roy of the Rovers*. Other strips weren't so lucky – least of all 'Rogue Driver' which was left to hastily kill off its title character who, after wilfully causing a mass pile-up during a Formula One race, inadvertently careered off the road to his death. Comics could be so cruel.

The Topper
(DC Thomson, 1953-1990, every Friday)

See: *The Beezer.*

Well, maybe not, but it seems *The Topper*'s fate is to be forever confused with its companion paper by misremembering readers. So, let's get it straight here: *The Topper* came first, and it was the one which featured 'Mickey the Monkey' and 'Beryl the Peril'.

Ever one for tradition, DC Thomson pressed a 'Big Crack Bang' (also known as a paper 'Whizz Bang!') inside that first tabloid-sized edition, dated 7 February 1953. However, its arguable that little enticement was required to get potential readers buying, as the front cover feature – the aforementioned simian Mickey – was handsome stuff. Drawn by comics legend Dudley D Watkins, the strip was almost entirely devoid of dialogue, and featured the dungaree-clad chimp exacting revenge on a guardsman who'd run his ornamental spear through the ape's football.

If that wasn't appealing enough, there was also Watkins' very own Oor Wullie standing alongside the comic's title, brandishing what we can only presume was the titular top hat in question. Curiously, however, he didn't actually appear inside the issue. What did was a strong mix of humour ('Uncle Dan: The Menagerie man'), features ('Easter Customs Around the World') and straighter, more illustrative pieces ('The Story of Treasure Island'). A fine mixture, designed to appeal to boys and girls, some have levelled the accusation at the publication that it lacked in terms of distinctive characters.

On paper, this argument certainly has some weight. Chief suspect was Beryl the Peril, drawn by Davy Law just two years after he'd first delineated Dennis the Menace for *The Beano*, the character was very much in the mold of the spiky-haired troublemaker (in fact her dad looked somewhat like Dennis' equally slipper-happy old man in early issues) although she was arguably more a victim of circumstance – accidentally flinging a tub of cake mix over her auntie in one issue – than the chief instigator of trouble. However, so popular did she eventually become that in 1986 she took over as *The Topper*'s cover star.

By definition more derivative was the decision for the paper to reprint a couple of US comic-strips – 'Fritzi Ritz: She'll Keep You In Fits' and the spin-off strip that came to eclipse it in America, 'Nancy'. While the latter could just about cut it in the world of British comics (the harmless adventures of a little girl), the former – being the tales of a New York 'flapper' – seemed decidedly odd alongside the likes of 'Captain Bungle: He Lives in the Jungle'. That, plus it was just plain weird to see artists being credited for their work in the pages of a DC Thomson comic (Ernie Bushmiller's name attached to both). And yet, 'Nancy' stuck with the paper through to the Seventies.

Another curious aspect was the comic's ever-changing logo which was constantly tweaked throughout the publication's life, meaning there was never really a distinctive *Topper* masthead. Somewhere along the way, Oor Wullie was also sacked from the job of mascot, even though he'd varied his shtick to include pulling a rabbit out of the hat, juggling with that head gear or, memorably, shamefully donning a dunce's cone and facing the corner.

With the likes of Beryl, Mickey, the sheep-bothering Foxy and special agent Nick Kelly drawing in the readers (although, less so 'The Whiskery Dicks'), *The Topper* flourished, prompting DC Thomson to create another comic in the same vein, *The Beezer*, in 1956.

Still going strong throughout the Sixties and into the Seventies, the publication absorbed fellow tabloid paper, *Buzz*, in 1975, benefiting immeasurably by incorporating the finest from that fallen title into its own line-up. Then, two years later it gobbled up *Sparky*, running its new acquisition as a pull-out supplement inside.

In 1980, there was a bigger change as the comic switched to the more familiar A4 size of its contemporaries. Poor old Mickey had long since been booted off the front by the likes of Nick Kelly and 'Danny's Tranny' (about a boy and his radio, lest there by any confusion). Now it was generic practical joke funster Tricky Dicky doing the honours. Inside, Kelly (who hosted the letters page, 'Kelly's Corner'), Foxy, Mickey and Beryl were still doing the necessary alongside other stories they'd picked up along the way: 'Ali's Baba' – a barely literate baby and his genie; 'Al Change' – a neglected child who dressed up as members of his own family while his dad was away; and 'Splodge: The Last of the Goblins', to name but three. But the new decade was biting hard.

In an effort to appear more modern, *The Topper* rebranded itself *Topper 89* as the Nineties approached. But despite a revamp for pretty much all of its characters, drafting in 'Pup Parade' from *The Beano* and even running a parody of *EastEnders* (the inevitably named 'Vest Enders'), the end was nigh. *Topper 90* followed, but sadly there was to be no '*91* as in September the comic was forced to join up with *The Beezer* to create *Beezer and Topper* (DC Thomson, 1990-3, 'Two comics in one!'). Alas, Mickey was nowhere to be seen. Nevertheless, this conglomerated publication did at least represent one final fun twist of the knife for all of those who could never tell the two publications apart anyway.

Tops
(DC Thomson, 1981-1984, every Thursday)

For nearly ten years, **Look-In** had ruled the roast when it came to juvenile TV-related publications. Granted *TV Comic* had been around for longer, but, bolstered by its association with listings magazine *TV Times*, the brightly coloured bible for ITV kids was a hugely popular proposition, which had easily seen off the likes of the low-rent *Target* thanks to its glossy production values and seemingly limitless access to the *Magpie* team.

But all that was set to change when DC Thomson entered the fray with *Tops* ('You'll like it – not a lot, but you'll like it!' came the endorsement from a big-head-little body caricature of Paul Daniels on the cover of issue one). A new early-teen-centric title that didn't owe allegiance to one particular channel (unlike the ITV-bound *Look-In*), here you could see – at last! – Little and Large rubbing shoulders with Russ Abbott.

'*Tops* is for young people, boys and girls, who want a magazine full of

TV, pop, adventure, fun,' ran the hyperbole. '*Tops* has got 'em all with a lot more besides!' That premier number kicked off in fine – and what we'd come to recognise as characteristic – style with a big picture of Adam Ant adorning the front. Inside, his life story was drawn in comic-strip form, and would be the first step along the road to the comic's full-blown obsession with the insect-themed pop star. Alongside that, Little and Large indulged in some fluffy comic-strip action; *Tiswas* favourite Sally James introduced her 'Almost Legendary Pop Interviews'; Todd Carty chatted about his schooldays; Paul Daniels hosted a 'Puzzle Page'; 'Spit's Bit' boasted a half-page funny featuring the salivating dog plus chums Charlie the Monkey and Cof the Cat; and Shakin' Stevens did the pin-up thing as required.

So far, so *Look-In*, however there were other innovations that were very much *Tops*' own. First up was the photo-strip 'The Witch of Westwood High', a feature that didn't derive from any ongoing TV series. Traditional comic-strips 'The Horse that Came from the Sea' and 'Kids' Army' were similarly original, although it has to be said in this instance both looked suspiciously like something from the DC Thomson back catalogue. Far more interesting was a strip adaptation of *The Professionals* ('It's Bodie – he's taken some beating'), which was notable for the post-watershed nature of its source – something *Look-In* would have no truck with.

Tops would go on to prove it had no such qualms in bringing juvenile-versions of other adult fare to its readers as the sketch-show *Not the Nine O'Clock news* turned into 'NOT The Pamela Stephenson Page', while *Minder* and *Hart to Hart* both got comic-strip outings.

But, despite the promise of such forbidden fruits, it soon became clear that what the readers really wanted was more Adam Ant. Thus, the dandy highwayman secured regular coverage via a series of ludicrous (but finely wrought) comic-strip tales, 'The Fantastic Adventures of Adam Ant', which cast him in the unlikely role of a kind of crime fighter who reappeared through the ages in different guises (an Edwardian sea captain in one, a red Indian in another and, apparently, as Lawrence of Arabia – if the cover of issue twenty-eight is anything to go by). So why was all this happening? Simply because a chap in a voluminous hood had decreed: 'You live now, Adam Ant, as you have lived many times throughout history, fighting evil wherever you may find it!'

Tops – © DC Thomson & Co., Ltd

Keen to play up the comic's telly preoccupation, along the way it was given a rebranding of 'will this do?' proportions, as 'TV' was slapped over 'Tops' at a jaunty angle on the cover to form *TV Tops*, and the paper continued to bring us more thrills, such as a *Hi-De-Hi!* strip ('Meet your Maplin's mates inside!'), 'Kartoon Kapers with the Krankies' ('When Wee Jimmy's the caddy, he's a hungry laddie!') and a *Buck Rogers in the 25th Century* adaptation ('Bi-di, bi-di, bi-di!'). All that, plus 'Your Page' where readers sent in their scribblings of – inevitably enough – Adam Ant, and even drew their own comic-strips; Fiona Gibson of Irvine introducing us to cartoon dog 'Walter', for one.

Alas, something wasn't working and despite a nervous reversion back to plain old *Tops*, the market just wasn't big enough to support two glossy weeklies banging on about *Metal Mickey*. When boys around the country woke up one morning to discover the newsagent had delivered them a copy of *Suzy* (DC Thomson, 1982-7) instead of *Tops*, they could only assume a huge mistake had been made. But in fact, 'Britain's Best TV Comic' had been folded into the 'super photo stories' and 'fun pics' of the girly publication.

Tornado
(IPC Magazines Ltd, 1979, every Monday)

For whatever reason, *Starlord* hadn't been deemed a success, however just five months after its passing, IPC brought us another *2000 AD* variant in the form of *Tornado*.

Destined to be as short-lived as that doomed sci-fi comic, there was the sense here that the company was very much going back to basics. Whereas *Starlord* had been printed on nice paper and sported pages of full-colour art, this new venture reverted to the good old-fashioned bog-roll quality stuff we were all familiar with.

More lo-fi than sci-fi, *Tornado* was the comic of choice for boys who wanted some of that IPC brand of adventure, but didn't go any great shakes on spaceships, cyborgs and stasers. Still seemingly obsessed with the idea of 'character' editors, the company bestowed the comic with a real cracker, who came with a personal endorsement from none other than Tharg himself. 'Over the long months I have been grooming and training an editor,' revealed The Mighty One. 'His mind capacity is fifty times that of a normal human; his physical strength is limitless. He has all the amazing powers of mind and body that he needs to edit a comic of *many* worlds.' And then: 'Earthlets, I present "Big E" and his comic – *Tornado*!' With the opening ceremony over, readers could cast their eyes on the new man, who, rather excitingly, appeared in photographic form. A fairly unimpressive ordinary bloke, sporting some kind of corset with 'E' emblazoned across it, a set of enormous gloves and boots, a cape and a pair of equally large pants over his body suit, Big E was – sadly – a bit stupid-looking.

The character was embodied by comic artist Dave Gibbons who would go on to enormous future success by illustrating the late Eighties graphic novel *Watchman*. It's probably a fair bet his time wielding the 'E' doesn't feature too prominently on his CV nowadays.

The first issue came with a free 'turbo-flyer' and advised us that 'five ace stories start today!' 'Victor Drago and the Terror of Troll Island' was moody fodder to kick things off. The titular 'tec inhabited a pleasingly hardboiled, dimly lit London of 1929 and proved himself as quick with his wits as he was with his fists. It's been rumoured that 'Drago' was originally intended to be a new adventure for Sexton Blake (the turn of the century sleuth and 'prince of the penny dreadfuls') but, for some reason, this idea was dropped shortly before publication. It didn't stop his car sporting the number plate 'SB192', though.

Next out of the bag was arguably the paper's strongest story, 'The Mind of Wolfie Smith'. Potential for reader identification here was strong, Wolfie being a gifted child whose parents didn't appreciate him. In fact, upon the first indication of his burgeoning mental powers his dad admonished him with a slap and a cry of 'crazy little beggar!' As his school began to realise the boy was nursing some prestigious skills (photographic memory, telekinesis – the usual) Wolfie grew fearful they'd bung him in an institution and went on the run.

'Angry Planet' (disgruntled Earth colonists on Mars, being shafted by The Man) and 'Triple T' ('Tornado's True Tales') couldn't really cut it by comparison. However, 'Wagner's Walk' – the story of three German soldiers escaping slavery at the hands of the Russians by trying to trek two-and-a-half thousand miles to India – felt suitably epic, and a nice change from traditional war stories.

Meanwhile, the back page brought us a pleasingly stupid superhero strip in the form of 'Captain Klep' who was 'faster than Anadin...more powerful than a 13-amp socket...able to jump long queues with a single bound'. His adventures would consistently amuse, and owe more than a little to the out-and-out parodic stuff you'd find in a copy of the US *Mad* magazine.

Sporting an impressive array of mouthy front cover strap lines ('We're ace, we're new, we're magic' said issue two, despite still having Tharg inside to hold Big E's hand) the comic was quick to add even more stories to the mix over the coming weeks. Most notable was the arrival of 'Black Hawk', the story of a Nubian ex-slave who befriends a bird of prey and is made a Roman officer. So popular did he become, he quickly muscled the lacklustre 'Angry Planet' from the centre pages.

Another, less impressive innovation, saw Big E himself break out into action as, in issue nine, he brought us a dopey photo strip wherein he physically assaulted a spy from a rival company who was trying to steal *Tornado*'s secrets. When his enemy attempted to lamp him with a handy iron bar, the superhero simply advised him: 'All editors have tough skins, but mine is super tough – and this fist is just as hard!'

Would that all problems could be laid out by a bunch of fives, but, after just twenty-two issues (the same total notched up by *Starlord*), Big E threw in the towel, and *Tornado* was consumed by *2000 AD*. Although Wolfie Smith, Black Hawk and Captain Klep continued for a time under

Tharg's guidance, none of them managed to secure the sort of foothold Johnny Alpha and Ro-Busters had enjoyed when they were transplanted from their own comic.

And for Dave Gibbons, it was time to put away those big pants for good.

Toxic!
(Apocalypse Ltd, 1991, every Thursday)

'I come to pollute your mind!' confessed notional editor Doc Tox inside the first issue of *Toxic!* 'I bring you stories to fry your brain – artwork to explode your eyeballs... Best read on an empty stomach – preferably someone else's'.

1991 saw the fall of *Crisis* and *Revolver* leaving comic creators in something of a quandary. Despite both titles garnering positive press, there just wasn't a large enough audience for this sort of 'mature' content.

And yet, with the juvenile end of the market fast imploding, UK publishers couldn't escape the nagging feeling that somewhere out there was an older reader who was ready to put aside *2000 AD* in favour of something a little more challenging. Certainly in the US it seemed as though the comic had well and truly 'grown up' with prestigious titles pouring out featuring sex and violence, stories of mind-bending complexity, chin-scratching Proper Artwork and numerous quotes from Aleister Crowley. When Batman checked himself in for a bit of word associative therapy in 1989's *Arkham Asylum: A Serious House on a Serious Earth* graphic novel, the resultant collage of fully painted pages and Lewis Carroll citations shifted nigh-on half-a-million copies, tantalising creators with the notion that somewhere out there lay a big, big audience. The fact that it had been created by a British duo (Grant Morrison and Dave McKean) proved the jig surely wasn't over just yet here at home.

So, how best to proceed? Pat Mills – who'd launched more than a few titles in his time – thought he knew; the trick was to go down-market. Forget about highfaluting notions such as social commentary and political point-scoring, what young adults really wanted was bad taste and gore.

Thus emerged *Toxic!* Riffing off the press reports that claimed the artform was growing up, it billed itself as: 'The comic throws up!' Sporting a lurid green masthead, its debut issue led with Mills' and Kevin O'Neill's ultra-violent bondage gear-wearing anti-hero Marshal Law. Here he was blowing a hole in some sort of dinosaur-cum-human hybrid, while pithily declaring: 'Consider yourself...*extinct!*'

The fruits of Mills' efforts to maintain ownership over the characters he created, Marshal Law had first appeared in 1987 in a US series published by Marvel US's mature imprint, Epic. Since then, he'd been reprinted in the short-lived Brit UK title *Strip* (Marvel Comics Ltd, 1990) before stepping out for a new run here. Judge Dredd with even more zips, the lawman patrolled a demented future world, bringing thinly veiled parodies of US superheroes to justice. Superbly and perversely rendered by O'Neill (the only artist, so legend has it, to be banned outright by America's Comics Code Authority), the whole thing was stacked with action and pithy one-liners ('Killing is my business – business is good'), but you couldn't escape the feeling it actually functioned best as a means for Mills to work through his hatred for the US comics industry.

Following on from the barbed wire and brutality was another story from the same writer, 'Accident Man'. Here we were introduced to a leotard-clad long-limbed assassin whose SP was to make his hits look like death by misadventure. With a habit of combing back his hair as he watched his latest victim dangle, in truth this was charmless stuff, aching to appeal cool (our man venturing into a nightclub to pick a fight with a pair of skinheads he accuses of being 'dickless') and depicting death in almost pornographic detail ('I thrust a single knuckle into each pit, disabling both his arms'). 'I don't see him as a person,' said the killer leaving behind another fresh corpse. 'I see him as a Bimota road-legal racing bike'.

A subsequent plot line involving lesbian eco-warriors and illegal nuclear processing attempted to smuggle in an undercurrent of worthiness, but coupled with fast cars and big-breasted female protagonists, the average reader was left more inclined to fumble with his flies than a Green Party pamphlet.

Next came 'Muto Maniac in Space Cannibals', yet another Mills-penned effort, given some distinction by the handsomely boxy art of Mike McMahon. An action-packed sci-fi tale set in – what else? – a dystopian future, it was all big guns and rebellion ('You're the only man I've met who's had a penis transplant to his head'), and billed as 'Space Jonah with an attitude', presumably in an allusion to 'Jonah' in *The Beano* (one of Mills' all time favourite strips).

The final story was a one-off of little consequence – or plot – entitled 'Once Upon a Time in the West', but was notable for being the only thing in the comic that originated from a different writer – it was Alan Grant on script duties here.

Issue two brought a couple more continuing features. 'The Driver' was an appallingly drawn fusion of *Mad Max, The Cannonball Run* and *Duel* (sounds great – it wasn't), while 'Bogie Man' was much more like it. A witty and likeable tale about mental patient Francis F Clunie, who thought he was really a Bogart-esque private eye, it played out his hard-boiled fantasy against a backdrop of modern-day Glasgow, and didn't stint on the Scottish colloquialisms ('He wuznae wearin' any clothes'). Written by 'Judge Dredd' regulars Alan Grant and John Wagner, this was little short of a comedy classic – the scene where Clunie threw a Scottie dog off a suspension bridge leaving its elderly owner to cry out 'Scotty – come back! Come back!' as it disappeared under the currents below being something of a highlight.

The character had actually first been seen in a four issue mini-series published by small Glaswegian outfit Fat Man Press in 1989, and would go on to secure another kind of immortality when Robbie Coltrane played him in a one-off TV drama in 1992. Certainly he stood head and shoulders above anything else in *Toxic!*

As the weeks passed, various other menacing and unlikeable anti-heroes jumped on board. 'Makabre' was an avenging dark angel who patently had something to get off his chest about religion (which he did in one episode by gouging out a vicar's eyes); 'Sex Warrior' empowered women by representing them as estrogen-powered fighting machines, socking it to an evil aged community who were intent on sterilising the younger generation; and 'Coffin' was some kind of African demi-god who was in the habit of ripping people's limbs off.

When issue thirty-one rolled around seven months after that first edition, it looked like business as usual, with 'next issue' boxes at the end of the strips and even a cut-out coupon to present to your newsagent to reserve future editions. The only clue that (suitably enough considering the publishing company's name) Armageddon was beckoning lurked at the bottom of the letters page, 'Dump Your Load'. With one reader enquiring after the identity of regular correspondent Nic Holland, notional editor Doc Tox replied: 'We have no idea who he is…but one thing's for sure, if he writes in again, we're going to have to cancel the comic.' Cue a missive from Mr Holland. 'Right, that does it…' declared the Doc.

In the final analysis, *Toxic!* had proven that – in all honesty – there was actually nothing that could be done to continue the lineage of the British weekly into a new age. Lofty ideals may not have helped *Crisis*, but getting down and dirty was, if anything, an even less effective ploy. Perhaps it was better if everyone retreated back to the confines of *2000 AD* then, which, against all the odds, was holding on in there, gradually 'maturing' its content to keep its aging readers from straying. Oh yes, the first appearance of bare boobs in the 'Galaxy's Greatest Comic' wasn't all that far off now.

TV21
(City Magazines Ltd/IPC Magazines Ltd, 1965-1971, every Wednesday)

'Dateline: 23 January 2065: Stingray Lost!'

In 1964, *TV Comic* was robbed of the delights of its *Supercar* and *Fireball XL5* adaptations when the licenses were withdrawn by AP Films (Merchandising) Ltd, a new arm of Gerry Anderson's empire. The reason for the move became clear the following year when the company jumped into bed with the News of the World's City Magazine publishing and distribution arm to launch *TV Century 21* (as it was originally called).

Developed as a top quality TV magazine which was set to sport a high proportion of Anderson-related content, the publication had been devised by Keith Shackleton and Alan Fennell. The latter not only had a background in the industry (he'd previously edited the aforementioned *TV Comic*), he'd also scripted the odd TV episode of *Stingray* and *Fireball XL5* in his time (and would go on to contribute to *Thunderbirds* and *UFO*).

In an age when *Eagle* **mk I** was clearly past its prime, *TV Century 21* was the good-looking new kid on the block. Tabloid sized, running to twenty pages – of which a generous eight sported full colour photogravure printing – and brimming with fantastic art, the whole thing really stood out from the crowd.

With each issue dated a hundred years hence, *TV Century 21* fashioned itself as a futuristic newspaper ('No.1 universe edition' ran the small print on that premier issue), with banner headlines of the 'Stingray Lost!' or 'New Rocket Engine Tested!' variety hurtling urgently across its cover, alongside lovely great pictures of something exploding in the latest Anderson TV series.

Of the marionette master's oeuvre, those two properties swiped back from *TV Comic* inevitably appeared here, along with a *Stingray* adaptation. While *Supercar* had to make do with black and white and a rather comical-looking representation, the other two were gloriously colourful and beautifully drawn.

Propping them up was 'Burke's Law', the comic's take on the US detective series, which was slotted in between the sci-fi fare with the explanation: 'The *TV21* Time Machine returns to 1965 for thrills and spills with Captain Amos Burke', and a suitably light and breezy version of *My Favourite Martian*.

Quick to join in the fun was Lady Penelope, whose self-titled strip turned up in a matter of weeks, despite the fact *Thunderbirds* hadn't hit our screens yet. The embodiment of 'elegance, charm and deadly danger' (because, let's face it, without the latter this wouldn't be much of an action strip), she was presented as a well-to-do adventurer who not only bashed spies for fun, but answered the occasional reader's query too ('Could you please tell me the age of Sean Connery who plays James Bond in the films?'). Unaware they were watching history in the making, *TV Century 21*'s audience even got to witness the first ever meeting between the doe-eyed one and faithful butler Parker.

Even more exciting, though, was the arrival of the Daleks from *Doctor Who* (alas, the Time Lord himself was tied up with *TV Comic*) in a back page serial written by the TV series' script editor David Whitaker. It was here excited youths first encountered the bulbous-headed emperor of the metal meanies and thrilled as the pepper pots took to the skies on individual hover platforms.

When a *Thunderbirds* strip arrived a year after launch, things could hardly get more exciting, and by now *TV Century 21* was out *Eagle*-ing *Eagle* – with several of that comic's best artists making the short walk from the publisher's HQ at Huton House on 161-166 Fleet Street to AP Merchandising at no. 167.

At the start of 1968, the publication's name was changed to the less cumbersome *TV21*, and the paper size was taken down an inch or two. Then it proceeded to go nuts over the latest bit of supermarionation fancy, *Captain Scarlet*: a character who proceeded to nab the front cover and even succeeded in jamming his spectrum insignia into the comic's logo.

In September the title merged with the less sci-fi hued and all together more downmarket **TV Tornado** which brought with it a 'Tarzan' strip and an adaptation of the Roger Moore *Saint* series. This was the start of a rocky road for *TV21*; from hereon in the publication would get progressively worse in appearance.

By now, Fennell was out as editor and the paper was being padded out with an increasing number of stories that hadn't originated on the small screen. The following year it rallied itself by joining forces with – deep breath, now – *Gerry Anderson's Joe 90 Secret Agent* (City Magazines Ltd, 1969), a title that had quickly become unsustainable when it was realised the big-lipped kid in the National Health specs was hardly proving a hit on screen. Turning this union into a proper relaunch, *TV21 and Joe 90* wiped the slate clean by reverting to issue one, but seemed to have lost the faith from the off.

The line-up now ran thusly: 'Forward from the Back-Streets' (a generic footie story about a promising hopeful from Glasgow); 'Land of the Giants' (a pretty nicely drawn version of the Irwin Allen TV pot-boiler); 'Joe 90' (given just one and a half pages of black and white action); 'The Adventures of Tarzan' (a supposed tie-in with the Ron Ely series, but in fact just a US reprint); 'The Kid King' (a half page funny), 'Star Trek' (the paper's new big hope, which had arrived with young Master 90, and was afforded the colour centre spread), 'Meet the Saint' (the daft name given to its *Saint* spin-off); 'Thunderbirds' (also demoted to black and white); and 'I've Got a Sports-Mad Dad' (hmm). Covers were now devoted to full-page paintings depicting some exciting event that was taking place within ('The space spies strike! See "Star Trek" inside'), but, alas, excitement was draining away fast.

As a mark of how uncertain times were, the paper size shrunk again with issue twenty-six, while all references to Joe 90 were removed come issue thirty-seven. In fact, by 1970 there wasn't a shred of Anderson to be found within its pages. In July 1971, News International sold off City Magazines to IPC, who wasted little time in padding out *TV21* with nonsense such as 'The Tuffs of Terror Island' (the tale of three shipwrecked brothers), 'Clancy Clott: Magician's Mate' ('Magical mirth', we were advised) and…'Spider-Man'? Yep, the webslinger supplied two black and white pages reprinted from his US title courtesy of good old Marvel comics.

'Star Trek', however, continued – now the only telly-related strip in the whole, *ahem*, enterprise.

Three months after City Magazines had packed it all in, the inevitable happened and *TV21* was swallowed up by the relatively new and thrusting

Valiant, which was eager to provide a home for those irritating Tuffs and, of course, Captain Kirk and crew.

And it had all started out so well. But, in about half the time it had taken *Eagle* to go from terrific to truly terrible, *TV21* had achieved the same feat – and how.

TV Action
(Polystyle Publications Ltd, 1972-1973, weekly)

OK pedants – prepare to split those hairs now. Does *TV Action* really deserve a separate entry in this book? A direct continuation of *Countdown*, even to the point of maintaining that comic's issue numbering, *TV Action + Countdown* (as it was originally titled) represented editor Dennis Hooper's efforts to distance the paper from what was now seen as the under-performing genre of TV sci-fi, and to instead align it with the new trend in straight-ahead fisticuffs.

Nonetheless, this being a Polystyle publication, there was still an above-average quota of spaceships and laser guns evident, thanks to the company's continuing links with Gerry Anderson, and its unwillingness to give up on a certain Time Lord who was actually still proving popular onscreen.

Indeed 'Dr Who and the Daleks' was now the paper's cover feature, as Jon Pertwee's version of the character continued to enjoy a run of superior strip adventures. Alongside the dandy Time Lord, the new comic (which hit the stands dated 1 April 1972), was promising 'blistering adventure' with its adaptations of US series *Hawaii Five-O* and ATV's school-based espionage thriller *Tightrope*. 'Big laughs' came courtesy of 'Motormouse and Autocat' while 'old favourites' *UFO* and *The Persuaders* put in an appearance. Rather thrillingly, the publication also offered kids the chance to win a colour TV 'for your family' by designing a new monster for the Doctor to face.

Aside from the advertised features, the weekly continued *Countdown*'s trend in factual articles by looking 'Towards 2000' and discussing the Thames barrier project. A later entrant in this series became quite breathless at the thought of exciting innovations in telephony: 'Soon you won't have to use a rotating dial...for the new phone of the future now being given a full-scale trial by the Post Office, has push-buttons instead'. A dizzying concept, indeed.

Meanwhile, 'Tech Talk' lifted the lid on holography.

The long-running adaptation of *Thunderbirds* was by now nearing its end, with the penultimate episode – drawn by former 'Dan Dare' art assistant Don Harley – appearing in this first issue, meaning from number three onwards, *TV Action* was content to fling out International Rescue reprints culled from the pages of *TV21*. And before long, it became the case that anything sci-fi appearing in the comic – apart from the good Doctor and *UFO* – was simply stuff lifted from that now defunct title. Thus, when Captain Scarlet and Fireball XL5 later reported for duty, their exploits were all too familiar.

Nevertheless, *TV Action* wasn't totally without innovation, and in July it announced the winner of that coveted TV, as Ian Fairnington's elephantine 'Ugrakkk' saw off competition from the likes of David Dickson's 'The Klos' (a gun-touting turd in a pair of jeans, going by the illustration), Alan Moore's 'Hyberdon' (a slothful-looking chap in a smock) and Carol Griffith's 'Waspid' (unsurprisingly, an overgrown wasp) to win the role of the new 'Doctor Who' baddy. A fine achievement, the exercise had even involved a bad-tempered Pertwee who acted as one of the judges ('"Good Heavens. How on Earth are we going to get through this lot?" exploded the tall elegant figure when confronted with the thousands of entries for our competition').

As the weeks rolled by, a *Mission: Impossible* strip joined the line-up, while all references to *Countdown* were finally jettisoned in January 1973. When sitcom *Dad's Army*, cartoon dog *Droopy*, hard-boiled detective *Cannon* and Wild West desperados *Alias Smith and Jones* also signed on, the fantastical element was pretty much shown the door. Meanwhile, the comic took to promoting just one 'big' story on the cover each week, which would then enjoy an extended page count inside.

Alas, it wasn't enough to keep *TV Action* afloat, and in September of that year the title was incorporated into the comparatively juvenile-centric *TV Comic*. This was bad news for the Doctor, who, after two years of superbly delineated adventures in both *TV Action* and *Countdown*, was now facing a humiliating return to his old inky haunts – where he'd first appeared in 1964. Coming along for the ride were Cannon and Captain Mainwaring's septuagenarian soldiers.

As for The Persuaders, Smith, Jones and the rest; it was time to start hanging around outside the **Look-In** offices in the hope a kindly writer would take pity.

TV Comic
(News of the World Ltd/Beaverbook Newspapers Ltd/TV Publications Ltd/Polystyle Publications Ltd, 1951-1984, every Friday)

The first British comic to theme itself around the goggle-box, *TV Comic* launched itself onto the world on 9 November 1951, sporting a line-up of characters plundered from the juvenile end of the airwaves.

The guv'nor during these early days, of course, had to be Muffin the Mule, in whom it seemed the publication had taken out a franchise option as not only did the clod-hopping wooden puppet nab the cover ('by arrangement with Annette Mills, Ann Hogarth and The Hogarth Puppets' of course) but his chums Peregrine Penguin and Prudence Kitten also got their own share of the comic-strip action inside.

However, the ass wasn't the only star to have his celebrity status exploited. While slapstick merchant Mr Pastry merited half a page (in a strip that was credited to the character's real-life alter ego Richard Hearne), the somewhat spurious 'Jack and Jill' were billed as being 'as helpful as Mr Pastry'.

In fact, when you looked closer, it did seem some of the links to television were rather spurious. Elephant and hippo double-act Tusker and Tikki for one. And likewise, the reprint of US strip 'Little Iodine'. Okay, that had at least spawned a feature film spin-off in 1946, but billing her as 'The TV Terror' didn't really cut the mustard.

Overseeing the enterprise was reassuring face Jennifer, the girl who helmed children's programmes on the BBC (although the comic's actual editor was cartoonist Blos Lewis). She referred to her readers as 'Muffets' in deference to the paper's top draw, and hosted a chatty little column called 'Let's Be Gay'. *Ahem.* The star shared her page with the donkey's creator Annette Mills, who brought us regular dispatches in the form of 'Muffin Club News'. 'Do you know what Orthopaedia is?' began one particularly scintillating report in September 1952.

Later additions to the line-up of puppeteered pals included Sooty, Noddy (who bumped poor old Muffin off the front) and Lenny the Lion, while the virulent marketing that was 'The Secret Sign of the Ladybird Adventure Club' (also see *Swift*) took hold of the back page. The arrival of 'Roy Rogers: King of the Cowboys' after a few years signalled the comic's willingness to venture outside the *Watch With Mother* slot for inspiration, while 'Red Ray: Space Raynger [sic]' seemed to be nothing more than a kiddie-fied knock-off of *Eagle* mk I's 'Dan Dare'.

As the end of the Fifties arrived, *TV Comic* had first been sold to Beaverbrook, and then passed onto TV Publications, part of the Rediffusion Holdings group who held the franchise for television broadcasting in London. Far more significant though, was the introduction of Mighty Moth, who – in what would become the paper's mainstay strip – spent his time avoiding the fly-swatter wielded by his oedipal-based nemesis, Dad.

In 1961, the weekly received a major overhaul, debuting that iconic red-on-yellow logo and turning into a rather knockabout publication which traded in the mumsy puppet animals for punch-ups betwixt Popeye and Bluto, gun-slinging action in the adaptation of Gerry Anderson's Nicholas Parsons-voiced series *Four Feather Falls*, and all out sitcom in 'Bootsie and Snudge'. However, the big event in each issue was now another Anderson property, 'Supercar' ('It flashes across the sky – it zooms through water – it speeds over land! It's the marvel of the age!' No hyperbole there, then).

As the Sixties continued, the title swallowed up *TV Express* (Beaverbrook Newspapers Ltd, 1960-2), and more sci-fi joined up, including *Fireball XL5* (appearing in the paper two weeks before its TV debut in 1962), *Doctor Who* (who was accompanied on his travels by 'grandchildren' John and Gillian), *Space Patrol* and *The Avengers*. The latter was surely quite a grown-up signing for the weekly, but represented the paper's desire to extend its age-range as the likes of *TV21* were now creeping into the market.

Despite that, *TV Comic* couldn't quite forget its puppet roots and Basil Brush began appearing in the paper, controversially sporting legs.

In 1968, Rediffusion lost their license for broadcasting in the Thames region and were forced to sell off TV Publications. However, they decided to form a new publishing arm and thus Polystyle Publications Ltd was created – the name that would appear in the small print of every edition of the weekly from issue 851 onwards.

As the Seventies dawned, Steed and company were still doing the do in 'The Avengers', despite the fact the TV series was no more, and had now been joined by Skippy the Bush Kangaroo (who communicated with human owner Mark via a series of 'Eeek!'s and 'Squeak! Squeak!'s), the fabulous Norman magician Catweazle ('Huff-snuff and double puff!'), a version of the Ron Ely *Tarzan* series and – what every comic was surely crying out for – 'Johnny Morris's Animal Magic' which brought us a colourful one-page funny every week.

The yin to this high-octane yang came in the form of a host of cartoon characters. Tom and Jerry, Road Runner, Deputy Dawg, Bugs Bunny (who no one, it seems, can draw properly), Pink Panther, Inspector Clouseau (known only as 'Ze Inspector' here) and the Hanna-Barbera versions of Laurel and Hardy all signed up. A real bran tub of a comic, its production values may have taken a tumble since the Fifties, but its line-up had never been finer.

In December 1973, it incorporated *TV Action* and regained the 'Doctor Who' strip that had been prised from it in 1971 when the Time Lord was sequestered by *Countdown*, the precursor to that comic. Then, a year later, it swooped upon *Tom and Jerry Weekly* (Spotlight Publications, 1973-4) scooping up its, er, 'Tom and Jerry' strip...which it had already been running anyway.

By now, you could expect to see hard-nosed US detective 'Cannon' side-by-side with 'Mighty Moth', while Captain Mainwaring's men in the 'Dad's Army' strip rubbed shoulders with Tarzan. On the toon front, Barney Bear and Droopy had also joined in the fun, ensuring this was still one of the most eclectic titles on the shelves.

The mix remained fairly static as the Seventies continued, until September 1976, when competition from *Look-In* began to bite. In a blatant marketing exercise, the title became *Mighty TV Comic* and it switched to a tabloid format, issuing free gift 'Mighty Midget' comics of reissued material, while also slinging a reprint of a US *Star Trek* strip into the line-up. Thankfully this phase didn't last long.

By November 1977, the 'Mighty' was dropped and the paper reverted back to its former size, although now it was only sixteen pages in length. Nevertheless, old material was continuing to invade, and no one was impressed when the Doctor stepped out of his TARDIS in 1978 sporting Tom Baker's head blatantly slapped on top of a reprint of an old strip originally featuring the Time Lord's second incarnation, Patrick Troughton.

That same year, the publication swallowed up the rubbish *Target*, meaning three police series were now joining the publication: 'Target', 'Charlie's Angels' and 'Kojak'.

As the Seventies ended, the paper found *Doctor Who* finally whisked away from them for good, with the BBC awarding the time travel license to Marvel Comics' *Doctor Who Weekly*. Luckily, the Eighties brought new thrills, such as 'The Dukes of Hazzard' who arrived with full cast present and correct (a permanently apoplectic Boss Hogg raging at Sheriff Roscoe: 'Bonehead! You couldn't catch a cold in a flu epidemic!') and greatly entertained readers with its distinctive mix of automobile acrobatics, hot pants and moonshine. Similarly, you couldn't deny the appeal of a *Battle of the Planets* strip, however reprints of old 'Ken Dodd's Diddymen' and 'Catweazle' strips must have left the kids scratching their heads, while adventures for not only the Bisto Kids but also British Telecom's annoying mascot Buzby were hardly page-turners.

With sales falling, not even a late arrival by 'Tales of the Gold Monkey' and 'The A-Team' could bale *TV Comic* out of trouble, and on 29 June, 1984, the shutters came crashing down. Where now could BA Baracus, Bugs Bunny and, of course, Mighty Moth go to meet under one roof?

TV Fun
(Amalgamated Press, 1953-1959, every Monday)

On 19 September 1953, the publishers who'd pioneered the whole 'multi-media' push with *Film Fun* (1920-62) and *Radio Fun* (1938-61) finally embraced the next big thing and brought us *TV Fun*.

Of course, in this case Amalgamated Press had been shamefully slow on the uptake – the News of the World stealing a march on them back in 1951 with *TV Comic*. However, the main thing was they'd finally got their act together and, continuing the *Fun* lineage, produced a paper devoted to stars of the cathode-ray.

Featuring a tremendously Fifties logo (beautifully neat fonts, and beams of light emerging from a TV screen) the first issue of the 'smashing new weekly!' led with 'It's me, playmates – Arthur Askey' on the front cover. Obviously a durable personality – he'd been *Radio Fun*'s star attraction in the late Thirties/early Forties. Whereas *TV Comic* concentrated specifically on children's characters, *TV Fun* was smart enough to realise kids' interests weren't confined to *Muffin the Mule* and the like, and bolstered its pages with grown-up entertainers such as 'popular star of stage, screen and radio' Jack Warner (who'd go on to feature in *Dixon of Dock Green*, a TV series spin-off from his 1950 film *The Blue Lamp*), 'The Pride of St Capers' Jimmy Edwards ('Wake up at the back there!')

and out-and-out sex appeal courtesy of 'The Cutie Queen of the TV Screen' Diana Decker (the US actress who specialised in dizzy blondes).

Rather fantastically, although all three were ostensibly appearing as themselves, they took on the personalities of the type of characters they generally played on TV. Thus, Warner battled wrong-doers, Edwards got involved in *Whack-O!*-like adventures as a mortarboard-wearing school teacher and the ditsy Decker found herself mixed up in various light-hearted domestic calamities.

Alongside these star-led features, the comic also dealt out strips which only had a tenuous link to the box. 'Put Your Question' was presided over by Ivor Poser, as a panel answered various queries ostensibly sent in by readers; 'Inventors' Circle' saw wacky gadgets being put through their paces by President Knutson-Tite; and 'The Traveller's Tales' brought us globe-trotting adventures with the eponymous Traveller. And then came 'Hoofer the Tee Vee Gee Gee'. Nope, there was nothing remotely telly-related about this character either – despite the name – although the nag was notable for being a (slightly) revamped version of *Radio Fun*'s 'George the Jolly Gee Gee'.

With the passing of weeks, more celebrities made their way into the pages of the comic. Issue ten had much to crow about when Beryl Reid consented to be interviewed by *TV Fun*'s 'ace reporter' Amanda: 'Sorry to have kept you waiting, Miss Amanda! Aren't I the absolute terminus!' was the star's disarming opening gambit. Former child star Sally Ann Howes ('The Sweetest Girl in the Golden West') featured in her own cowboy strip and a dashing-looking Max Bygraves also got the star treatment ('He's Arrived – and to Prove It, He's Here!').

Nine months after launch, the comic absorbed *Tip Top* (Amalgamated Press, 1934-54) and *Jingles* (Amalgamated Press, 1934-54) in one fell swoop becoming – for a short period of time – the unwieldy *TV Fun, Tip Top and Jingles*. Thankfully, this madness was dropped after a scant few weeks.

And still the stars poured in! Shirley Eaton ('The Modern Miss in Merry Moments') booted Diana Decker off the back cover for her own series of similarly themed adventures, starlet of small repute Sally Barnes became 'Our Little Lady Make-Believe', a future *On the Buses* face had his formative years turned into comic fodder with 'The Adventures of Reg Varney as a Boy – and What a Boy!' and *Life With the Lyons* spawned a strip spin-off: 'Roar With the Lyons'.

Nearing the end of *TV Fun*'s life, Arthur Askey was replaced on the front by a rotating stock of strips wherein a featured personality – such as Max Bygraves, Joan Regan and Jack Warner – took turns to 'tell' a story…or, more accurately, have their mug shot reproduced alongside an unrelated yarn. However, on the inside the comic made its most thrilling signing yet in the form of a *Wagon Train* serial. Counteracting this excitement, though, was the creeping proliferation of text, as features covered more and more pages, while the strips themselves became unhealthily wordy.

In 1959, the comic received a whole new look, as Amalgamated was taken over by the Mirror Group's Fleetway division. A major change of direction took hold and now billing itself as *TV Fun and Romance in Pictures*, the paper was transformed into – choke! – a girls' comic. 'Romantic songster' Dean Martin brought us tales of 'First Love', the front-page strip was gushingly entitled 'Sweet Words of Love', while Pat Boone was roped in to introduce 'Summer Heartbreak', a 'wonderful romantic story in pictures.' Capping off this new spirit of slushiness was a slight change in name on 12 September, as *TV Fun* bowed out to make way for…*TV Fan*. As if the alteration of just one letter didn't make it obvious enough, the change proved to be a pretty half-hearted effort. It continued the issue numbering from *Fun*, but only managed to eke out another twenty-one editions of barely TV-related pap before it was swallowed up by *Valentine* (Fleetway, 1957-74).

TV Fan was survived by *Radio* and *Film Fun* – something of an indictment of Amalgamated's take on the telly.

TV Tornado
(City Magazines Ltd, 1967-1968, every Tuesday)

A bit of a makeweight in the over-populated genre of television-related comics, *TV Tornado* was a plodding mix of text stories, brand new content and stuff filched from America, as City Magazines Ltd formed an unholy alliance with those kings of the cheap TV spin-off annual, World Distributors Ltd.

Black and white under the covers, there was always the danger readers could be tricked into having a peep inside by dint of the rather fetching full colour paintings it sported on the front – even if the subject depicted often didn't feature inside.

Issue one arrived dated 21 January 1967, and came with a free 'Batchute'. Yes, you too could own a miniature Adam West hanging off a small striped canopy. Inside, things got off to an underwhelming start with 'Flash Point by Ed Storm', the comic's talking-shop, if you will. Here the apparent able seaman chatted about the world of TV, punctuating each paragraph with an irritating 'Flash!' in an effort to pump up the excitement. And then, when he ran out of gossip, he pulled out a few dopey did-you-knows to pad his way to the end of the page (a classic from issue seven: 'This week's saying: *put on the dog*. It means trying to act superior').

Text stories loomed all too large here, with readers doubtlessly feeling short-changed to discover the emotional-looking exchange that was taking place between Batman and Robin on the cover related to a caper in prose, as did *The Man from UNCLE* feature and Superman story, both of which had also been bigged up on the front.

Meanwhile, a trio of strips were flown in from the States as United Features' efforts: 'The Phantom', 'Flash Gordon' and 'Tarzan' were scatter-bombed throughout. At least 'Voyage to the Bottom of the Sea' originated in the UK and was drawn by *TV Tornado*'s editor (and 'Marvelman' creator – see *Warrior*), Mick Anglo.

Later additions to the paper included still more TV signings who looked great on the cover, but were only represented in text inside, while US strips 'The Green Hornet', 'Magnus, Robot Fighter' ('Tut, tut! One should never lose one's head,' he quipped in an episode, after decapitating a 'bot with a swift karate chop to the neck) and 'The Lone Ranger' also elbowed their way in. However, when it came to sheer élan, none of them could hold a candle to *The Saint* adaptation, which depicted a suave-looking Roger Moore in the title role, foiling nasties without so much as upsetting his quiff.

Things did improve a little later on in the year, when *TV Tornado* incorporated its sister title *Solo* (City Magazines Ltd, 1967) from 23 September. A co-production with Gerry Anderson's Century 21 Publishing – formerly AP Films (Merchandising) Ltd – it had also bandied about *The Man from UNCLE* within its pages, and in fact drew its name from that programme's lead character, Napoleon Solo. Although its first few weeks had been stuffed full of material taken from the US, excitement had briefly broken out when the Mysterons invaded some months before making their TV debut in *Captain Scarlet*. As a result, when it merged with *TV Tornado*, those disembodied menaces came along too.

Despite that, the combined forces of these also-rans was never going to be enough to secure the daft comic any form of longevity, and the following year it was swallowed up by *TV21* – rather sullying that fine organ in the process.

Valiant
(Fleetway Publications/IPC Magazines Ltd, 1962-1976, every Monday)

Hewn from the same redoubtable stock of British boys' comics that had also brought us **Lion** and **Tiger**, *Valiant* wouldn't last as long as either of those (although it would eventually consume the former) yet it was still a supremely sturdy publication all told. A confident mix of killings, comedy and, er, crows, it would donate more than its fair share of memorable characters to the Fleetway/IPC roster of eccentrics.

Issue one arrived in October 1962, playing up the *numero uno* status with a beaming Captain Hurricane ('Royal Marine Commando' – in case we thought he was just donning the beret and khakis for kicks) declaring: 'Thumbs up for No 1' in huge text, with a far more modest 'Meet me on page two' sneaking into the bottom right-hand corner of the page.

Rather excitingly, the comic arrived with not one, but two free gifts. First up was that old standard, the 'Football League Ladders', which allowed boys to chart the progress of their fave team via the means of fiddly cardboard flaps. Then there was the 'Pocket Rocket'. Nowadays, doubtlessly a euphemism best kept out of the juvenile market, back then it referred to a miniature plunger device ('A gentle twist will help get a better result', *fnarrr, fnarrr* etc.) that would propel a small plastic projectile a good few centimetres.

Come page two, and indeed we did meet the windily named military man. Rather a far cry from the barrel-chested berserker readers would become familiar with, we were presented with an origin story of sorts that saw the character serving on board a Naval vessel, SS *Sweetness*. When it was torpedoed by a German U-boat, the Cap and his deckhand Maggot clung to the debris as the evil vessel emerged to allow its German occupants a chance to gloat, before leaving the two to 'swim or drown' as it disappeared back under the waves. Thankfully, a passing boat picked them up, but by now Hurricane was nursing a grudge. 'This day, Maggot, you and I have declared war!' he roared.

Signing up with the Royal Marines, his opportunity for vengeance presented itself three panels later when – two years on – he had another encounter with the sub. Getting into one of his famous rages he tore the vessel apart with his bare hands, but decided not to leave his nemesis bobbing about in the water. 'I'll show you the proper way for a fighting man to behave when he's got his enemy well and truly licked! Drag the rat aboard!'

With the tables sufficiently turned, this was the start of something big: 'Our private war has only just begun!' exclaimed the Cap, his hand placed in an avuncular fashion on the diminutive Maggot's shoulder. And thus was laid in all that was required to furnish *Valiant* with a regular whirlwind of mayhem across the rest of its run.

Following on came 'The Nutts', a comedic one-pager that declared itself to be about 'the family with nuts in the belfry! Get ready to laugh!' Refreshingly down-at-heel, this bordered on kitchen sink drama, as the clan bickered over what to watch on TV ('Never mind about your football! I want *Coronation Street!*') before getting in a panic when the landlord approached looking for his rent ('Hide, quick!').

Next up was 'It Really Happened', a cavalcade of 'fact is often stranger than fiction'-type stories and then Wild West action with 'Hawk Hunter and the Iron Horse' – the tale of a seventeen-year-old who'd been brought up by Indians before realising 'in his heart he was white'. He was quickly enlisted by General Grenville M Dodge to safeguard the construction of his railroad against the native Americans, and the two embarked on a journey across the country in a huge steam train, the 'Iron Horse' of the title.

Electing for more comic relief, we then had 'Paladin the Fearless'. A very Disney-esque piece of work, it owed something to *Asterix the Gaul*, as a gifted child was raised by a woodcutter to help resist the onslaught of Viking invaders. This was followed by another classic-in-the-making: 'The Steel Claw'.

The sentient body-part that crept around seemingly of its own volition dispensing mayhem was an enduring image in British comics, but this was probably its definitive outing. In a superbly rendered introductory episode, lab assistant Louis Crandell helped his boss Professor Barringer in an experiment to create what was rather vaguely referred to as 'a new ray for medical purposes'. Stuck with a right hand made of metal following some previous laboratory accident, Crandell found himself centre stage in another cock-up, getting zapped by a dose of 'ultra-high voltage'. Although, upon first glance, it looked as though the dogsbody had been vaporised leaving only his metallic mitt behind, in fact his flesh had temporality turned invisible. Returning to corporeal form, he quickly realised that every time he ran a high voltage through his artificial hand, the same thing would happen – and thus made a direct bee-line for the bank to pull off a robbery – 'I'll put my steel hand into my pocket. The bank assistants won't see anything!'

At this stage in its life, 'The Steel Claw' was a noir-ish effort, the lead character described as having a 'sallow' and 'bitter' face, and likely to express himself in fruity dialogue of the 'by thunder!' variety. A confused chap, by anyone's definition, over the years he'd turn from crime to crime-fighter, enjoying a brief flirt with out-and-out superheroics (donning a nutty skin-tight costume to boot), before heading off to South Africa in light of a suspicious public at home (well, could you blame them?). However the strip changed, though, it remained one of *Valiant*'s defining features.

Maintaining the interchange with laffs, 'Percy the Problem Child' was next out of the bag – a smart-arse teen who spent his page setting stupidly chirpy mental challenges, before giving the answers in inverted text at the end of the strip. The centre pages were then given over to a biog of Admiral Nelson (what was this, *Eagle* mk I or something?) which segued into the letters page, 'It's All Yours'.

Following a couple of half-page humour strips ('Hey Presto: The Saucy Apprentice' and 'Shorty the Sheriff'), it was India-based excitement in 'Blade of the Frontier'. Here, the 'tall, broad-shouldered' Captain Brett Blade of the Khyber Lancers ran into trouble when four Wazir tribesmen mistakenly concluded he'd killed three of their 'brothers'. Annoyed they may have been, but in all honesty they didn't represent that much of a threat – the eponymous captain ducking behind a rock causing them to declare: 'It is magic! The white man has disappeared!'

Wolf cub scout 'Sixer' and feathered family 'The Crows' stepped out for a further page of humour, with slum-dwelling boxer 'Kid Gloves' then fulfilling the plucky, disadvantaged sportsman role.

The comic entered the final lap with some more 'believe-it-or-not' type facts about soccer and 'crazy inventions' before presenting its final strip, 'Jack O'Justice and the Siberian Giant' – an atmospheric tale of an eighteenth-century swordsman who fought crime accompanied by his 'girl comrade' Moll Moonlight.

'Famous Fighters', a series of features dedicated to men renowned in history for their murderous qualities, provided *Valiant* with its back cover pay-off, thrilling boys with its fearsome portrayal of 'The Red Indian'. Next week it was to be 'Britain's paratroopers...the Red Devils!'

From this convincing debut, things steadily improved as, the following year, the comic proved its mettle by absorbing *Knockout* mk I (Amalgamated Press/Fleetway 1939-63). The merger brought the paper two important characters who'd serve it well over the years.

Billy Bunter ('The Heavyweight Chump of Greyfriars') was the legendary creation of Charles Hamilton who'd first appeared in *The Magnet* story paper in 1908. When his title had folded into *Knockout* in 1940, he'd continued his porky ways unabated – and now, he was set to do the same in *Valiant*.

Even better than the morbidly obese 'fat owl' was 'Kelly's Eye'. While Bunter always seemed rooted in the turn-of-the-century ('Yaroo!'), this was a fantastically exciting, globe-trotting venture that wreaked of Sixties glamour and roll-neck sweaters. Premiering in 1962, the strip featured Tim Kelly, who'd become invulnerable when he wore the Eye of Zoltec – a big shiny gem – around his neck. Inevitably, a panic would ensue every time he mislaid the stone, or the chain on his necklace broke – both of which happened surprisingly often. Intent on using his power to fight crime, he initially travelled the world socking it to an array of exotic-looking bad guys, but early into his run with *Valiant*, he met time-traveller and Edwardian frock coat-devotee Doctor Diamond (who in no way infringed upon *Doctor Who*'s copyright, doing the time and space thing in an oversized clock rather than a police box) and the pair voyaged through history tackling an array of nasties including Diablo – a bloke who'd managed to get his hands on what we're calling The Other Eye of Zoltec.

As the Sixties continued, *Valiant* gradually junked the lion's share of its comedy stuff, while infusing its adventure fare with a welcome streak of whimsy. By June 1968, Captain Hurricane was a red-faced lummox with a nice line in alliterative exclamations ('Great jumping jellyfish!'), The Steel Claw was battling the Federation for Extortion, Assassination and Rebellion (FEAR) and Tim Kelly was fighting uppity Red Indians back in the Wild West. Meanwhile, 'The House of Dolmann' had come along in 1966, bringing us the adventures of a master puppeteer and his ingenious walking-talking mechanical dolls who, together, also fought crime. In a similar vein was 'Mytek the Mighty', the story of a King Kong-like robotic ape who was used to foil the nefarious schemes of evil dwarf Gogra ('Ha, here he comes – the lumbering metal oaf!').

Less far-fetched were the comic-strip adventures of the nineteenth-century detective Sexton Blake, and the down and dirty 'Raven on the Wing'. The latter was something of a minor classic, following the fortunes of a faintly satanic-looking gypsy boy, who played barefoot for lowly first division club Highboro' United. An often gloomy strip, it mixed Romany curses with last-minute goals and boasted evocative dialogue from the title character of the 'Oi ain't got time to argify, master' variety.

In April 1971, another merger was on the cards. The title about to bite the bullet this time was *Smash!* (Odhams Press/IPC Magazines Ltd, 1966-71). Its main contributions to the conglomeration was the battling Bash Street Kids-style strip 'The Swots and the Blots' and 'The Incredible Adventures of Janus Stark'. This iconic strip centred on a painfully thin Victorian escape artist whose defining features were his propensity for wearing black, shockingly large eyebrows, luxurious self-confidence ('My perceptive senses have never failed me yet!') and mal-leable frame which allowed him to fit into the tightest of cavities. Inevitably, this skill was put to good use – yep – fighting crime.

Just six months later, *Valiant* made another acquisition and absorbed the once great *TV21*. Despite carrying illustrious strips based around *Doctor Who, Land of the Giants* and *Joe 90* in its time, all it managed to get placed in the new line-up was the silly monster-fest 'The Tuffs of Treasure Island' and its adaptation of *Star Trek*. For Kirk and company, nestling between the footy antics of Raven and the jokes and stamp adverts of the 'It's All Yours' page must have represented new life and civilizations of the like they could never have imagined.

In 1972, another colourful character joined the ranks in the shape of 'Kid Pharaoh'. Cursed to sleep 'while darkness reigns' back in ancient Egypt, Zethi was awoken in the modern day, whereupon a tangle with some thieves prompted him to declare: 'I shall oppose evil in modern Britain, just as my father did in ancient Egypt', before he got waylaid by the excitement and glamour of wrestling instead. A nifty mover in the grapple arena ('Now for a pin-fall!') how comics fans yearned to see him get into a headlock with *Tiger*'s Johnny Cougar – now that really would have been a fight.

However, if we're talking worlds collide-style encounters, then few could hold a candle to the clash that took place in 1974. Swallowing up *Lion* in May of that year had to represent *Valiant*'s most high profile takeover yet and thus the comic really put out the bunting to celebrate. Not only did it launch a competition to win five hundred 'North Pacific Sky Flyer Planes' (simple models, not a full-scale jet, you understand), but it also staged an historic meeting between Captain Hurricane and *Lion*'s Steel Commando inside. 'Stone the blinkin' crows, look at that!' roared Maggot. 'It's the *Steel Commando!* I've 'eard 'undreds o' stories abaht that fightin' Ironsides!'

A fine idea it may have been, but the marriage wasn't set to last, despite the batman's think-bubble assertion that 'from now on, the fireworks are *really* goin' ter fly between them two!' Mere months later the metallic military man was nowhere to be seen.

Others joining up included the ageless but suicidal Adam Eterno, highway patrolman Zip Nolan and comedy strip 'Mowser: The Priceless Puss!'

Although it was all good solid stuff, by the middle of the decade *Valiant* was looking a little bit old-fashioned, particularly in comparison to a new high-octane publication, **Battle,** which launched in 1975. As a result, that comic's co-creator, John Wagner, was tasked with shaking up the paper (while his colleague Pat Mills went on to launch **Action**). Thus, *Valiant* got a sudden infusion of hardcore violence and bastardry.

Leading the charge was the Wagner-created tough New York cop Jack McBane, better known as 'One-Eyed Jack'. Hard as nails and utterly without mercy – here lay the seeds for *2000 AD*'s Judge Dredd.

In April 1976, *Valiant* made its final takeover, gobbling up the reprint title *Vulcan* (IPC Magazines Ltd, 1975-6) which was represented as a 'mini mag' pull-out section for a couple of weeks before being dropped altogether. By now, the comic was looking increasingly schizophrenic. Alongside Jack McBane there was the wolfhound 'Paco' tearing the throat out of his broken bottle-wielding owner, and the all-out nihilism of Sgt Joe 'Death Wish' Bannon. But none of these sat comfortably alongside the buffoonish behaviour of Captain Hurricane, the cakes 'n' caning in 'Billy Bunter' and the craziness of 'The Nutts'.

Less than sure-footed in the new era of mega-violence, it was probably for the best that, come 16 October 1976, the title was swallowed up by *Battle*. 'One Eyed Jack' – a born survivor if ever there was one – found a new home within its pages, but for the gentler characters whose relationship with violence had always been singularly bloodless, this was the end of the line.

Victor
(DC Thomson, 1961-1992, every Monday)

In the early Sixties it was still apparent boys were crazy about war and sports stories, but it seemed patience for the old-fangled story papers had finally run out.

Thus, it was time for DC Thomson's first ever boys' comic (i.e. with strips and nothing but – well almost): *Victor*. When that premier issue hit the news-stands, the front cover belied the high-octane action that lay in wait inside. Instead, it was more intent on bigging-up the free 'super squirt ring' that came with issue one, depicting one chucklesome lad spraying water over a less effusive friend's face.

Inside, that issue brought us a reliable mix of stories featuring a pot-pourri of old and new characters – a move that would be copied by latter-day whipper-snappers *Buddy* and *Spike* some twenty years later. Chief among them was Sgt Matt Braddock VC, plucked from the pages of *Wizard* mk I (DC Thomson, 1922-63) for the terse prose piece 'I Flew With Braddock'. Alongside him there was just one other text story, 'Come Away the United', and a feature on Lester Piggott, 'When he was a Boy'. Otherwise, it was top comic-strip action, including Second World War miscellany in 'The Raid on General Rommel'.

It wasn't long before the template for success was established, and classic *Victor* strips came flooding through as the prose stuff was quickly dropped altogether. Favourites included 'Cadman the Fighting Coward' (a superb re-working of George MacDonald Fraser's famous Flashman character, and a classic comics anti-hero); 'The Hammer Man' (the humorous adventures of dim-witted blacksmith Chell Puddock and his titular tool); and 'Joe Bones: The Human Fly' (plucky, bare-footed rock climber, sent on numerous dangerous missions during the Second World War by the sinister, bowler-hatted Lord Plimpton).

Other DC Thomson old timers also made the grade, such as 'Gorgeous Gus' (from *Wizard* mk I), 'Morgyn the Mighty' (the strong man first seen in *Rover*, 1921-61) and, best of all, 'The Tough of the Track' (also from *Rover*). The latter came to be the quintessential *Victory* story, telling the travails of welder-cum-championship runner Alf Tupper.

Victor – © DC Thomson & Co., Ltd

The inspiration for the character was thought to lie in real-life figure Alf Shrubb. An apprentice brickie from the start of the twentieth century, Shrubb discovered his prowess for running when he raced three miles across Sussex fields to summon help putting out a burning cottage. His spectacular career subsequently took him to Ibrox Park in Glasgow where, in 1904, he broke numerous world records during one historic run.

For his part, Tupper was the salt-of-the-earth member of athletics club Greystone Harriers, who existed on a diet of fish and chips – one typical morning's training run ending with the athlete popping into his local chippie to declare: 'I'll have a sixpennyworth and a bit of fish, Seth, and wrap them in the sports page. I'll see if there's anything about running in it.'

Inevitably, his racing engagements would necessitate our man taking on some despicable posh type from a well-to-do club and being spiked by said rival halfway around the track ('Good try mate – but not quite good enough!') or breaking off to rescue an imperiled steeplejack ('Bloomin' Ada!') if the course was cross-country. Whatever the distraction, Alf was perennially first across the finish line, letting rip with his iconic cry, 'I ran 'em all!' One episode saw him venture to Edinburgh for a competition, only to leave his comfortable B&B in the middle of the night to sleep on the city's craggy Arthur's Seat because the bed had been too soft for him. That's the sort of man he was.

Aside from Alf, there were two other perennial features. The first was the one-page funny, variously dedicated to 'Cap'n Hand and his Mutinous Band', feuding hillbillies 'The Ruffies and the Tuffies' (a rebrand of *The Beezer*'s 'The Hillys and the Billys') and – best of all – *The Topper*'s crap Mexican bandito 'Figaro' (named because his portly frame made him look like a figure 'O', geddit?). A strip from an early Seventies issue about a prolific Australian batsman entitled 'Johnny Gets the Runs!' is sadly not eligible for entry here.

The second stable item was the front cover heroics detailing real instances from the First and Second World War (although, usually the latter). Only given the memorable name of 'A True Story of Men at War' in the Seventies, these were gung-ho history lessons from land (denoted by the title appearing in the silhouette of a grenade), air (the outline of an RAF badge) and – less frequently – sea (Royal Navy button). It was here *Victor* established the fact that when the 'Krauts' bit the bullet, they'd go out with an '*AAAARGH!*' while the 'Nips' met their maker to the tune of '*AIEEEEEEE!*'

During its run, *Victor* probably brandished the headline 'Today! *Two* great papers in *one*!' more than most, as it swept up falling DC Thomson titles by the bucketload. That roll call of mergers in full, then: **Wizard mk II** (1978), *Hotspur* (1981), *Scoop* (1981), *Buddy* (1983), **Champ** (1985) and *Warlord* (1986). As a consequence, come the end of the Eighties, it was the only DC Thomson boys' comic still standing.

But times were getting tough, and sales were falling. In a last throw of the dice, *Victor* relaunched itself in 1991 (boasting 'Free! Zany laces!' – whatever they were). Now carrying features on real-life football stars, mountain bikes and 'the latest videos' alongside the regular strip fare, it just wasn't enough. Eighteen months later, with no one else to merge with, *Victor* folded, taking the long lineage of DC Thomson's boys' comics with it.

Warlord
(DC Thomson, 1974-1986, every Thursday)

Stories of warfare had always proven popular in boys' comics, so why not go the whole hog and produce a weekly that was entirely dedicated to combat?

Warlord was exactly that proposition, and – in the eyes of many – had a profound effect on the British comics market during its run. With little time for whimsical stories, the plucky exploits of unlikely sports heroes or sci-fi drama, the comic was one thin slab of bloody action. Heroes perpetually spoke through gritted teeth, while death came in various flavours of lead and bayonet. With its devotion to destruction, it set a new bar for acceptable levels of violence and – despite many of its tales being set in the Thirties and Forties – dispensed in the main with the 'chocks-away' brand of dialogue for more gritty, modern stuff ('Ain't seen a Jap for hours'). Yes, the Seventies trend for ultra-violent comics started here.

Issue one plugged the war-and-nothing-but angle with its free gift of eight golden replica medals and a 'super holder'. It also placed Union Jack Jackson – a Royal Marine 'temporarily' attached to the 'Yanks' – on the front, running straight towards the reader with gun blazing. However, despite bagging the cover, he was far from being the star attraction here. But we'd get to that soon enough.

Jackson's exploits were the first to greet boys inside, as the plucky Brit showed lumbering Yanks a few tricks on the battlefield. Constantly moaning that the 'Limey' was showing the US boys up was the red-necked

O'Bannion who – despite his uncouth ways – grew to become good 'buddies' with the hero.

Next to be dispatched into combat was hoary old RAF hero Matt Braddock who'd been delivering death from the skies for decades now, most recently in the pages of *Victor*, but before that at the behest of *Wizard* mk I (DC Thomson, 1922-63).

Far more interesting than 'Bomber Braddock' was the 'Weapons in Action' series. If clever-clogs critics wanted to accuse comics of obsessing over military hardware, they need look no further than this. Some instalments read almost like pornography ('Its long barrel and high velocity made it extremely accurate. The .55 calibre bullet was capable of piercing armour plate at 500 yards') as tales of conflict placed the men secondary to the clumps of metal they brandished.

And then came the main event, in the form of debonair secret-agent Lord Peter Flint, codenamed 'Warlord'. An own-brand James Bond, this dashing Second World War operative was in some ways self-consciously old school (referring to colleagues as 'old boy' and in his first story advising an enemy soldier: 'Sorry old chap, can't stay to argue' as he laid him out with a punch to the neck). On top of this, Flint was bequeathed with an interesting double life.

While society at large saw him as a gadabout playboy who refused to sign up ('Take this white feather, Lord Flint,' said a snooty socialite proffering the item, 'the sign of cowardice'), he was actually serving the country in his eight-page self-contained strips wherein he would swoop in, steal important intelligence from the 'Hun' and then make good his exit, leaving an unfeasibly large number of baddies dead, or at least maimed, in his wake. Boys just loved his exploits.

Following in his shadow we then had 'Spider Wells' (the travails of a First World War wannabe-pilot who accidentally killed his cruel stepfather) and 'Young Wolf' a sort of 'secret origin' – if you will – of *Wizard* mk I's Wolf of Kabul.

The free gifts followed thick and fast (a mighty sixteen replica medals in issue two, a polystyrene glider in three and a secret sign ring in four) as an extra story, 'The Long Walk' (a bomber crew go down following a raid, and have to make their own way back to Blighty, lugging their top secret bombing sights with them) also joined the line-up. However, what was becoming increasingly obvious was just how popular Peter Flint was. As such, a bog-standard letters page (called – what else? – 'Fire Away!') was hastily scrapped in favour of the peerless hero's 'Calling All Warlord Agents!'

A kind of recruitment drive for a pre-pubescent *Dad's Army*, the Warlord himself (helpfully identified not just by a cut-out of his head, but also a 'Lord Peter Flint speaking' caption) would set his readers top secret missions such as: 'Plan out an hour's walk or hike in your area. On this hike, use your eyes to watch and observe – and write down the number of things you see beginning with the letters "B" and "C".' Here, he also printed encrypted messages which could only be understood by the legion of lads who'd sent off that 15p postal order to become one of his special Warlord Secret Agents and, in return, received a wallet, identity card, secret codebook, ominous-sounding special instructions and a metal badge. Soon, the whole page was awash with mysterious numbers as mentor and pupils traded recon info in covert form.

Make no mistake, it was a real-life battleground out there for the comics' readers, as revealed by one letter from a 1976 edition wherein a junior agent reported some 'anti-Warlord agents' had tried to obtain from him Lord Peter's cipher info. After giving them false information, the rotters tried to force the resourceful youngster into giving up his secrets. Luckily, this was one tough nut to crack: 'I defeated their leader in hand-to-hand combat to protect the code,' boasted the true-believer. Oh yes, our boys would certainly be ready when the balloon went up.

So popular had *Warlord* become that just four months after its launch, IPC responded with their own similarly themed publication, *Battle,* and then, two years on, DC Thomson hit back with a bona-fide *Warlord* spin-off, *Bullet.* Even though this venture proved short-lived (and was absorbed by its parent in 1978), the comic continued on through the Seventies and into the Eighties peddling its spectacular brand of blood and thunder. Surely this was the only paper around that ran strap lines across the pages of its strips that read: "'I'll split you in two!'", "'Sorry to spoil your fun, Krauts!'", "'Trust me – or shoot me!'" and "'Rocket strike!'"?

Peter Flint certainly proved to have staying power, as did Union Jack Jackson, while along the way we met fellow gun-touting heroes such as 'Bring-'Em-Back Bert', 'Cannuck King: The Fighting Lumberjack' and 'Korea's Strangest Fighting Team!: The Best of Enemies'.

Warlord's eventual death in 1986 is probably best attributed to the general downward trend in the comics market, rather than any real problems with the publication itself. That said, perhaps war was beginning to look a little *passé* as, a few years after it was incorporated into *Victor*, its new home started to anxiously diversify away from carnage, killing and sticking it to the Krauts in favour of football, skateboarding and celebs.

Warrior
(Quality Communications Ltd, 1982-1985, monthly)

Dez Skinn is a bit of comics legend, all told. Not only did the man edit **Whizzer and Chips**, he also created ***Doctor Who Weekly***, regularly broke bread with Stan Lee during his stint at Marvel UK and, best of all, brought the world *Warrior*.

A good half a decade ahead of its time, this was the first British paper that actually allowed its writers and artists to retain copyright on their creations, and represented the industry's first credible stab at something that would preoccupy it for the latter half of the decade: adult comics.

It was all possible thanks to Skinn's entrepreneurial streak. He'd set up Quality Communications Ltd and could therefore run the outfit anyway he saw fit. His plan was to produce a *2000 AD* bothering sci-fi title (which, indeed, poached a ton of that title's creators) that would allow its team to stretch their muscles a little bit.

The first issue may have sat in development hell for ten months, but as the man himself explained in his very first *Warrior* editorial, 'being a totally independent publishing group...we wanted to get everything right, so the on-sale date had been luxuriously pushed back further and further until we all felt happy with the characters, the costumes, the stories, everything.' Now he was hopeful that 'while the large comics publishers' – hello IPC and Marvel – 'seem to be in a period of creative regression, we hope our attempt, our one little magazine in a sea of others, will spark off enough interest to get things moving again.'

The 'fantastic first issue' (a strapline Skinn had used three years earlier on *Doctor Who Weekly*) proudly advertised it contained 'new stories from Britain's top comics creators', and majored on a central image of 'psychotic cyborg' Axel Pressbutton. 'He's back!' ran the breathlessly copy. Er, from where exactly? Although the majority of readers were probably unacquainted with the slap-headed nutter who sported a scythe in place of his left arm, he'd actually previously appeared in a little-known London-based rock magazine *Dark Star* before enjoying a few adventures in the pages of serious inky music journal *Sounds*.

Continuing the theme of dodgy acquisitions, a strap down the left-hand side of the front cover also advised us Skinn had rescued 'Father Shandor: Demon Stalker' from *Halls of Horror* (Quality's Hammer films tie-in title). More intriguing was a buff bloke's silhouette with a question-mark emblazoned across his chest. 'From present-day Britain – *a hero reborn.*' Who, from the mighty annals of British comics, could this possibly be?

'Britain's top super-adventure character is back after eighteen years' ran the detail on the contents page for a strip that – at this point – was merely billed as 'A Dream of Flying'. When the big reveal finally came, it left readers pretty much none the wiser. 'I'm Marvelman…' crowed the hero. 'I'm back!!' Again: from where, exactly?

The character had been created in 1954 by publishing company L Miller & Son who, until that point, had been producing British editions of the US *Captain Marvel* comic. However, when the American Fawcett Publications decided to scrap the title following repeated legal action from DC Comics (who claimed the Big Red Cheese was nothing but a rip-off of their own Superman), the Brits refused to roll over and die. Instead, artist Mick Anglo was tasked with creating a Captain Marvel clone who would continue in his stead. Thus, whereas young Billy Batson would utter the phrase 'shazam' to be transformed into 'The World's Mightiest Mortal', when Micky Moran let slip a 'Kimota' (atomic spelled backwards…nearly) he'd become 'The Mightiest Man in the Universe' – Marvelman.

Although it would be wrong to say Marvelman fast entered the British public's consciousness, he did notch up an impressive three hundred and forty-six issues in his time.

However, the revival was actually the least of the strip's appeal. What was more important was the superb artwork from Garry Leach and the quality script from Alan Moore. A writer who'd go on to redefine the boundaries of comics, this was the first real chance for the then IPC stalwart to push the limits of the medium. OK, so some of the prose was a bit on the purple side ('His power courses through his veins like molten silver'), but it was uncommonly intelligent stuff as a grown-up Micky (now Mike) found himself plagued with memories of his superhero past.

Other strips in that first issue proved less arresting. 'The Spiral Path' was a drab tale of druids and sub-Tolkien nasties which featured unappealing dialogue such as: 'You're looking at the armies of Cormac, Caradoc and Artuc combined' (which is presumably a bad thing). 'The Legend of Prester John' may have been beautifully drawn by John Bolton, but this quest set during the Crusades was similarly densely written, and full of pompous characters telling each other boring stories.

Slightly better was 'Father Shandor: Demon Stalker' which came from the same creative team, but had the good sense to throw in a few demons alongside the pomposity, while 'Laser Eraser and Pressbutton' was just straight down the line sci-fi which would have better suited *2000 AD* if it hadn't been for a perspiring ball of alien perversity known as Zirk who, at one point, mused: 'I would like to see one of your human females...*thrash!*'

All these efforts had 'second-stringer' written over them, thanks to the long shadow cast by Alan Moore, who not only contributed the aforementioned Marvelman, but also what became one of the classic British comic-strips of the era, 'V For Vendetta'.

Starkly delineated by David Lloyd, right from the off the story established many of the 'rules' for the adult comics boom of the mid-Eighties. Here, Moore ditched the traditional conceits of 'sound effects' and think bubbles in a bid for naturalism – although he did still persist with a slightly overbearing caption-based commentary. The story told of a post-holocaust Britain in 1997, which was being ruled by a fascist government. Standing against them was a bloke in a stovepipe hat, cape and Guy Fawkes mask, who gradually picked off all personnel that were connected with a long since abandoned concentration camp.

From the start, this was determinedly grim fare, with poverty-stricken heroine Evey forced into prostitution ('Uh...would...would you like to...uh...*sleep* with me or anything?') but told with a compelling cinematic quality. Soon, themes of child abuse, depression, censorship and – well – just having a really bad time, were coursing through the story. The only thing that would actually strike a bum note would be Moore's ill-founded assumption a nuclear war was survivable – 'To the best of my current knowledge, this is not the case,' he sportingly admitted later.

By the end of *Warrior*'s first twelve months, the mix of strips remained pretty much the same, with Moore's dual efforts continuing to dominate.

In 1983, Quality printed a *Marvelman Special* which drew the attention of Marvel Comics, who felt the character infringed upon their trademark. Keen to avoid a legal wrangle with his former employers, Skinn decided to drop 'Marvelman' from *Warrior* with issue nineteen, while the two parties came to some agreement. Unfortunately, it was to be the last readers would see of the character for a long time. Robbed of one of its star attractions, the monthly found itself floundering. While 'V for Vendetta' was still going strong, 'Big Ben: The Man With no Time for Crime' proved a poor replacement for Mike Moran and company as *Avengers*-style espionage with a bowler-hatted hero merged with confused science fiction. Issue twenty-two brought an English language reprint of European strip 'Bogey' in the paper's new 'Comics International slot' and suddenly it felt as though the makeweights were now running the show.

Warrior's final issue arrived in February 1985. Celebrating the fact it had recently won fourteen Eagle Awards (the comics industry's own BAFTAs), the cover was decked out like an edition of that ornithology-themed publication. Aside from publishing further excerpts from the company's protracted legal correspondence with Marvel ('Quality Communications Limited has no intention of producing any further magazine bearing the title "Marvelman". We have no desire whatsoever to be confused with your client's publications') there was no hint that the curtain was about to fall. Indeed, now that **Captain Britain Monthly** had come along, Skinn was feeling buoyant about the mature comics market. 'Maybe we'll become a growth industry yet!' were his final words for the publication as, behind the scenes, falling sales took their toll and *Warrior* closed up shop.

Thankfully, 'V for Vendetta' found a new life overseas, with DC Comics reprinting all the episodes thus far seen, before Alan Moore and David Lloyd finally finished the whole thing off in May 1989.

Against all odds, 'Marvelman' also made a comeback. Now cunningly rebadged 'Miracleman', his adventures thus far were also reprinted, this time by US publishers Eclipse in 1985. There he continued until the company went bust in 1994, by which time Alan Moore had signed over his share of the character's rights to fellow scribe Neil Gaiman. Then, at a bankruptcy auction in 1996, US artist/writer/publisher Todd McFarlane picked up the company's remaining assets for a knock-down price which, as far as he was concerned, meant he now owned MM. Gaiman thought differently...and so did Alan Davis who'd taken over drawing the strip from Garry Leach back in *Warrior*'s early days, also picking up a share in the character. Not only that, Dez Skinn now claimed the entire rights had reverted back to him...before original Marvelman artist Mick Anglo crawled out of the woodwork to insist that, actually, the whole Marvelman/Miracleman franchise was rightfully his and Skinn had never secured the property in the first place. The resultant five-way stand-off has kept Mick Moran from uttering that nuclear-tinged catchphrase for the last few years.

Despite the lineage of legal grappling, *Warrior* is still best-remembered as the hugely influential title that launched an unfettered Alan Moore onto the world, prompted *2000 AD* to pull its socks up and set in motion the whole idea that comics in this country could indeed tackle grown-up topics, and do so with real credibility. **Deadline**, **Crisis** and **Revolver** were all on their way.

Whizzer and Chips
(IPC Magazines Ltd, 1969-1990, every Monday)

The legendary *Whizzer and Chips* is probably only overshadowed by **Buster** in the IPC funny comics hall of fame, but even though it didn't manage to beat the cloth-capped kid's title in terms of longevity, for many it remains the ultimate in humour titles.

Blessed with the totally arbitrary, but somehow utterly ace, premise of sporting two rival publications between its covers, readers were expected to align themselves with either the Whizz-Kids or the Chip-ites, depending on their preference. '*New!* Two comics for only 6d!' ran the headline, but to be strictly accurate, what you were getting here was actually two half-sized publications for the price of one. With the conceit being that kids were supposed to discard the section of the paper they hadn't sworn to honour (because, if you supported one of the titles then you had to hate the other, by law), in reality no-one ever actually did this, and besides, most people threw their lot in with the Whizz crew anyway, simply because *Chips* was always hidden away somewhere inside (a colour 'front' and 'back' page denoting its start and finish), making it seem rather like the poor cousin, or the unwanted result of a comics merger foisted upon *Whizzer* by IPC execs.

Why the Whizz-Kids and the Chip-ites were at war was never sufficiently explained, but it's worth remembering that, despite the later venom poured upon the rival publication by *Whizzer* frontman Sid (of

'Sid's Snake' fame), the serpent-rearing chap actually headlined the 'other' paper upon *Whizzer and Chips*'s launch in October 1969 (whereupon the title came free with twelve 'super stickers', featuring a variety of 'Sid Says' slogans such as 'Sid Says: England for the World Cup' and '...Support your local bobby'). Nevertheless, he soon crossed over to *Whizzer* from where he'd pen his propaganda-spewing editorial which would generally include something along the lines of: 'That'll drown any feeble *Chips* chuckles!'

His own strip – which would go on to inspire 'Victor and his Boa-Constrictor' in *Viz*, fact fans – paired him up with the huge, zig-zag patterned Slippy the snake, and together the pals would get up to all manner of hi-jinks, the reptile generally saving the day by using his supple body to imitate an over-sized letter of the alphabet. It was amazing how often a big 'S' was required to fill out a shopkeeper's sign and the like.

Sid's opposite number, and *Chips* cheerleader, was the hapless lad Shiner. Originally appearing in a strip billed as 'Shiner and his Mum' (who, in the early days, remained a constant, nagging thorn in his side), the hooped-jumper wearing tyke was well-meaning enough, but always ended up sporting a black eye thanks to various mishaps. You could bet that, pretty much every week, come the last panel of his adventures, he'd be there holding a raw steak against his throbbing optic.

From the start, *Whizzer and Chips* hit readers with a hugely impressive line-up. Highlights that would serve the paper for many years included 'Odd Ball', the tales of a spherical shape-changing creature from the planet Bounco; 'Wear 'Em Out Wilf' who dealt out entropy-based entertainment; 'Champ' (later to be redefined as the definitive article when the strip was renamed 'The Champ') which followed the exploits of a skinheaded would-be overachiever ('I'm the greatest!') whose efforts to break records normally ended in – what else? – disaster; and 'Parker the Parky', a particularly demented take on the familiar archetype of the grumpy park keeper, this one not averse to wielding a shotgun if his gander was really up.

Four years into its life, the title proved its worth by swallowing up *Knockout* in June 1973 whereupon it became *Whizzer and Chips incorporating Knockout*. Although it would quickly drop all reference to its new acquisition, it benefited greatly from the inclusion of the likes of ghost train escapee 'Boney', 'Pete's Pockets', 'Joker' (who, after a long and quietly fought campaign would wrestle the front page off Sid in the mid-Eighties), 'The Toughs and the Toffs' and the supremely haughty 'Fuss Pot' ('H'mmph! These sweets I bought had better be good! Fuss, fuss!') who quickly established a place for herself as *Chips'* back cover star. In the meantime, the comic had also developed a few more of its own stories, including 'Harry's Haunted House', Charlie Brown look-alike 'Loser' and – best of all – the supremely ugly 'Sweet-Tooth' which detailed a confectionary-mad lad's battle for chocolates and the like against rival gobbler Greedy Greg.

Cor!!'s loss to *Buster* in 1974 didn't hurt either, as *Whizzer and Chips* provided a new place of rest for the now homeless 'The Slimms'. Suddenly, it looked as though the title was turning into a greatest hits compilation of IPC's best characters, and that was no bad thing, because – despite the rampant pick 'n' mixing – the paper maintained its essential character, with *Chips* personalities regularly kicking up an alarm by running sorties into *Whizzer* territory. Anyway, if things were looking complicated now, wait until we got to the Eighties.

More merging was on the cards in 1978, when this time the title picked up the pieces for *Krazy*, retaining the services of 'The Krazy Gang', '12½p Buytonic Boy' and 'Micky Mimic' for a time. By this stage, other classic strips were in full swing, such as 'Store Wars' (capitalist Mr Superstore versus small trader Mr Bloggs – guess who regularly came out on top?) and 'Happy Families' (featuring the always-feuding Happies of Wimble Walk). By the time the title's tenth birthday came around in 1979, the Whizz-Kids and Chip-ites were in ebullient mood, offering readers not just a Boris the Spider toy, but also a miniature replica of its first ever issue.

As the Eighties arrived, and its stablemates began to drop out, the paper still appeared to be in top form. Now it trained its sights on the almost equally legendary *Whoopee!*, the inevitable takeover bid reaching fruition in April 1985. With *Whoopee!* having previously engulfed *Shiver and Shake*, *Cheeky* and *Wow!* it was getting increasingly difficult to trace the true parentage of the comic's various personalities. In all, *Whizzer and Chips* had now absorbed characters from six different comics via mergers, as well as pilfering from *Cor!!*'s stock.

By 1986, a random sample shows the publication was carrying 'Sweeny Todd' and 'Lolly Pop' (both originally from *Shiver and Shake*), 'Toy Boy' and 'The Bumpkin Billionaires' (from *Whoopee!*), 'Bleep', 'Boy Boss' and 'Creepy Comix' (*Wow!*), 'Mustapha Mi££ion' and 'Calculator Kid' (*Cheeky*), and 'Joker' (*Knockout*'s sole survivor, but now on the back cover from where he could eye up his ultimate goal). Of course the title kept its own creations coming too, and by the time it had undergone something of a relaunch – which involved a larger page size and better paper quality – it looked like 'Lazy Bones', 'Bottom' (can you believe it? The arse-based exploits of a young teen), 'Junior Rotter' (JR off of *Dallas* in the form of a mischief-making kid), 'Town Tarzan', 'Phil Fitt' and the others might have secured the comics continuation through the Nineties.

Well, maybe not. There's no denying issues from 1990 were in the main characterised by some distinctly poor-quality artwork, while the comic's efforts to embrace current pop culture was looking increasingly desperate; the less said about 'Watford Gapp: He's the King of the Rap!' and the *Bread* inspired antics of 'Scouse Mouse and the Scallywags', the better – although 'The Ossies' wasn't half bad ('Strewth!'). Still, at least Shiner and Sid kept up the feuding – from March 1990, a boxing-glove wielding Shiner: 'D' you know why Sid reminds me of someone who inherited a fortune in March? 'Cos he's as mad as a March heir! Har, Har!' Scathing.

Nevertheless, it was becoming clear things couldn't go on like this, and on 17 October 1990, the curtain finally came down. With only one other IPC humour title now left on the shelves, *Whizzer and Chips* finally learnt how it felt to be on the receiving end of a takeover, advising its readers that, from next week, all your favourite characters would be found in the pages of *Buster*.

A sad – but inevitable – finale for one of IPC's funniest titles and most enduring polymaths.

Whoopee!
(IPC Magazines Ltd, 1974-1985, every Monday)

When it started, it may have had one of the more insipid logos on the news-stands and sported a paper size that was slightly smaller than its IPC stablemates, but *Whoopee!* would prove to be a pretty durable proposition.

Launched a year after **Shiver and Shake** – which was already proving to be no great, er, shakes – the title weighed in with a packed and very generous forty pages, decreeing across the front of its first issue like some 'Gouranga'-spouting disciple, 'Get happy – get this paper'. In addition, it also offered up a far more practical reason for your endorsement, namely that the comic was 'for fun – and cash to be won!' You can't say fairer than that.

With a huge array of stuff on offer inside, the title presented a winning mix of traditional and modern fare. In the tried-and-tested camp were a few variations on the patented IPC 'chalk and cheese' strips. 'The Upper Crusts and the Lazy Loafers' and 'Ivor Lott and Tony Broke' (who appeared in issue two as 'star guests' on loan from *Cor!!*) both essayed the ever-popular class war format, while 'Clever Dick and Dozy Mick' told tales of the former's ill-fated attempts to capitalise on the latter's lack of mental agility.

Elsewhere, 'Bumpkin Millionaires' did *The Beverly Hillbillies*, albeit relocated to the UK with a bunch of West Country corn-chewers adjusting poorly to the jet set life following a win on the football pools ('I've finished mowing the Persian carpet, ma! T'were a bit thick!'); 'Little Miss Muffit' regularly 'muffed' any activity she attempted (for the sake of clarification, that means she continually messed things up); 'Ernie Learner' took on new hobbies with aplomb, but always came unstuck, usually infuriating all around him into the bargain ('Oh well, I didn't make a bandsman...but I am a *banned* man! Sigh!' exclaimed our hero in one issue after another ill-fated scheme); 'Toy Boy' was nothing to do with Eighties pop star Sinatta's 'love toy', rather it detailed the exploits of a plaything-obsessed little lad; 'Pop Snorer' was narcolepsy-related hilarity involving a constantly kipping dad; and 'Daisy Jones' Locket' brought us the trials and tribulations of the titular girl and her genie, who'd emerge from her necklace to interpret his mistress' wishes all too literally.

Of the more cutting-edge fodder featured in these early issues, highlights included 'Spy School' ('Today, boys, we're going to learn all about the art of getting information from the enemy!'), the truly disturbing 'Evil Eye' (a disembodied optic organ that could appear anywhere at will and make previously law-abiding people turn bad...and this was supposed to be humour?), 'The *Whoopee!* Holiday Guide' (dispatching 'our traveller' to various locales around the world for different regional based laffs), 'Ad Lad' (a young Les Gray from Mud lookalike, obsessed with getting his face on telly) and the rather fantastic 'Hee Gee and His Nag' (the theatre of modern marriage played out by two domesticated horses).

Against this backdrop of zaniness, devoting the centre spread to serious strip 'The Lone Ranger' seemed an odd decision. Far more suitable was the back cover 'Wanted' pin-up feature; top Ken Reid portraits of hideous rogues originally sent in by *Whoopee!* readers. But, the creativity didn't stop there. 'Kid Cartoonist' was a full page drawn by the comic's fans. A neat idea that inevitably resulted in some of the most appallingly realized stuff ever seen in print, it also netted budding artists three quid if their efforts made it into print.

Seven months later, change arrived as the comic picked up the tab for the failing *Shiver and Shake*, and the two titles merged. The result was an influx of new characters into an eight-page *Shiver* pull-out section and an immediate axing of 'Wanted' in favour of similar feature 'World Wide Weirdies' (one issue featuring Stephen Sylvester's suggestion of a creepy London landmark, 'The Houses of Horrorment'). Along the way, the publication had also increased its paper size to correspond with other IPC titles.

From the incorporated comic, *Whoopee!* really took infamous infant 'Sweeny Toddler' to heart ('Cor! It's fun making people go all of a jelly!') Accompanied by his dog Hairy Henry, the child – originally drawn by comics legend Leo Baxendale – appeared in some of the nuttiest strips committed to paper, packed with background jokes and even gags between the panels. Anything went as far as he was concerned – well almost. A strip which depicted the character filling his nappy did fall foul of IPC's censors, but by 1978 he was even gracing the cover of his new title.

As the Seventies drew on, *Whoopee!* finally ditched its lame wide-eyed logo and infused the comic with a new swathe of characters. 'Super Mum' came from the pen of Dicky Howett and proved an immediate hit with its silly adventures of the headscarf-wearing matriarch; Smiler proved you could have the most scant USP ever (in that all he really had going for him was a fixed grin) and still end up hosting the comic's letters page; 'Dick Doobie: Back-to-Front Man' challenged readers' patience by forcing them to both invert their copy of the paper and look at it in a mirror to understand what he was saying; and 'Dads as Lads' spotlighted a couple of fathers reminiscing about their youth. From the original line-up, however, 'Toy Boy' and 'Bumpkin Billionaires' were still hanging on in there.

In 1980, it was *Cheeky*'s turn to do the pull-out thing as it too merged with the now seemingly indomitable publication, the deal sweetened by the chance for readers to win a Corgi 'Friscodisco' DJ unit. Three years later, *Wow!* joined the fold, although it wasn't lucky enough to be afforded its own section, despite the fact the occasion merited a hugely impressive front cover with characters from both titles meeting over a banquet table. 'Something to celebrate!' they declared. 'No.1 comic combination'.

With the zeitgeist-surfing Pacman-inspired 'Snack Man' now on the cover and the comic's portfolio boosted by its recent acquisitions, *Whoopee!* appeared to be in pretty good nick and celebrated its five-hundreth issue in November 1983. But, unfortunately, time was running out for the comic and come Easter 1985 it was to be *Whizzer and Chips* that was laying on the excited 'two-in-one' roundelay as it swallowed up the eleven-year-old funny paper in light of falling sales.

Nevertheless, up until 1992, *Whoopee!* annuals still appeared every Christmas, while the late Eighties saw a reprint comic *The Best of Whoopee Monthly* flourish for a brief period. Ah well, it hadn't been a bad run, all told.

Wildcat
(Fleetway Publications, 1988-1989, fortnightly)

Winter 1988 was an exciting time for The Mighty Tharg. In September, he'd dedicated his regular *2000 AD* editorial to ushering in a new age of adult publications with the launch of *Crisis*. A month later, here he was introducing a 'ghafflebette new comic to be published by those nice folks at Fleetway...designed for the younger Earthlets among you.'

Winter 1988 was an exciting time for The Mighty Tharg. In September,

On paper, it may have looked as though *Wildcat* was a no-brainer – sci-fi thrills for the junior audience – but in fact it was a decidedly dicey proposition. With the comic audience aging dramatically in the Eighties, it just didn't seem as though there was a new generation coming through to pick up the habit. As a result, juvenile publications were dropping like flies and, in truth, it flew in the face of all evidence to tailor a new publication to what was the once traditional eight to twelve-year-old target group.

As a result, despite the fawning press that greeted the arrival of Pat Mills' politics and pontificating in *Crisis*, *Wildcat* was actually the ballsy proposition here.

Going great guns to nab as many readers as possible, Fleetway flagged up its arrival with the production of a free preview comic ('Not for sale')

which it appended to copies of *2000 AD*. The front cover laid out the big concept: 'In the year 2500, life on Earth will cease to exist!' it said, as a meteorite storm bombarded the planet. Inside, we were in familiar territory with a black and white strip that felt almost retro in its execution. Sans those now fashionable artist and writer credits, what we got was a slice of old school science fiction that owed rather a lot to sci-fi series *Space 1999*.

Sick of being laughed at by unbelievers who didn't buy his prophecies of doom, four-square hero 'Turbo' Jones (and get that name!) recruited a team of people to join him setting up a new life away from the soon to be destroyed planet. Making up the numbers was generic mercenary Loner, feisty female Kitten Magee and dopily designed stretchy armed android Joe Alien.

Together, along with a crew of faceless humans and cute robots, they'd travel the galaxy in their spaceship Wildcat, looking for a new world to call their home.

Boasting 'long six-page stories, based on and around the Wildcat space craft – stories to astound you!', aside from being pleasingly glossy, the other way the title was set to differ from its Seventies forebears was in its conceit of having all its stories linked to the comic's central premise. Thus, when issue one proper arrived there were separate self-titled strips for each of the main characters in which they'd shuttle off from the mothership to investigate different sectors of whatever planet their sensors indicated held out good prospects for life. Alongside this there was a different one-off tale every issue, based around various personalities also present on the vessel.

With a letters page entitled 'Time-Warp Datalink', free alien stickers to collect and a host of inoffensive, clunky-looking monsters, in truth you couldn't really get more traditional than this. However, despite being set some five hundred years in the future, it was clear *Wildcat*'s time had already passed. While, in the short term, *Crisis* looked like it had identified a sustainable audience base with the older teens and twentysomethings, those pesky prepubescents just weren't convinced by this venture – not in the brave new world of Super Mario Land on the Game Boy, *Batman* at the cinema and Jive Bunny on the decks.

After just twelve issues, the comic was forced into a hasty consolidation with *Eagle* mk II, a redoubtable and similarly juvenile publication that was heading into a rather desperate final four-year period of constant relaunches as it too struggled to stay afloat.

All in all it had been a worthy effort, but also a complete and utter failure. For the last new traditional adventure comic (to date) to be launched in this country, it was a sorry way for the genre to go out.

Wizard mk II
(DC Thomson, 1970-1978, every Monday)

Here's a rare case of a comic getting revenge.

The original, highly impressive run of the boys' story paper, *Wizard* (DC Thomson, 1922-63) – which had brought us characters such as Wilson, Limp-Along-Leslie and Gorgeous Gus – came to a close when the title was forced to merge with *Rover* (DC Thomson, 1922-73). However, seven years later on Valentine's Day 1970, *Wizard* enjoyed a Second Coming, now in the form of a fully fledged comic proclaiming itself to be a 'great *new* picture story paper for boys'. Bundled with a free 'sure-shot shooter', this was to be another typical DC Thomson mix of war, sport and sci-fi, but with a particular emphasis on football.

Thus, the comic's centre pages were given over to 'The *Wizard* Football Special – Thirteen Pages of Strips and Stories'. Here we had a 'light-hearted look at the world of football' (inevitably titled 'It's a Funny Game…'), a remembrance of a fine real-life performance on the pitch (in this first issue centring upon Berwick Ranger's legendary goalie Jock Wallace), a comic-strip profile of a soccer star's early life (George Best here, but future editions were devoted to Jimmy Greaves and Peter Bonetti), a fact file on a chosen team (Arsenal) and a fun text-based tale ('The Owl of the Albion'). Augmenting these items were two strips, 'The Voice That Ran the Rangers' (an anonymous telephone caller who eerily left nuggets of info like, 'The floodlight pylon at the north-east corner of the ground is in some danger') and 'Cool Kragg: The Team Maker' (a forever calm player-manager who was leading third division Burhill United to success).

If you weren't particularly taken by soccer, there was still some treats on hand. 'Slave of the Ring' followed the fortunes of Johnny Nelson, forced to box by his cruel stepfather (what was this? *Mandy*?!) who pocketed all his winnings; 'Scrappy: A Boy All Alone' (an orphan making his way on the harsh slagheaps of Midlands town Wiggton); 'Out of the Ice He Came' (an explorer who'd been lost in the Antarctic for decades, secretly helping out the progress of a new expedition); and 'Soldiers of the Jet Age' (rocket-pack action in the United Nations Task Force of future Britain 1990).

Perhaps fearful it was already looking a bit passé, it wasn't long before *Wizard* overhauled its front cover, which originally featured a compendium of sports-related facts accompanied by whimsical cartoons, and instead concentrated on full page pictures depicting a suitably bloodthirsty sequence from one of that week's strips. It also dumped the soccer pull-out section, although it continued to give the sport a good run with its continuing profiles and strips such as the 'Cocks of the Common', a tale about a bunch of store workers hoping to win a local footie tournament.

And then, in January 1973, the comic took care of an old grudge by swallowing up a fellow title that was now ailing. Yes, it must have been a grim day in the *Rover* offices when the comic was forced into the care of *Wizard*, the very title it had consumed ten years previously.

By the mid-Seventies, football had been dropped still lower in the mix, as *Wizard* became pretty much indivisible from other boys' comics. By the time it reached the end of its run, it was nigh-on impossible to tell it apart from the likes of **Bullet** or **Hotspur**, save for its occasional innovations like a small record review slot tucked away on the same page as a text story (the Dave Clark Five's *25 Thumping Great Hits* was 'ideal for parties and boisterous record-playing sessions,' if you must know). It was therefore no great jolt when the titled finally folded into the pages of **Victor**.

Still, it had stitched up *Rover*, so that was mission accomplished.

Wow!
(IPC Magazines Ltd, 1982-1983, every Thursday)

OK, so *Jackpot* hadn't worked out. After two and a bit years it had been forced into a partnership with **Buster**, so, what to do now?

A scant five months after that title's demise, here was the answer. But, on first glance, *Wow!* was much the same sort of thing all over again, bar a few zeitgeist-surfing features.

Issue one arrived clutching one of four free 'funny face' gifts (in much the same way *Jackpot* had dished out six various practical jokes – were kids expected to shell out for multiple copies to get the full set, or something?), while also offering readers the chance to win probably one of the dullest toys ever marketed, Bluebird's Savings Bank. 'It's been called the "Bank with a Brain",' we were told, and – here comes a snapshot of the tumultuous times we were living in – 'it will accept the new £1 and 20p coins when they are issued.'

Inside, 'your friend' the Editor could only really muster up the fact *Wow!* was 'Britain's newest comic' by way of a selling tool, but in fact it did have more going for it than that. With IPC always more on the ball in regard to pop culture than DC Thomson, the publication was packed with allusions and references to the worlds of TV, music and technology.

Here was would-be comedian 'Kid Comic' ('Hey, Grandpa, want to hear a funny poem?'), whose bedroom was festooned with posters of Basil Brush, Morecambe and Wise, Benny Hill and The Two Ronnies (we know this, because their names were written underneath); a gothic take on the famous BBC sitcom in 'Hi De Hi, Hi De Hooooo' (based in Hauntins' holiday camp) complete with lookalikes of Gladys Pugh, Ted Bovis and Peggy Ollerenshaw; the first in a series of 'Competition Stories', 'Space-Invaders', which dwelt on a sentient arcade machine and offered up the chance to win an Atari console ('Readers – how many Space Invaders are there in this picture?'); and 'KBR' ('Kids' Band Radio').

This strip mined the nascent CB radio craze and was packed with jargon-filled dialogue such as: 'All the sevens from steamy Sid! The fairycakes have gonked on my chunker. I'm fruiting down summerside hill!' Unfortunately, it was poorly rated by the comic's female readership when *Wow!* took a straw poll in November, prompting the Editor to desperately assert: 'It's disappointing…but support *is* growing…the story is being talked about, and the novel language is being picked up and used by more and more children.'

Meanwhile, 'Adam and his Ants' reworked 'Andy and his Ants' from *Cor!!* to max-up the pop-crossover quotient – cut to the Giggleswick Adam Ant fan club: 'It's great having the same name as Adam! I wish I could sing like him though!' said the eponymous character before discovering his Prince Charming-alike crooning attracted the attention of a swarm of insects.

Aside from these strips, the paper also boosted its celeb status with a centre page spread devoted to a certain breathless Antipodean artist-cum-musician-cum-all-round entertainer. '*Wow!* It's Rolf' was top stuff, featuring a startled photo of Mr Harris himself, the chance to win a set of his Magic Brushes (you had to hand it to *Wow!*, it wasn't stingy with the merchandise), some hi-jinks with – yes! – Jake the Peg ('Is it cricket to be used as a wicket?' puzzled the three-legged wonder as a ball belted off his shin), a Rolf comic-strip and, inevitably, a guide to making one of his patented 'Rolf Rollers' – a two-stage animation concocted by rolling one layer of paper around a pen and then flipping it backwards and forwards over a sheet below.

Similarly effusive was the *'Wow!* Star Turns' page which lumped in pictures of Big Daddy, Kojak, John McEnroe and the like under the pretext of providing celebrity-related puzzles and gags.

But it wasn't all famous faces from off the telly, *Wow!* also sported a fine selection of standard funny stuff. 'Shipwreck School' soon earned itself front page status with its tales of a Robinson Crusoe-esque educational establishment, 'Penny Dreadful' did the requisite naughty girl stuff; 'Bill and Coo' took the unpromising concept of a boy and his pet pigeon and made it mildly entertaining; 'When I Was Young' brought us mock biogs of the formative years of such characters as Dracula and King Kong; 'Country Cousin' retrod 'Richie Wraggs' from *Jackpot*'s footsteps with more yokel-goes-to-big-town stuff; and 'Spare-Part Kit' was wish-fulfilment fodder about a child from the country of Zoblobnia who donned a bionic body suit to perform all sorts of physical miracles.

Other strips that joined the paper along its run included 'Boy Boss' (superbly drawn by Frank McDiarmid, which we know because he regularly snuck his signature in between panels); standard 'versus' doodles in 'The Goodies and the Baddies'; a *Two Ronnies*-style mock headline feature entitled 'Here is the News' ('The world's best husband-and-wife trampoline act have just had a son. He is reported to be a bonny, bouncing baby!'); 'Gulliver's Troubles', the tale of an extremely tall boy, and the paper's response to the readers' aforementioned desired for 'odd men out' strips; and *Whoopee!*'s 'The Upper Crusts and the Lazy Loafers'.

In the meantime, Rolf had hopped off after filing his last centre-spread in issue twenty-six, declaring: 'It's been great being with you during the last six months – let's hope we meet again some time!' Presumably he'd finally flogged a sufficient quantity of those Magic Brushes. He was replaced by the lively 'TV Quiz Kids', with the likes of 'Robot Robinson', 'Michael Aspirin' and 'Tommy Void' presenting non-television related 'complete this gag' questions (although, to be fair, Mr

Aspirin did do the occasional teaser wherein he 'mimed' a TV title; his version of *Clapperboard* being particularly neat).

However, *Wow!*'s life was to be a short one, and just over a year after it started, an 'all-star get-together' was on the cards as the paper joined forces with the similarly effusive-named ***Whoopee!***. Despite that, it went out in style, still off-loading the merchandise by offering kids the chance to win a selection of Tomy electronic games.

British Comics Today

This is a book with a sad ending.

Although, when you think about it, pretty much every single entry contained within has finished up on a bum note. Time after time, we've seen formerly bright-eyed, enthusiastic publications quickly (and sometimes not so quickly) succumb to poor sales and falter into oblivion or, more frequently, a shot-gun marriage with a better-selling stablemate.

That was OK, though. The capriciousness of those comic-reading kids, who quickly bored and hankered after something new, kept creators on their toes. While titles dropped like flies, there was a continual churn of new publications to replace them – especially in the Seventies. Almost every Saturday brought a new launch to pore over. New chums to meet, free gifts to covet – why on Earth would we still be interested in last week's stock?

But, like a snake consuming its own tail, the circle gradually grew smaller, with less to sustain it as the years rolled by. What caused the comic-reading audience to fall away over the Eighties and Nineties isn't clear, but there are a few doorsteps upon which the blame has traditionally been laid: television, home video, computer games – pretty much every other media, really. Whatever the reason, somewhere around the mid-Eighties it seemed adolescence was brought forward by half-a-decade, with eight-year-olds becoming more concerned about their own image than whether or not Winker Watson's latest wheeze would raise the ire of Mr Creep. Allegiances were now sworn to pop groups, rather than the Whizz-Kids or Chip-ites, and you didn't stay up late shining a torch under the bed covers at a copy of *Champ*, when you could be sneaking a look at the *The Young Ones* on telly instead.

The result? At the time of writing just five titles featured in this book are still in publication: *2000 AD*, *The Beano*, *Commando*, *The Dandy* and *Judge Dredd Megazine*. In each case, they're selling a fraction of what they once shifted, and resigned to their status as a lower shelf oddity in WH Smith, bought variously by nostalgic thirtysomethings, OAPs searching out a treat for the grandkids, war-obsessed forty year-olds or hardcore Forbidden Planet-frequenting enthusiasts.

But, aside from this admirable quintet, British comics today are pretty much dead in the water.

Collecting

Nowadays the real action has slid from the high street newsagent into the realms of the collectors' circuit, where old comics shift for Lord Snooty-sized stashes of cash. In 2004, an anonymous investor in Essex bought *The Dandy* issue one, complete with free gift and the original four-page flyer advertising the new comic's arrival, for a record-breaking £20,350. Six months earlier, the same bloke had shelled out £12,100 for one of the twelve surviving editions of the first issue of *The Beano*. That's serious money, but, to be honest, few comics in the British market ever reach such heights (American publications, however, are a different story...).

Obviously, it's those number ones which are really collectable, particularly if they're still sporting that imminently loseable free gift. A premiere *Dandy* sans Express Whistler could only muster up a paltry £7,261 in 2004, while a space spinner can easily put over £100 onto the price of a *2000 AD* prog one.

If you're really serious about this comic-collecting lark, then the place to be is the Comic Books Postal Auctions website (*www.compalcomics.com*). This is where the big money changes hands, and at the time of writing, some of their recent first issue sales include:

 Buster – £371
 Commando – £338
 Beezer – £243
 Topper – £242
 Eagle mk I – £183
 TV Century 21 – £182
 2000 AD – £154
 Lion, Tiger and *Boy's World* – £126
 Valiant – £104
 Victor – £81
 Hotspur – £73
 Hornet – £43

All of the above were generally in top-notch condition when sold, another factor that can seriously affect the price. One careless coffee ring on your *Valiant* number one and you can wave goodbye to £20 or so.

If the sums of money look daunting (and they are) there are, thankfully, other places online specialising in second division prices. Of course, eBay (*www.ebay.co.uk*) looms large here, that communal car boot sale where pretty much anything goes. The funny papers are such a mainstay of the auction site it has its own section for UK comics and annuals. It's here you'll really get to see the ebb and flow of the market in full effect, with certain items immediately picking up interest upon listing (in the main, anything related to *The Dandy*, *The Beano*, *Action*, *Misty*, *Eagle* mk I and *Scream*), while others do well to muster up a couple of quid (a copy of *Swift* number one recently making less than a fiver, for example). Providing you bid late, avoid being stung by ridiculous postal charges and read the item description carefully, the canny collector can come away with some top bargains.

More rigid, but less stressful, is the curiously named 26 Pigs (*www.26pigs.com*). Aside from being a fantastic factual resource (thanks to its A to Z 'library'), it's also a friendly and easy-to-use market place, where you pay set prices for comics sold by private collectors. With a stock of over 40,000 British publications up for grabs, it's a godsend for those former *Beezer* readers desperate to finally get hold of that specific issue in 1984 which Mr Newsagent somehow forgot to put aside for them.

Of course, there are dozens of other websites also happy to flog you the back issues your mum threw away, but the above two are the ones the author of this book came to rely on most when he needed a *Look-In* number one, like, fast.

If you're not afraid to use up a little shoe leather, you could also shoot along to one of the many comic marts which run periodically around the country. These generally small affairs usually take place in universities, hotels, town halls and the like, and while they give you the chance to actually get your mitts on the goods before handing over the cash, they're generally weighted more towards American produce and can prove disappointing if you're expecting to come face-to-face with a big stack of must-have early *Mandys*.

Likewise, the annual Bristol Comics Expo is usually worth a visit – particularly if you're interested in meeting some of the industry's writers and artists, while The London Film and Comic Con is held every year at Earls Court, and usually boasts the patronage of various creators, plus some guy who apparently appeared in one of those *Star Trek* spin-offs. Again, old British fare is generally not particularly well represented, but it's still worth a look.

One Last Thing

In his fantastic tome, *The International Book of Comics* (Hamlyn, 1984), Denis Gifford rounds off his introduction with the following brilliantly cheeky comment: 'Every comic in this book comes from my collection, and if your own favourite is missing, perhaps it's because I haven't got it. Send it to me at once!'

The author of this publication has a different spin on that. Now keen to offload the groaning stack of titles he's amassed while putting this thing together, he invites any reader who's seen something mentioned in this book that they're aching to own to email him on *graham@kibble-white.com*. If he's still got it, he'll be quite happy to part company with it for a reasonable price.

So, drop him a line at once!

Credit Note

All images used with the kind permission of DC Thomson, Egmont UK Ltd, IPC Media and Rebellion A/S (*www.2000adonline.com*).

Plate Section

Plate 1   *2000 AD* – Artist: Brian Bolland. Judge Dredd & Strontium Dog created by John Wagner & Carlos Ezquerra. Nemesis the Warlock created by Pat Mills & Kevin O'Neill. Rogue Trooper created by Gerry Finley-Day & Dave Gibbons. Nikolai Dante created by Robbie Morrison & Simon Fraser. All © 2005 Rebellion A/S

Plate 2   *Action* – © (1976-1977) Egmont UK Ltd

Plate 3   *Beezer* – © DC Thomson & Co., Ltd

Plate 4   *Champ* – © DC Thomson & Co., Ltd

Plate 5   *The Crunch* – © DC Thomson & Co., Ltd

Plate 6   *2000 AD*'s *Diceman* – Artist: Glenn Fabry. Nemesis the Warlock created by Pat Mills & Kevin O'Neill. © 2005 Rebellion A/S

Plate 7   *Emma* – © DC Thomson & Co., Ltd

Plate 8   *Jinty* – © (1974-1981) Egmont UK Ltd

Plate 9   *Judge Dredd Megazine* – Artist: Glenn Fabry. Judge Dredd created by John Wagner & Carlos Ezquerra. © 2005 Rebellion A/S

Plate 10   *Krazy* – © (1976-1978) Egmont UK Ltd

Plate 11   *Mandy* – © DC Thomson & Co., Ltd

Plate 12   *Nutty* – © DC Thomson & Co., Ltd

Plate 13   *Plug* – © DC Thomson & Co., Ltd

Plate 14   *Shiver and Shake* – © (1973-1974) Egmont UK Ltd

Plate 15   *Tornado* – © 2005 Rebellion A/S

Plate 16   *Wow* – © (1982-1983) Egmont UK Ltd

Other images

Page 39   *Battle* – © (1975-1988) Egmont UK Ltd

Page 48   *Beano* – © DC Thomson & Co., Ltd

Page 53   *Buddy* – © DC Thomson & Co., Ltd

Page 56   *Bullet* – © DC Thomson & Co., Ltd

Page 58   *Bunty* – © DC Thomson & Co., Ltd

Page 65   *Buster* – © (1960-2000) Egmont UK Ltd